D1065517

SAVING THE BREAKOUT

SAVING THE BREAKOUT

The 30th Division's Heroic Stand At
Mortain, August 7–12, 1944

Alwyn Featherston

With a foreword by
Maj. Gen. Ellis Williamson, U.S. Army (Ret.)

★
PRESIDIO

*This book is dedicated to all who served
during World War II,
but especially to those who had the dirtiest,
least glamorous, most dangerous,
and most important job of all—
the combat infantrymen.*

CONTENTS

Maps

FOREWORD

The 120th Infantry Regiment was my home. I joined it as a seventeen-year-old high school trombone player and served in it for eleven years. I was an enlisted man for five and a half years before I was commissioned. In the next five and a half years, I commanded platoons, commanded two different rifle companies, was the S-3 (operations officer) of the 3d and the 1st Battalions and then of the regiment, commanded the 1st Battalion, and was the last commander of the 120th Regiment before it returned to North Carolina state control in 1946.

I was serving as S-3 of the 1st Battalion when the 30th Division landed in France and we began to battle our way through the hedgerows. It seemed like the grind would never end. Each few yards were fraught with wounds and death and tears.

The 1st Battalion was commanded at that time by Lt. Col. Hugh I. Mainord, one of the finest soldiers that anyone will ever know. He was a fine gentleman, a National Guard veteran of World War I, and he was old enough to be my father. He told me that he knew he was too old to last long commanding a frontline infantry battalion. He was praying to God that he would be able to keep up his physical strength long enough to hold the unit together through its first really tough fight. He did better than that. He carried us until we all were convinced that we could stand up under anything that was thrown at us.

One morning, after about four weeks in the hedgerows, he and I were walking along a small trail toward one of the frontline rifle companies. He looked at me with glazed eyes and said, "Butch, I've just got to rest a moment." With that statement, his knees slowly buckled. and he very, very slowly knelt to the ground, completely unconscious. I called for a litter, and two men carried him to a field hospital.

A couple of hours later, the regimental commander came to see us. He told us that Colonel Mainord was being taken care of and that it appeared that he would recover. He then told me that I was to command the battalion until higher headquarters could send us another lieutenant colonel!

There I was, a, twenty-six-year-old captain, with relatively little military training, commanding an outfit of almost a thousand men. Every company commander in the battalion was older than I.

I held my command only a short while—just before and during the St.-Lô breakout. As far as history records, the massive carpet bombings from the air on July 24 and 25, 1944, were probably the key to our breaking out of the Normandy hedgerow area. As far as we were personally concerned, the two great tragedies of the war were the St.-Lô breakout when our own aircraft dropped bombs on us, and the massacre at Malmédy, when we found the bodies of so many American soldiers who had been shot down in cold blood after being captured.

The blast of a bomb had blown me out of a trench and thrown me several feet. I, like many others, was bleeding and dazed. Some of our people were killed outright. One of my personal friends was buried alive and died before we could dig him out. Many others were wounded.

We were still trying to gather ourselves together when up walked our assistant division commander, Brig. Gen. William K. Harrison. He was known to almost everyone in the division. He was always out among the troops.

He called out, "Butch, how many men can you get together right now?"

I answered "about fifty" but told him we'd need time to find individual weapons.

He said, "Let's you and I go. Tell the others to follow as soon as they can."

We had not gone far before men started catching up with us. Going along with General Harrison was one of my most rewarding hours. We didn't make the breakthrough by ourselves, but we did show some tankers the way through. They made the dash, but, by golly, we got them started by walking in front of them for over two miles.

Lieutenant Col. William Bradford arrived soon after the St.-Lô breakout and assumed command of the 1st Battalion. I expected to return to my job as battalion S-3. That was not to be. The regimental commander told me that I had to leave the outfit that I had become so fond of. He told me my promotion to major should be coming through any day and that I was to take over as S-3 of the regiment.

That bothered me, as I had always thought of the regimental staff as pencil-pushing, rear-echelon people. Of course, I went back and made a discovery. In the frontline units, one can do a little about enemy gunfire, either shooting back or spreading out and finding cover. In the regimental headquarters, you are *there*. There is little danger from flat-trajectory fire, but the artillery and mortar fire comes in just as often and many times is unheard until too late. One has to stay put and just take it.

After the breakout, we were supposed to get a little rest. We were told to occupy a hill mass that had been held by a unit of the exploiting force. We rushed up the hills and made a fantastic discovery— their positions were facing in the wrong direction for the situation as we knew it.

It was getting dark, so we made what adjustments we could and settled in for the night. During the night, we were hit by a strong armored counterattack designed to cut off the entire exploiting force. None of our units was actually overrun. However, enemy forces came through every seam in our line.

This was Mortain, which turned out to be one of the decisive battles of the war. If we could just hold Mortain, our exploiting forces could continue to be reinforced and supplied.

There are many fantastic stories to tell about this battle. There was the one and only bayonet fight that I heard of in World War II, certainly the only one I participated in. A telephone operator at the regimental switchboard picked up a bazooka and knocked out a tank—without leaving his seat! At one point, our only regimental reserve was our attached engineer company. We converted the engineers into riflemen, and I personally placed them in strongpoints of five men each. I told each group to hold its position or I would [deleted]. One soldier was heard to say he feared that crazy captain more than the Germans.

We held on for all we were worth, and after a real knock-down-drag-out fight, a regiment from another division earned a Presidential

Unit Citation for getting to the hill where we had been for a week. Of course, we were also royally recognized for our actions.

Our higher commands also deserve much of the credit for the battle. They supported us in every way, but they should be praised most for having faith that we would hold and permitting the main attack to continue.

That's real generalship.

Maj. Gen. Ellis Williamson
U.S. Army (Ret.)

*Major General Williamson transferred from the National Guard to the regular army and stayed in the service after World War II. He landed with the leading elements of, the marines at Inchon during the Korean War. He commanded the 173 Airborne Brigade, the first U.S. Army ground troops to fight in Vietnam. He later had a second tour of duty in Vietnam commanding the 25th Division. He served as chief of the Military Advisory Group in Iran. He had already received notice of his pending promotion to lieutenant general when ill health forced his "premature" retirement after forty years of military service.

PREFACE

In the early morning hours of August 7, 1944, the spearheads of three German panzer divisions rolled out of the fog and darkness to strike positions held by a single American infantry division in and around the small French town of Mortain. The six-day battle that followed was one of the most dramatic and important actions of World War II. General of the Army Omar Bradley wrote in his memoirs: "In his reckless attack . . . at Mortain, the enemy challenged us to a decision, the most decisive of the French campaign. It was to cost the enemy an Army and gain us France." Bradley's judgment was confirmed by three of the highest-ranking German generals captured after the war—Alfred Jodl, Wilhelm Keitel, and Albrecht Kesselring—who told Allied interrogators the Mortain counterattack was "an astonishing failure" and cited it as one of the two decisive events in the western campaign.

Yet, inexplicably, the American victory at Mortain has been all but forgotten. The battle is unknown to the general public and is usually disregarded or misunderstood by historians. Most accounts of the campaign in France give it scant mention. For instance, in his *History of the Second World War*, respected British analyst B. H. Liddell Hart manages to dismiss the German counterattack in two sentences without even identifying Mortain. The West Point Military History Series contains a brief, badly distorted account of the battle in its volume on the European theater. Even the best recent studies of the French campaign include little about Mortain beyond what Martin Blumenson revealed in *Breakout and Pursuit,* the official U.S. Army version published in 1961. Whereas the other major German counterattack in the west, the Battle of the Bulge, has been the subject of countless books and articles, both scholarly and popular, there is not a single English-language book devoted to the Battle of Mortain.

I will attempt to correct the two major misconceptions that continue to distort most accounts of the battle.

The first is the mistaken belief that General Bradley was forewarned of the German counterattack at Mortain. Even before F. W. Winterbotham's 1974 claim in *The Ultra Secret* that British cryptographers had given the Allied command five days' warning of the German plan, many historians credited Bradley with anticipating the blow and laying a well-prepared trap for the Germans. This view, reinforced by Winterbotham's sensational claims, has persisted, despite evidence that the codebreakers' warning came too late for Bradley to act. Unfortunately, it is a view shared by many veterans of the battle, who blame Bradley for "sacrificing" the National Guard's 30th Division to save the regular army's 1st Division. Actually, as the evidence will show, the Germans achieved almost complete tactical surprise at Mortain, hitting the newly arrived 30th Division before its deployment was complete. Had Bradley anticipated the German attack, surely he would have laid a far better trap, one that wouldn't have cost so many lives and put the entire Allied position in Normandy in such jeopardy.

The second Mortain "myth" regards the role played by air power in stopping the German assault. According to most modern accounts of the campaign, the German attack was halted only by the timely arrival of rocket-firing Typhoons from the British Second Tactical Air Force. German commentators are fond of blaming their defeat on the intervention of Allied air power, perhaps because that explanation preserves the image of German tactical superiority on the ground. However, once again, the evidence is at variance with the popular view. Although air power made an important contribution to the victory at Mortain, the German thrust had already been brought to a halt *before* aircraft appeared over the battlefield in the early afternoon hours of August 7. In reporting their failure to advance, German officers on the spot first blamed American artillery and antitank fire, and only later complained of the murderous attacks from the air.

The fact is that the victory at Mortain was won not by Bradley's brilliant generalship, nor by Allied air superiority, but by the tenacity and courage of the American infantryman. Surprised, outnumbered, and often overrun or surrounded, these men fought the most celebrated divisions in the German army to a standstill. The key to the victory was the heroic performance of the 30th Infantry Division—not the generals or colonels back at headquarters plotting the battle, but the junior officers and sergeants who stepped forward in the crisis and fought their isolated companies and platoons with little direction or help from above.

The Battle of Mortain is important not only because of the decisive role it played in the rapid liberation of France, but because it demonstrated what kind of fighting force the U.S. Army had become by the late summer of 1944. The inferior quality of the American GI has become a popular theme for revisionist historians. It is now accepted as axiomatic that, man-for-man, the Germans were superior soldiers and that the almost uninterrupted string of American victories in Europe was due only to overwhelming numerical and material advantages. One military historian went so far as to calculate the discrepancy between the two armies, using a complex mathematical formula to define precisely the German qualitative superiority. On average, reports Col. Trevor Dupuy, one German solider was worth 1.55 Americans.

The best answer to those perceptions was given by the 30th Division at Mortain—by the "Lost Battalion" of the 120th Infantry Regiment, which held out for six interminable days on Hill 314, cut off and surrounded by superior forces; by the 1st Battalion of the 117th Infantry Regiment, which erected an impenetrable barrier blocking the *Schwerpunkt* (main axis) of the German counterattack on the road to Juvigny; by the antitank platoons of the 823d Tank-Destroyer Battalion, whose men stuck by their inadequate guns in the face of terrible odds on roadblocks at L'Abbaye Blanche and St.-Barthelmy; by the stubborn GIs who refused to be pushed off Hill 285; and by the gunners of the 30th Division's artillery battalions, who often had to pause in their support missions to fight as riflemen to keep from being overrun.

GI cartoonist Bill Mauldin, writing in 1944, characterized the American soldier this way:

They are normal people who have been put where they are, whose actions and feelings have been molded by circumstances.

There are gentlemen and boors; intelligent ones and stupid ones; talented ones and inefficient ones. But when they are all together and they are fighting, despite the bitching and the griping and the gold-bricking and mortal fear, they are facing cold steel and screaming lead and hard enemies and they are advancing and beating the hell out of the opposition.

I have tried to tell the story of these men, as often as possible in their own words. I hope that the reader will accept such men as Reynold Erichson, R. Ernest Frankland, Ronal Woody, John Whitsett, Murray Pulver, George Greene, and the dozens of other voices I have quoted as representative of the Americans who fought and died and won at Mortain. Their story is a dramatic tale, an account of how a collection of civilians from all walks of life and from all over the United States evolved into the finest infantry division in the European theater, and of how, in the crisis at Mortain, they met and defeated the most renowned troops in the German army.

It is the story of a remarkable American victory that has been too long forgotten.

<u>ACKNOWLEDGMENTS</u>

This book would have been impossible without the help of a great many people.

Many thanks to Saul Solow and Frank Towers of the 30th Division Alumni Association, who helped me contact most of the veterans interviewed for this book. In addition, the families of Capt. Reynold Erichson and Lt. Col. Ernest Frankland were extremely helpful in obtaining material related to these two important officers.

Much valuable assistance was provided by the staff at the National Archives in Suitland, Maryland, and the United States Military History Institute in Carlisle, Pennsylvania.

I would also like to thank Carlton Harrell, Edison McIntyre, Elliott Warnock, Bob Whitaker, and John Stokes, who all provided the author some needed help and encouragement in the early stages of the project.

But most of all, I would like to thank the veterans of the 30th Division, who so generously shared their memories with me. It's their story. I only hope I did them justice.

CHAPTER 1: OLD HICKORY

When Adolf Hitler's blitzkrieg crashed into Poland on September 1, 1939, the United States Army consisted of just three skeleton divisions and a total active manpower (including the Army Air Corps) of 188,565 men. It was the world's nineteenth largest army, ranking behind Portugal's, but slightly ahead of Bulgaria's. By contrast, Poland put fifty-two divisions and some 2.5 million men in the field against the Wehrmacht, yet was crushed in less than a month. The rapid collapse of the Poles created no panic in the United States. Surrounded by weak neighbors and wide oceans, Americans felt free to indulge their traditional distaste for standing armies.

The majority of the American men who would, in a few short years, confront the German army on the field of battle were still civilians in 1939—students, farmers, factory workers, businessmen, clerks, soda jerks, and salesmen. Reynold Erichson, who would play a large role at Mortain, was working his family farm near Miles, Iowa. The former high school basketball star was a tall, blond young man of twenty, more interested in the girl next door than in the news from Europe. Ronal Woody was enjoying the return of prosperity in Richmond, Virginia. He had a good job with the American Tobacco Company, making enough money to support his wife and mother, while still saving toward the purchase of the new Buick sedan he had his heart set on. Ernest and Walter Frankland were running the auto supply store their father had founded in Jackson, Tennessee. Their good friend Ben Ammons was writing for the *Jackson Star*. Robert Bradley was a painfully shy premed student at the University of Maryland and one of the youngest members of the American Rocket Society. Murray Pulver, an erect, soft-spoken young man with dark hair and a poker face, was working in a hospital in upstate New York and still dreaming of a career as a professional baseball player.

The war seemed very far away through the winter and spring of 1940. Newspapers labeled the lull in the fighting after the fall of Poland as the "Phony War" or the "Sitzkrieg." America's rearmament had begun, but at a leisurely pace. There was little sense of urgency. Most of the military funds appropriated by Congress went to the navy and to the air corps's heavy bomber force. There was still no need for a powerful army. No hostile nation could invade the United States as long as the U.S. Navy and the friendly Royal Navy of Great Britain were the undisputed masters of the seas. And it was unthinkable that the United States might once again send a large expeditionary force to intervene in another European squabble.

The fall of France in June 1940 shattered the nation's complacency. The French army, regarded at that time as the world's premier fighting force, proved helpless against the German juggernaut. The French collapse left Great Britain isolated and apparently vulnerable to invasion. Italy entered the war on Germany's side. The Soviet Union, extremely unpopular in America after its war with Finland, was on good terms with the Fascist dictators. Suddenly, Axis domination of Europe was a very real possibility, a situation that all but the most ardent isolationists understood would jeopardize the security of the United States.

The time had come to rebuild the U.S. Army.

The Luftwaffe was just beginning its aerial attack on Great Britain when the United States Army held its 1940 summer maneuvers in Louisiana. Elements of the regular army (now grown to 267,767 men) were joined by citizen-soldiers of the National Guard for the war games. No German observers were present, a circumstance that probably spared the U.S. Army a good deal of embarrassment. The panzer leaders would have been amused to see trucks masquerading as tanks, stovepipes used as mortars, and soldiers carrying wooden boards shaped like rifles. Almost a year after the futile sacrifice of Polish cavalry against German armor, the U.S. Army's mock combat opened with a clash between the 1st and the 23d Cavalry divisions, the latter a National Guard unit that had to rent its horses for the occasion.

Despite the comic-opera aspects of the war games, the Louisiana maneuvers were an important training ground for the still-tiny U.S. Army. "We took it seriously, even with all the make-believe weapons," recalled Hubert Pennington, a young National Guardsman from North Carolina. "The way the war was going in Europe, we all felt we'd be in it before long."

Pennington would be in it sooner than he expected. Before leaving Louisiana in August, members of four National Guard divisions were notified they would be called to federal service in September. The other fourteen National Guard divisions would follow within a year. The initial call-up was designed to minimize the impact on the nation's economy. Hence three of the first four divisions came from rural states: the 41st (Idaho, Montana, Oregon, Wyoming, and Washington); the 45th (Oklahoma, Colorado, Arizona, and New Mexico); and the 30th (North Carolina, South Carolina, Tennessee, and Georgia).

"It is the feeling of the War Department that the next six months include the possibility of being the most critical period in the history of the nation," Gen. George C. Marshall, the army's chief of staff, said on a national radio broadcast on September 16. "For the first time in our history we are preparing in time of peace against the possibility of war. We are starting to train an army of citizen-soldiers which may save us from the tragedy of war."

Marshall warned his listeners that it would take some time for American industry to produce the weapons those soldiers would need. However, he insisted the coming war would not be won by tanks, airplanes, and other munitions: "I fear we expect too much of machines. The finest plane or tank or gun in the world is literally worthless without technicians trained as soldiers—hardened, seasoned and highly disciplined to maintain and operate it . . . The decisive element remains the same little-advertised, hard-bitten infantry soldier with his artillery support."

Only one day earlier, Sunday, September 15, in a great battle of men and machines, Britain's Royal Air Force (RAF) had beaten back the Luftwaffe's last major daylight raid on London. Pennington and the other members of his National Guard company were reading accounts of the great air battle as they waited at the guard armory in Durham, North Carolina, to receive their orders. For Pennington, a tall, slender eighteen-year-old, the dramatic reports from London made stirring reading.

"If I'd had the courage, I'd have deserted, jumped a tramp steamer, sailed to England, and joined the RAF," he said.

Pennington had enough trouble just joining the National Guard. "My mother was very much against it. I had to join secretly. The nights we had drill, I'd tell her I was going to the YMCA to play basketball. I finally had to confess when we went away to summer camp. Boy, did she squeal about her baby!"

Pennington was far from the "hard-bitten soldier" General Marshall wanted for his new American army. A self-described mamma's boy, Pennington looked forward to the federal service as a great adventure: "I could be a man, surrounded by other men. I could be profane. I could be as mean as hell and get away with it." Apparently, his enthusiasm was shared by many of the guardsmen. The four infantry regiments that made up the 30th Division were oversubscribed. When several thousand men were released due to age and marital status, eager volunteers vied to fill the vacancies.

Those men were proud of the unit they were joining. The 30th Division was created just before World War I and served with distinction in that conflict. During four months of fighting in 1918, soldiers of the 30th earned more than half the decorations awarded American troops by the British. Members of the division also earned twelve of the seventy-eight Medals of Honor awarded during World War I. Many GIs in the new 30th were direct descendants of the doughboys of the old 30th. Sergeant James Kelly, the 1st Platoon guide for F Company, 120th Infantry, was the son of Sgt. Wade Kelly, who had held the same position when the 30th fought the Boche (Germans) in Belgium. The father of Pvt. Frank Williams of D Company, 120th Infantry, was killed with the same company on November 11, 1918, the last day of World War I.

"We were brainwashed as children," Pennington recalled. "We all had relatives who served in the 30th. I had an uncle who was in the 105th Engineer Battalion. He was a large, profane, rough character. He used to brag about how the 30th cracked the Hindenburg line. I loved his war stories."

The 30th Division was known as the "Old Hickory Division" in honor of Gen. Andrew Jackson, who was born near the North Carolina–South Carolina border and rose to political power in Tennessee. The division's red and blue unit patch featured a large *O* surrounding a stylized *H* with the Roman numeral *XXX* forming the crossbar. The first soldiers to receive the patches in 1918 didn't understand the symbolism and inadvertently sewed them on sideways. The mistake became a part of Old Hickory's tradition and persisted throughout World War I.

Tradition was important to the Southerners who voluntarily joined the National Guard division. They kept alive the memory and the customs of the famous units that made up the division—units like the 120th Infantry Regiment, which traced its lineage to the 1st North Carolina Infantry of the Civil War. The regiment's unofficial motto was "First at Bethel; Fartherest at Gettysburg; Last at Appomattox." On a hot July day in 1863, when Gen. George Pickett's Virginians were stopped on the bloody slope of Cemetery Ridge, Lewis Armistead's Tar Heels fought their way to the crest, briefly cracking the Union line and establishing what came to be known as the high-water mark of the Confederacy. Company F of the 120th was a direct descendant of the Mecklenburg Minute Men, who helped crush Maj. Patrick Ferguson's Tory force at the Battle of King's Mountain in 1780. Company L was even older, tracing its roots back to the Parkton Rangers, formed to fight Indians on the frontier long before the revolutionary war.

The 117th Infantry Regiment was heir to the tradition of the original "Tennessee Volunteers," so-called because when the state was asked to furnish two thousand men for the Mexican war, more than ten thousand answered the call. Several of the regiment's companies claimed descent from the militia force that routed the Shawnee Indians at the Battle of Kanawha in 1774. Others claimed a direct tie to the small group of Tennessee riflemen who fought with Andy Jackson—Old Hickory himself—at the Battle of New Orleans. Another ancestor was Col. John Sevier's Washington County company, which fought alongside the Mecklenburg Minute Men at King's Mountain, just as another generation of young men from Tennessee and North Carolina would fight side by side in the low hills of Normandy in 1944.

The 30th Division assembled at Fort Jackson, just outside Columbia, South Carolina, in the fall of 1940. The old World War I camp, located on a rolling, wooded site crisscrossed by roads named for Confederate war heroes, was overgrown after years of idleness. The regular army's 8th Division, also forming at Fort Jackson, grabbed the few permanent structures on the base. The first arrivals from the 30th

Division found themselves sleeping under the stars. "You'd go to sleep on the ground in a sleeping bag and the next morning you'd wake up and find a bulldozer pushing dirt all over you," recalled Layton Tyner, a private first class from Raleigh, North Carolina.

The soldiers had to rebuild the camp even as they began their training. One of the first jobs was to erect rows and rows of Sibley tents—large pyramids of canvas built on square wooden platforms. Each tent would hold half a squad. The only permanent wooden structures on the base were the mess halls and a handful of rough frame houses thrown up for the ranking officers. Even the stockade was a small tent city, surrounded by a high barbed wire fence. Once the tents were up, the troops began their next project: clearing a large flat field as a parade ground. "The place was overgrown by small scrub oaks, maybe six, eight, ten-foot high," said Claiborn Byrd, a second lieutenant from Pennington's company. "The whole division was put to work clearing it off. We didn't have any excavating tools; just our trenching knives and some small shovels. When we got finished, there wasn't a thing on it except dust. Every time somebody would sneeze, there was a dust storm." The troops nicknamed the site the Dust Bowl and dreaded the endless hours drilling there.

Morale, so high at first, declined as the crisis faded and the novelty of the military experience turned into drudgery. The off-duty situation didn't help. There was little to do in camp. Nearby Columbia, the state capital and site of the University of South Carolina, didn't need or want the GIs. The new soldiers found themselves unwelcome at most of the city's nicer establishments. For instance, a large sign was posted on the front door of the Wade Hampton Hotel: No Dogs or Soldiers Allowed. Most of the town's classier establishments shared those sentiments. "The division there before us were a bunch of bums," Tyner explained. "They had even raped a couple of girls. Naturally, the townspeople weren't happy to see us. We'd have to change into civilian clothes before leaving the camp. If you met a girl, you told her you were a traveling salesman making the run from Charlotte to Atlanta. Only when you got to know her could you tell her the truth."

A few establishments welcomed the soldiers. A cathouse on Washington Street, known as the Rocking Chair, was always busy. The price was two dollars, quite a sum for a private earning just twenty-one dollars a month. "I'll bet some of those girls retired as millionaires," recalled one veteran. Actually, there wasn't all that much for a soldier to spend his money on. Beer was ten cents a bottle and cigarettes were dirt cheap at the post exchange, when they weren't being handed out for free. The army provided the rest: food, clothing, and shelter. True, the shelter was a canvas tent and the clothing was a leftover World War I uniform, complete with Smokey-the-Bear hats and puttees, but the food was plentiful and better than many of the depression-era guardsmen were used to.

There were also a few pleasures in camp. Lewis Cole, a sergeant in D Company, 120th Infantry, remembers the nightly battle of the regimental bands. "Each regiment had its own song," he said. "Ours was 'Roll Out the Barrel.' The 117th always played 'She'll Be Comin' Round the Mountain.' The crest of the 118th had a blue bonnet on it, so they always played 'Put on Your Old Blue Bonnet.' "

All three bands played the popular tune "I'll Be Home in a Year, Dear," in recognition of the fact that the call-up was only supposed to last a year. However, as the fall of 1941 approached, it became clear that the newly trained soldiers wouldn't be released. Many accepted President Roosevelt's decision to extend their service indefinitely. But many others were disgruntled and a few were openly rebellious.

That wasn't the only source of conflict. The 30th was sharing Fort Jackson with the regular army's 8th Division, which was being brought up to strength by the addition of draftees, called up under the nation's first peacetime Selective Service Act. There was considerable friction between the two divisions. The "Old Hickory" soldiers discovered that their unit histories didn't count for much with outsiders. There was, they learned, an unwritten hierarchy within the service: at the top were professionals of the regular army, who looked down on the National Guardsmen, who in turn looked down on the draftees. The situation resulted in some healthy competition on the athletic field and some unhealthy fistfights off it.

"It was like the Civil War again," recalled John Whitsett, a National Guardsman from Reidsville, North Carolina. "We felt like the regular army was made up of fellows who couldn't get a job in civilian life. They resented us because we used to get paid a dollar a day, while they were only getting twenty-one dollars a month. None of us had any use for the draftees. I once had to walk a two-hour [punishment] tour when an officer heard me call one a 'BBB'—that's a breeze-blown bastard."

The task of turning these disparate elements into a combat force capable of meeting the war-tested Wehrmacht fell to Lt. Gen. Lesley J. McNair, a fifty-seven-year-old artilleryman from Minnesota. Appointed chief of staff of General Headquarters in 1940, McNair became commander of Army Ground Forces in March 1942. He designed and oversaw the training program that would expand an out-of-date force of a quarter-million men into an efficient, modern army of almost eight million soldiers. McNair's strategy was to give thorough training to the small army on hand, then break up the trained units and use them as cadres to form larger units. His training program stressed physical endurance and employed realistic exercises whenever possible. Immediately after the first American troops saw action, combat veterans were rushed back to the States to serve as instructors.

McNair also redesigned the organization of the U.S. Army for modern warfare. He gave the standard U.S. infantry division a new shape for World War II. The "square" division of World War I had contained four infantry regiments, divided into two brigades. In order to get a leaner, more mobile division, the army began experimenting in 1937 with a three-regiment division. McNair stripped away one infantry regiment from each National Guard division (using many of the orphan regiments as cadres for new formations). His "triangular" division included three infantry regiments of approximately 3,000 men each, supported by four artillery battalions (each with twelve cannon) and a variety of specialist companies (headquarters, engineers, signals, antitank, quartermaster, and medical). Each infantry regiment contained three battalions; each in turn was divided into three rifle companies (each with an assigned strength of 212 men), supported by a heavy-weapons company and a headquarters company. Special units, such as tank-destroyer battalions and antiaircraft batteries, would be attached to divisions as needed.

In the reorganization, the 30th Division lost the 118th Infantry Regiment from Georgia, which was shipped off to garrison Iceland, and the 121st Regiment from South Carolina, which was rushed to the West Coast soon after Pearl Harbor. Even worse, the two remaining regiments, the 117th and 120th, were stripped several times for cadres, reducing the division's manpower from a high of 12,400 men in June 1942 to barely 3,000 men two months later.

The dispersal of Pennington's company (D Company, 120th Infantry) provides a good illustration of how the 30th was used to speed the army's rapid expansion. "The first exodus came when they began to expand the air corps," Pennington said. "Privates could transfer over and become flying sergeants. We lost a lot of guys right there."

Lieutenant Byrd, who left the company to join the 30th's first antitank platoon, saw the dispersal differently. "We were allowed to pick the candidates for the first cadre," he said. "We got rid of a lot of deadbeats and goof-offs. Then they got smart. The second cadre, they selected themselves. The third cadre, they let us volunteer. We lost a lot of good men then, because by that time, it looked like the 30th would remain a training formation and never get into combat."

Major General Henry Russell, the 30th's National Guard commander, estimated that more than a fourth of the men in the original division ended up as officers. Warren Giles, who enlisted in the guard as a private and ended his military career as a two-star general, did a careful study of his original company from Athens, Tennessee. Of the 108 men who reported to Fort Jackson in 1940, three eventually became generals, three reached the rank of colonel, seven became lieutenant colonels, five ended up as majors, four as captains, and five as lieutenants.

The men of D Company, 120th Infantry, ended up everywhere: Harvey Everett transferred to the 1st Armored Division and saw early combat against the Germans in Tunisia; Bill Rowe was sent to China, where he trained troops in Chiang Kai-shek's army and helped build the Ledo Road; Truman George became a jumpmaster in the 82d Airborne; Ed Tiller joined the military police and ended up as a member of Gen. Dwight Eisenhower's bodyguard; Lt. Dan Edwards was sent to the Pacific, where he served on the staff of Lt. Gen. Robert Eichelberger and was awarded the Distinguished Service Cross on New Guinea; Walter Rigsbee, the baby of the company (he was sent home when the army learned he was only sixteen, but he returned to Fort Jackson after his seventeenth birthday), joined the 45th Division in Italy and was captured during the ill-fated Rapido River crossing; Sgt. Lewis Cole went to artillery school, rose to the rank of captain, and commanded an antiaircraft battery in North Africa; Lt. Claiborn Byrd trained with the rangers and became a lieutenant colonel with the 100th Division, which saw action in southern France.

*   *   *

Pennington and three of his buddies made a short move, leaving the 120th to help reactivate the 119th Infantry, a World War I unit brought out of mothballs to become the 30th's third infantry regiment. Pennington, the once-frail mamma's boy, had grown into a husky man after two years of army chow and training. He had also become a competent soldier, a sergeant in the 119th's Cannon Company. However, he was becoming discouraged by the endless training routine. American troops were in combat in North Africa and the South Pacific, yet the 30th remained a training pool for incoming recruits.

"I didn't see how they could fight the war without me," Pennington said. "Some of us were outraged the war might pass us by. Then one day an officer lined us up and told us to look at the men around us. 'Those are the men you're going to die with,' he said."

The 30th's escape from duty as a replacement pool was due to a vigorous lobbying effort by Maj. Gen. Leland Hobbs, the new division commander. He was actually the division's third commander in less than a year. Major General Russell had brought the 30th into federal service. The aging National Guard officer was the brother of a Georgia senator and, like many of his officers, was a wealthy and influential man in civilian life. The division's top commanders were replaced in the spring of 1942 in a "purge" (to use Russell's word) that to this day excites the bitterness of National Guard veterans.

"They just wanted to open up command spots for their West Point buddies," said Flossie Roberts, a lieutenant from Raleigh, North Carolina. "They said the National Guard officers were too old and too soft. Let me tell you, I served in World War II and Korea, and the best officers I ever saw were National Guard officers."

Walter Johnson, the West Pointer who would command the 117th Infantry in 1944 and 1945, agreed that the National Guard veterans in his unit were "damn fine officers . . . the best." General Russell, in defending his performance as commander of the division, pointed to the Tennessee and Carolina maneuvers in 1941. During one scenario, Old Hickory was matched against two regular army divisions commanded by J. Lawton Collins (the same Lightning Joe who would command the VII Corps at Mortain). The chief umpire ruled that the 30th "had simply outguessed and outmaneuvered the remainder of the Corps." In a later scenario, which matched the 30th against the 2d Armored

Division, commanded by the already-celebrated George Patton, a detachment of Russell's infantry surrounded and captured three tanks, one of which left the area in defiance of a ruling by the umpires that it would be destroyed if it attempted to escape. Russell later learned that Patton, who had offered his men a bounty of twenty-five dollars for the capture of an "enemy" general, was inside the offending tank. "Patton had a lot of fine qualities," Russell later wrote, "but fair play in maneuvers wasn't one of them."

Despite the success of the 30th Division in maneuvers, Russell and his top commanders were removed as McNair and Marshall ruthlessly purged the higher-ranking civilian-officers from all the National Guard divisions. According to Russell, no guard officer would be allowed to rise above the rank of lieutenant colonel. Indeed, the most prominent guard veterans to remain in the 30th were a pair of lieutenant colonels from Jackson, Tennessee. Ernest Frankland was given command of the 1st Battalion of the 117th. Frankland's brother Walter was named the 30th Division's supply officer (G-4).

Russell was replaced briefly by Maj. Gen. William Simpson, who oversaw the dispersal of three-fourths of the division's manpower before turning over the remnants of the division to Hobbs on September 12, 1942. Leland Hobbs was a big, bluff man, a professional soldier with friends scattered throughout the army's high command. Hobbs had been a football and baseball star at West Point. His classmate and close friend Omar Bradley recalled, "He had a big, strong jaw and a stubborn streak a mile wide. Nobody could get by him on the football field. His division [became] a reflection of his character. Hobbs was a hard charger."

Hobbs graduated in 1915, a member of the famous "class the stars fell on" (which included Bradley, Eisenhower, and so many other future generals). Hobbs saw his first combat action that fall in a skirmish with Mexican bandits in Sonora, Mexico. To his intense disappointment, the young officer didn't get to France until a few days before the end of World War I, and he didn't see combat in that conflict. Between wars, Hobbs taught at West Point and served in a variety of infantry assignments before finally inheriting command of the 30th Division.

It was Hobbs, an emotional and often theatrical leader—some of his men called him "Hollywood Hobbs"—who obtained a promise from McNair to refrain from further manpower calls on the 30th. The division would be allowed to remain intact to train for eventual deployment in combat. However, that deployment would not come quickly. First, the replacement-filled Old Hickory Division would have to be retrained almost from scratch, a sixteen-month process.

By the time the 30th arrived at Camp Blanding, near Gainesville, Florida, in October 1942, the division had lost much of its regional character. The 120th Infantry Regiment contained only a small core of men from the North Carolina National Guard unit that had given it birth. The remaining handful of Tar Heels were outnumbered by the draftees and the enlistees from all parts of the country.

The changes started at the top. Colonel John Manning, the National Guard commander since 1937, was replaced during the purge by forty-six-year-old Col. Hammond Davis Birks, a round-faced, balding professional soldier from Chicago. Birks was not a West Pointer but had studied at the University of Chicago. He was commissioned a second lieutenant in 1917 and remained in the service after World War I.

"Whenever [Birks] looked at the promotion list, he would shake his head and say, 'That's what happens when you're not a ring man,' " James Lyles, the 120th's sergeant major, recalled. "He always felt he was being passed by because he was not a West Pointer."

Veterans of the 120th have mixed opinions of Birks. Some felt he was, like Hobbs, a bit of a glory hound. Others respected his personal courage and his aggressiveness. "He was fearless," Lyles said. "He constantly exposed himself to fire, but he never got a scratch. He led a charmed life in combat."

The small cadre of holdovers were joined at Camp Blanding by a host of newcomers. Among them were Ronal Woody and Robert Bradley.

Woody, a newly commissioned second lieutenant, had given up his job with American Tobacco to enlist soon after Pearl Harbor. He was almost rejected: "I was so excited during my physical, my pulse rate went over the limit," he explained. "I had to talk the doctor into checking me again." Left behind in Richmond were Woody's wife, his mother, and his beautiful new Buick sedan.

Bradley could have avoided service and continued his premed studies at the University of Maryland. However, he found it increasingly difficult to concentrate on books with America at war. "It seemed to many of the students that we should be doing something to help the men in the Armed Forces," he later wrote. Bradley quit school and requested service as a combat medic. After a brief training stint at Camp Lee, Virginia, he joined the 30th Division at Camp Blanding. The same process was going on in the 117th Infantry, which lost its National Guard commander, Col. R. H. Bond, while gaining a large contingent of draftees.

"We got a whole bunch of boys from up in the mountains of North Carolina," recalled Sgt. James Waldrop, a National Guard veteran from Jackson, Tennessee. "I remember some of them made a little whiskey back home. 'Course, we had a few from Tennessee who made some, too. I think those boys used to get together and compare notes."

Moonshiners aside, the division's most important newcomer was Brig. Gen. William Kelly Harrison, who assumed the newly created job of assistant division commander. Hobbs stole the highly regarded Bill Harrison from the War Plans Division, where he had worked closely with one of the army's rising stars, Brig. Gen. Dwight Eisenhower. The contrast between the huge, pompous, profane Hobbs and his quiet, diminutive, religious assistant couldn't have been more pronounced. Hobbs was an extrovert—"always bragging or complaining," according to one contemporary—who ran the division from a distance, whereas Harrison was a tight-lipped disciplinarian who relished the detail work Hobbs detested. The two men would complement each other well, even though Harrison ended up with little respect for his commander, whom he labeled "strictly a barracks soldier."

"Eisenhower said they were the best command team he had," said Roy Snow, a guardsman from Raleigh, North Carolina. "All I know is, Billy Harrison was the brains and guts of our division."

It was Harrison, the son of a prominent U.S. Navy officer and the grandson of a Confederate cavalry general, who assumed direct control of the 30th's training. He started by trying to instill his own philosophy of leadership. First, a commander must impart his orders precisely, so that each man knows exactly what he is expected to do; second, a commander must set a personal and visible example for his men; third, a commander must hold his officers and men accountable for following his orders exactly.

Harrison made certain his own performance was the embodiment of those three principles. "I used to make a regular inspection of the troops, both in training and in combat," he said. "If I found a squad that hadn't bothered digging slit trenches, I didn't scold or berate the men. I just fined the lieutenant twenty-five dollars out of his next pay. He and his men got the message. If something was being done in a superior manner, I called up whoever was running the outfit and congratulated him. You see, I tried to get everybody to realize I wasn't looking to find fault; I was looking for things to commend. I was on their side." As Harrison got that message across, morale in the division began to rise.

"We knew two things about him," reported Capt. Saul Solow, one of the 30th's new officers. "He was tough and he was fair. He had our total, unreserved respect."

Waldrop, who remained with the 117th as a platoon sergeant, spent many hours at Camp Blanding talking to the assistant division commander. He found Harrison unlike almost every other soldier in one respect.

"I never heard him use a curse word," Waldrop said. "He'd say 'sugar' where another man would say 'shit.' I can remember one incident, during the Battle of the Bulge. I was stuck in a jeep, being held up by an 88, when another jeep came grinding up in the snow, making a lot of noise, bringing down fire on us. I started cursing the driver of that jeep out: 'You stupid son of a bitch . . .' Then I saw it was General Harrison. Boy, did I start apologizing fast. But he just laughed and said, 'Forget it, Jimmy.' "

Profanity in the heat of combat was one thing. Harrison was less tolerant of casual profanity. It was the one thing he disliked about his old friend Dwight Eisenhower.

"I'd known Ike since West Point," Harrison said. "He could hardly say a whole sentence without taking the Lord's name in vain. He'd say 'My Jesus Christ . . .' incessantly."

Harrison, who taught Sunday school every week until the division was shipped overseas, didn't need profanity to get his message across.

"The General didn't storm and rave," recalled Capt. Robert Kline. "He just quietly and effectively made his point. And let me assure you, nobody in the area missed the point, either!"

The 30th Division spent seven months at Camp Blanding before moving to Camp Atterbury, Indiana, for advanced training. There, more newcomers arrived, including a newly commissioned second lieutenant from

Iowa, Reynold Erichson. The tall, blond farmer had left his sweetheart—
the girl next door had become his fiancée—to enlist in the army less
than a month after Pearl Harbor. After a brief stint as an enlisted man,
Erichson was selected to attend officer candidate school at Fort Benning,
Georgia. He joined the 120th Infantry Regiment in time to participate
in maneuvers with the Second Army in Tennessee, where the 30th was
credited with knocking out several "enemy" battalions with a tricky
double-envelopment maneuver. Erichson's first taste of mock combat
was far more realistic than the 1940 Louisiana war games the old-timers
remembered.

Realistic or not, the extended training process was discouraging to
some impatient officers. The lengthy wait was more than some men
could stand. Lieutenant Woody, who passed up a chance for promotion and a soft stateside job as a finance officer, got into trouble for
demanding a transfer to a unit overseas: "Five of us went in to see
Colonel Birks and ask him to send us to a combat outfit," Woody said.
"He threw us out of his office. That was my downfall with Birks. After
that, every time my promotion [to first lieutenant] would come up,
he'd knock it down."

Birks's angry response was predictable. Even before assuming command of the 120th, he had worked to save some of the regiment's best
men from the army's personnel department. While serving as the 120th's
athletics officer in early 1942, Birks formed a partnership with Lyles
to hide first-rate officers in obscure billets. The three-hundred-
pound top sergeant, nicknamed Mini-butt (later shortened to Mini),
was promoted to warrant officer and became the regiment's personnel officer. Together, he and Birks were able to retain a small but
well-qualified cadre for the 120th: men like Ellis Williamson, a National Guardsman from Raleigh who began his service career as an
enlisted trombone player in the regimental band and ended it as a major
general; men like Robert Hobgood, an enlisted clerk in the early days
at Fort Jackson, who was promoted to lieutenant and developed into
a top-flight company commander.

Obviously, Birks believed that Woody was worth saving. Four of
the five officers who barged into his office demanding a transfer were
shipped out to the most obscure backwater billets Birks could find.
But he held on to Woody, keeping him in the doghouse until the day
when the impatient young officer's skills would be needed.

That day was coming closer. In early February 1944, the 30th Division was shifted to Camp Miles Standish, outside Boston. The troops were alerted to prepare for overseas movement.

"Every day we'd pack up, secure everything, march out, march around all day, then march back into camp again," recalled John Whitsett, who had become a sergeant in the 120th's Headquarters Company. "After a few days of that, I figured I'd outsmart them. I used a piece of stovepipe to fill my pack and left all my heavy stuff like blankets and spare clothes in my locker. My pack was so light I could walk all day. I figured it was just another practice embarkation. Only this time, we got outside camp and didn't stop. We boarded a train that took us right to the dock. We marched off the train, up the gangplank, and right on board the SS *Argentina*."

The rest of the division was split between the SS *Brazil* and the SS *John Ericsson*. The three transports left Boston on February 12, 1944, in the midst of a blinding snowstorm. The convoy they joined was the largest to sail from the United States up to that time. Despite several submarine scares, the 30th Division reached Great Britain with no problems on the voyage worse than the bad food, overcrowding, and seasickness. The 120th Regiment disembarked at Glourock, Scotland, greeted by the odd strains of bagpipes playing "The Beer-Barrel Polka." Trains carried the unit south to Bognor Regis, a resort on the Channel coast, where the troops endured more training.

The division received a major addition in England when the 823d Tank-Destroyer Battalion was attached to bolster the 30th's inadequate antitank capabilities. The 823d would stick with Old Hickory from Normandy to the Elbe.

As the first days of summer approached, every man in the 30th knew that the invasion of France was imminent, but only the divisional staff knew that the target was Normandy. The 30th Division was not assigned to the initial assault. It was to land on Omaha Beach as soon as the beachhead was established. On June 5, 1944, one day after the fall of Rome, General Hobbs gave a speech to the men of the 120th Regiment, telling them, "You will remember this day." What Hobbs didn't know was that because of bad weather, the landings would be delayed twenty-four hours.

On D day, June 6, the American army landed two airborne and three infantry divisions in France. The 4th Division stormed ashore against light resistance on Utah Beach. Both the veteran 1st Division and the untested 29th Division, a National Guard unit that still retained its Maryland-Virginia character, suffered heavy losses assaulting the bluffs protecting Omaha Beach. To the east, the British and Canadians established a firm lodgment and began what was expected to be a quick dash to Caen. The men of the 30th were told they would be the next American division sent to Normandy.

The individual units were taken to their staging area near Southampton, where the men were issued two hundred francs, a supply of cigarettes, and several boxes of K rations. At the embarkation ports, the troops received their final briefings, checked their equipment, and waited for the moment they had been preparing for—some for almost four years.

The moment of truth had finally arrived for Old Hickory.

CHAPTER 2: AN EXPENSIVE EDUCATION

The 30th's gunners preceded the division's riflemen to Normandy. One of the first units to cross the English Channel was the 230th Field Artillery Battalion. Normally attached to the 120th Infantry Regiment, the battalion and its twelve 105mm cannon were rushed to Omaha Beach on June 7 to support the 29th Division, which had lost much of its artillery in the surf on D day.

Sergeant John Whitsett's antitank platoon was also given an early introduction to combat. The National Guard veteran watched his unit load at Southampton just three days after D day. Three trucks towing 57mm antitank guns drove directly on board a massive LST (landing ship, tank). Whitsett followed in the platoon's jeep. The GIs traded their K rations for a chance to visit the seamen's mess. It was a toss-up as to which Whitsett enjoyed more, the hot navy chow or the spectacle of the sailors experimenting with the packaged army rations the GIs found so boring and tasteless.

Whitsett's crossing turned serious only as the LST approached Omaha Beach. "The first thing I saw were all these sunken ships," he recalled. "I thought we'd lost our whole navy. But one of the sailors told me we'd sunk them ourselves, on purpose, to make a breakwater." The artificial harbor was not yet complete, and Whitsett's platoon had to disembark into the surf. "The guy maneuvering the craft let us off too soon. I drove the jeep off the ramp and it immediately went under-water. Everything was waterproofed with this stuff—it looked a lot like clay—so the engine kept running, even though I couldn't hear it under the water. I was trying to drive standing up with the water up to my neck."

Despite the mishap, Whitsett's platoon cleared the beach without loss and halted in a nearby field to remove the waterproofing from the equipment. Fortunately, the first items cleaned were the three antitank guns. The process had just been completed when Whitsett looked up and saw a German tank at the edge of the clearing.

"A goddamn tank!" he shouted, pointing at the panzer.

"I forgot everything I had learned. No distance to target. No direction. No order for type of ammo. None of that—I just pointed." Whitsett's gun got off the first shot and missed the tank by a hundred yards. "His turret was turning to knock out my gun when the gun on my left hit him on the side and he blew up. I realized then how lucky I was. I knew I'd better get myself together if I wanted to live."

Whitsett was fortunate to survive his first exposure to combat. Many didn't. The men of the 30th quickly learned that when they crossed the English Channel, they were crossing into a different world.

Some didn't even get ashore before the lesson was driven home. The ship carrying Sgt. Floyd Montgomery's platoon to Normandy was attacked by German E-boats. An escorting destroyer drove off the enemy gunboats, but in the process, the small transport was sprayed by gunfire. Nobody was hurt, but the platoon came under fire again when it disembarked as the Germans were shelling the beach. Private First Class Leo Temkin's introduction to the war came as he waded ashore at Omaha: "I saw heads floating in the water. Dead GIs from D day. It scared the life out of me." If that wasn't enough, his unit's first casualty was the squad's very popular sergeant.

An LST transporting three batteries of the 113th Field Artillery Battalion hit a mine in mid-Channel. The ship survived, but three members of the battalion were killed, eight were wounded, and twenty were reported missing. That was a severe blow to the division's only 155mm gun battalion.

Lieutenant Ronal Woody's arrival was more uncomfortable than dangerous: "We sat out in the Channel, in water up to our waist, on these flat barges, while they waited to take us in. Then they didn't take us in close enough. One little fellow next to me jumped off and went 'bloop-bloop-bloop' under water. I grabbed him by the seat of his pants and pushed and pulled him on in, then turned him loose." It didn't take long before Woody got his baptism of fire: "It was combat by the time you got to the top of the hill. They were firing tracers over the top of our heads."

The 30th's Service Company was landed on Utah Beach by mistake. Captain Layton Tyner, a National Guardsman from Raleigh, North Carolina, organized a convoy to drive the twelve miles down the coast road to Isigny, where the division was concentrating. Along the way, his convoy passed through Carentan, just as American paratroopers were driving the last German defenders from the town. The confusion was so great—and the newly arrived soldiers so green—that Tyner's men didn't even realize they were passing through the middle of a firefight.

The beachhead was still so narrow that German mortars could reach the boats unloading in the surf. General Bradley decided to use the 30th Division to push the enemy back from the narrow corridor connecting Utah and Omaha Beaches. On the night of June 13, the 120th Infantry Regiment took over the front line from the 101st Airborne, which had been in place since its scattered drop the night before the D-day landings. Supported by fire from battleships offshore and by the 230th Field Artillery Battalion (back from its brief tour with the 29th Division), the 120th launched its first attack on the morning of June 15, driving the Germans two and a half miles south to the Vire et Taute Canal. Most of the regiment's casualties were inflicted by enemy artillery and land mines. A strong German counterattack was broken up by the 3d Battalion, which first threw back an infantry attack in hand-to-hand combat, then broke the assault by calling in artillery to within twenty-five yards of its front lines.

"After the ranging shots, we got the order to 'Fire at will!'" said Lt. Ed McArdle, the executive officer of one of the 230th's four-gun batteries. "Then we got the word, 'Keep pouring it on.' We had everybody, including officers, packing ammo. Those tubes turned bright red from the heat. One colonel [with the 120th] said he thought it was the fire of the whole corps. He couldn't believe one battalion could shoot that much ammo."

The Germans were impressed, too. One prisoner of war told his interrogator the 30th Division artillery was "terrific, firing three hundred shots to our one. Its firing is terrifyingly accurate. It could hit a pencil with three shots."

The 120th Regiment's two-and-a-half-mile gain was a significant advance over terrain broken by hedgerows. The tall, dense shrubs were usually grown atop high dirt embankments and divided the fields into small areas, often no larger than a building lot. Sometimes the hedgerows and supporting banks were double, leaving a ready-made trench between them. The formidable shrubbery proved impenetrable to men and vehicles, including tanks. The *bocage,* as the hedgerow country was known to the French, proved highly advantageous to the German defenders, turning each field into a separate battlefield and negating the American advantages of mobility and air power. For the riflemen, life in the *bocage* became one long nightmare.

"We lived from hedgerow to hedgerow," recalled Royce Spann, a private first class in Company C of the 120th Infantry. "We didn't know what hot food was. We lived on K rations when we could get them. Sometimes we got nothing but a candy bar. We always slept two to a foxhole in one-hour shifts. One guy would stay awake in case somebody came up. It would be suicide for both men to sleep at the same time. We were that close. One time we occupied a German slit trench just behind a hedgerow; then we looked up and saw the barrel of an 88 sticking through over us. I can tell you, we backed up fast."

The German 88mm rifle was a fearsome weapon, especially to tankers, who knew that the high-velocity shell could penetrate the armor of their Shermans at almost any range. For the riflemen, there were other horrors: land mines, mortars, a multibarreled rocket launcher known as a screaming meemie, and a wooden rifle bullet that would hit a man and splinter into a million pieces. At least, that was what the GIs thought when they found the wooden bullets in abandoned German trenches. "Everybody believed it at the time," said Dr. William Allen, a surgeon with the 117th Infantry. "It was supposed to make a horrible wound when it hit you. But I never saw a casualty from one. Later, I found out they were for launching rifle grenades."

There were other imaginary fears. A rumor spread that German snipers were imitating the call of the hoot owl to communicate in the dark. Nervous GIs took a fearful toll on the inoffensive night-owl population of Normandy. The division was rousted on several occasions by reports of poison gas attacks. "The gas alarm went off the night before St.-Lô," said Lt. Roy Snow, a guard veteran. "I've never been more scared. Everybody was scrambling for his gas mask and I couldn't find mine. Luckily, it turned out to be a false alarm." The July 20 gas alarm, which spread to most of the troops in Normandy, was triggered when a demolition team was exploding some captured German ammunition, and the fumes caused discoloration of the gas-detecting paint on some nearby vehicles.

It was just another lesson for men who learned fast or died.

"We were learning the nature of fear and how to handle it," said Maj. Warren Giles, the 117th Regiment's intelligence officer. "[The troops] learned some important lessons: the ability to distinguish sounds that occur in battle, the ability to evaluate the relative danger of various types of fire, and to remain cool in the face of fire."

The enlisted men weren't the only ones who had to learn how to deal with combat. When the 30th first took up its positions in Normandy, the order came down from division headquarters for the men to engage in calisthenics every morning beside their foxholes. The German response was to lob artillery toward the exposed GIs as they exercised. "The calisthenics plan didn't prove too successful," one unit historian observed laconically.

It didn't take the men of Old Hickory long to learn how to remain cool in the presence of Bed-check Charlie, a lone German bomber that would fly over the lines soon after sundown each night and drop a few bombs. Charlie was regarded as little more than an inconvenience, like the swarms of mosquitos that bred in the flooded river basins or the rain that fell with dismaying regularity during June and July, turning foxholes into quagmires. For a man unable to bathe or obtain clean clothes, the mud could be as much of a nuisance as the enemy.

"All you could do was wait for your muddy clothes to dry, then try to slap the dust off," said Sergeant Montgomery, a farm boy from Alabama. "We learned to survive on a canteen of water a day. That was all we had to shave, bathe, and drink."

For Snow the miserable conditions were worse than the enemy. "The first night we landed, I got pinned down in the dark. I was lying in a pile of cow dung. That cow must have had scurvy. You can imagine what it smelled like. I had to wear those filthy clothes until July 28th."

Private First Class Spann remembers getting one break during this period. His platoon was pulled off the line and sent to a rest area for a shave and a shower. "They had a little tent-shower with an alarm clock," he said. "You got exactly one minute in the shower, so you had to do some fast washing." The clean GIs then had to put their filthy uniforms back on and return to the front. Their break was less than twenty-four hours. Another veteran of the hedgerows claimed that his platoon beat the system. Just as the alarm went off, a flight of German planes buzzed the rest area. The service troops dove for their slit trenches, but the dirty GIs continued to shower for precious minutes until the planes, which they had recognized as a recon flight, flew away.

Sergeant Hubert Pennington, a platoon sergeant in the 119th's Cannon Company, made frequent visits to the front line as an artillery spotter, but he usually slept and ate a few hundred yards behind the line, where conditions weren't quite so bleak. "We lived a much better life than the riflemen," he said. "All a rifleman did was move from hole to hole until he died."

Pennington was a holdover from the 30th's National Guard days, but as the division's casualties mounted in the hedgerows, more and more replacements arrived, and Old Hickory moved even further from its regional roots. Some of the newcomers had combat experience. Private John Weekly, a twenty-year-old from Glanville, Ohio, came ashore on D day with a ranger battalion. His unit took so many losses it was disbanded, and Weekly ended up in Company H of the 120th Infantry. But he found losses heavy in the 30th, too. "The night I went in, I was an ammo bearer. By daylight, I was second gunner." Everett Kelly, a West Virginia farmer, also landed on June 6, surviving the hell of Omaha Beach with the 29th Division. He's still not sure why he was shifted to the 117th Infantry Regiment.

The 30th got another veteran addition when the 743d Tank Battalion was assigned to support Old Hickory with its Shermans. The unit had won a Presidential Unit Citation for its performance on D day, when the battalion helped turn the tide on Omaha Beach with the handful of amphibious tanks that survived the deadly swim to the beach.

However, the veteran replacements were exceptions. Most of the newcomers were as raw as the men of the 30th had been just a few weeks before. Private Paul Nethery, a truck driver from Louisville, trained with the 97th Division but joined Company E of the 120th Infantry on the Vire Canal. Private Ken Parker, a Detroit office worker, joined Company B of the same regiment. He was pleased to find the old hands talkative and friendly, but he was surprised to discover that the combat veterans rarely cursed. Why? he asked one old-timer. "Probably most of the guys figure that swearing won't change your luck any," he was told. "Might even hurt it. But wait until we get in a real tight situation, when we're really desperate. Then you'll hear 'em let rip. Can't seem to stop them."

Parker's company commander, Capt. Howard Greer, was one of the few North Carolina National Guard officers to remain in the 120th. However, his platoon commander was another newcomer, Lt. Murray Pulver. The onetime baseball fanatic from upstate New York had entered the army in 1940 with the New York National Guard. His division, the 27th, was rushed to the West Coast one day after Pearl Harbor, then spent most of 1942 defending Maui, Hawaii. Pulver graduated from officer candidate school in 1943, then was assigned to the 75th Division, which was training at Fort Leonard Wood in Missouri. He was one of two dozen officers stripped from the 75th a month before D day and rushed to Europe to serve as infantry replacements.

The sudden transfer from Missouri to the Vire Canal came at an inconvenient time for the young officer, whose wife was expecting their first child in June. It was July 1 when Pulver joined the 30th, and the anxious officer had heard nothing from home since leaving the States.

A few days after joining B Company, Pulver got his baptism of fire— but not from the enemy. An American sergeant, distraught over the loss of many of his friends in a recent skirmish, grabbed a Browning Automatic Rifle (BAR) and began to fire it wildly in all directions, pinning down his own squad. When one of the company's veteran officers refused to go after the shell-shocked sergeant, Greer sent Pulver. The young officer cautiously edged his way along a hedgerow until he was close enough to hear the sergeant cursing and yelling for the "dirty Krauts to come out and fight!" Pulver shouted back, "Sarge, if you'll hold up a minute, I know where there's a whole bunch of Krauts." The firing stopped and Pulver heard the sergeant eject an empty magazine. Before he could reload, Pulver leapt forward and grabbed the gun by the barrel. It was so hot the young officer badly burned his right hand through his leather gloves. But the sergeant collapsed in tears and Pulver was able to take the gun away from him.

*   *   *

The 30th Division made little progress for several weeks after the drive to the Vire Canal. Its job was to hold the southern boundary of the beachhead while other forces drove west to capture the port of Cherbourg and clear the northern tip of the Cotentin Peninsula. However, on July 7, a major attack involving all three corps active in Normandy was launched in an attempt to break the stalemate in the hedgerows. Old Hickory was given a major role in the offensive.

The 117th Infantry Regiment, which had staged demonstration river crossings at Camp Benning in 1943, was to lead the assault across the Vire River. The 2d Battalion jumped off at 0430 and quickly seized a foothold on the far shore. The regiment's other two battalions followed at dawn. However, the 3d Battalion stalled soon after the crossing, forcing the 1st Battalion to back up at the crossing site under heavy German fire. Lieutenant Colonel R. Ernest Frankland, the 1st Battalion's commander, crawled through a muddy ditch to the river, where he spotted a 3d Battalion officer on the other side. Shouting across the narrow river, he asked what was the delay. The officer shouted back, explaining he had no orders.

"Orders, hell!" Frankland yelled. "We've got to move."

His outburst evidently got results, because the 3d Battalion cleared the riverbank, allowing the 1st Battalion to cross. By 1000 hours, the entire 117th Regiment was formed on the south side of the Vire and moving east. Casualties were heavy, including Frankland's exec, Maj. Wilfred Chandler, who was killed during the river crossing, but the regiment reached its objective, the high ground around Les Landes, by 2100 hours.

The 1st Battalion of the 120th Infantry was designated to spearhead the attack across the Vire et Taute Canal toward the key intersection at St.-Jean de Daye. Although the terrain was particularly difficult—because of the flooded lowlands, engineers had to construct several causeways for vehicles—the 1st Battalion needed just nine hours to cover the three miles to its objective.

The rapid advance appeared to indicate a crack in the German defenses. That night, the 3d Armored Division attempted to pass through the lines of the 30th Division for a quick dash to St.-Lô. However, limited by the single bridge over the Vire River and the constricted area of the bridgehead, the quick dash turned into a massive traffic jam. When the tankers tried to leave the crowded roads and move cross-country, they found their way blocked by the thickest concentration of hedgerows in Normandy. The confusion gave the Germans time to rush the Panzer Lehr Division into the breach. The veteran armored unit was able to set up its roadblocks and bring the advance to a halt.

There would be no quick, easy armored dash to St.-Lô. Instead, the city had to be taken by the infantry in one of the most bitter, bloody actions of the war. The 30th Division fought its way up the high ridge west of the city against the German 5th Parachute Division. The paratroopers considered themselves elite troops, but they could only slow, not stop, the advancing GIs. The 30th paid a heavy price for its gains, especially among junior officers. Company C of the 120th Infantry lost three company commanders in one four-hour stretch. By nightfall of July 17, eight of the twelve company commanders who had crossed the Vire et Taute Canal with the 120th Infantry ten days earlier had become casualties.

Lieutenant Pulver, still awaiting word of the birth of his child, was forced to take command of B Company's two lead platoons during the advance. He rushed to the front, arriving just as a German tank appeared, its gun blazing and paratroopers advancing on both sides. Pulver shouted for a bazooka team. Only one man appeared, Pvt. Werner Goertz, who explained that the bazooka gunner had been killed and he didn't know how to fire the unfamiliar device. Pulver ordered Goertz to load, then took the weapon himself. The lieutenant had had a dry practice run with a bazooka in England but had never fired a live round. He knew that the weapon was notoriously inaccurate. The small shaped charge had to score a solid hit on a vulnerable spot to penetrate a panzer's armor.

"By the time I was ready to shoot, the enemy tank was about one hundred yards away," Pulver recalled. "German soldiers were moving along both sides of the tank, firing their rifles at us. I took careful aim and sent the missile on its way. Bull's-eye! Lucky for me, I hit it in the right spot. The tank exploded and started to burn. Some of the enemy soldiers close to the tank were killed. We took care of most of the rest with our rifle fire. A few got away."

Pulver's day was far from over. He was ordered to attack the next hedgerow. Shouting "Let's go!" Pulver jumped over the barrier, landing in a hole on top of three stunned Germans. Before any of his men could follow him over the hedgerow, Pulver captured four more prisoners. Soon after the platoon secured the position, a call came from Company C for a bazooka team. Pulver and Goertz crawled over to the next field to see what they could do. Captain Robert Hobgood, the company commander, pointed out a panzer behind a stone wall fifty yards away. Pulver was about to fire when the tank's machine gunner opened up on their position. The first shells splattered to the left, giving Pulver time to duck. When the gun traversed to the right, he popped up, fired the bazooka, then ducked again. Pulver failed to see his second direct hit of the day, but the machine gun stopped firing and soon the tank's ammunition began exploding. Unfortunately, the last burst of fire from the tank's machine gun had killed Hobgood, the onetime company clerk who had become one of the regiment's finest combat officers.

Pulver, who was untouched, was awarded the Distinguished Service Cross for his efforts that day—two confirmed tank kills and the single-handed capture of seven prisoners.

The heavy toll in company commanders finally rescued 2d Lt. Ronal Woody from Colonel Birks's doghouse. Woody had been assigned to the 30th's pioneer battalion and spent his first six weeks in France as a demolitions specialist. That changed one night during the St.-Lô offensive.

"It was about two or three in the morning and I was down in a good, warm foxhole, reading *Stars and Stripes* with my flashlight," Woody recalled. "A runner came up and told me to report to headquarters on the double. That wasn't unusual, except he told me to bring all my gear. When I got there, Colonel Birks said I was to take over Company G. I was their fourth company commander that day."

Lieutenant Colonel Peter Ward, the regimental exec, spoke up and said, "This means a promotion for you, too."

Woody responded angrily. "I told him I didn't give a damn about a promotion—'When I could have worn a silver bar in the States and been proud of it, I was going around with a dirty gold one.'"

It was a perilous nighttime journey from the regimental command post up to the 2d Battalion's headquarters. A frightened runner refused to make the trip in the dark, so Woody made his own way by following the telephone line connecting the regimental command post to the battalion CP. Woody reached Lt. Col. Eads Hardaway at his command post in a barn and learned that Company G was split up and scattered along the front. After another dangerous trip in the darkness, Woody got close enough to hear one of his platoons lobbing hand grenades at the Germans. Woody crawled up alongside a hedgerow and waited until he heard some American voices. Then he rolled over the barrier and announced himself to his new command. He spent the rest of the night consolidating the company. The next morning, Hardaway sent up a relief company, and Woody was able to spend the day getting to know his new command.

St.-Lô was finally captured on July 18. The once-lovely medieval town was almost totally destroyed in the process. The U.S. First Army lost more than 11,000 killed, wounded, and missing in the eleven-day battle. The 30th Division suffered 3,934 casualties, almost 40 percent of its total strength. The toll among the frontline rifle platoons was even higher—close to 75 percent, according to one surviving officer. To say that Old Hickory was decimated at St.-Lô would be a gross understatement, since to the Roman soldiers who coined the word, *decimated* meant that a unit had lost 10 percent of its strength. A German general, reviewing the carnage around St.-Lô, called it "a monstrous bloodbath, such as I have never seen in eleven years of war."

Lieutenant General Omar Bradley, commanding the First Army, feared that the situation in Normandy was turning into a World War I–type stalemate. When Gen. Bernard Law Montgomery had outlined his plan for the campaign to the American commanders on April 7, he projected the breakout from Normandy to begin on D plus 20, from a position that the Allies had still not gained by D plus 50. "Bradley understood the situation of the moment," Gen. Dwight Eisenhower wrote, "and as early as June 20 had expressed to me the conviction that the breakout would have to be initiated from positions near St.-Lô, rather than from the more southerly line originally planned. He sensed the task with his usual imperturbability and set about it in a workmanlike fashion."

Bradley devised a bold plan to break the deadlock. His idea was to hit the German defenders with a massive aerial bombardment on a narrow front. Three infantry divisions would rush forward, punching a hole in the enemy line. Major General J. Lawton Collins, commanding the VII Corps, would then rush two armored divisions and the motorized 1st Infantry Division through the breach. The scheme was originally limited to a modest goal, the capture of the port city of Coutances. But Bradley and his staff soon expanded their aims. In the final version, Collins's tanks were to race south to seize Coutances and establish blocking positions on the eastern flank, opening the way for Maj. Gen. Troy Middleton's VIII Corps to drive down the coast highway to Avranches, the gateway to Brittany.

Bradley called his plan Cobra. It depended on good weather (the heavy bombers needed perfect visibility), proper terrain (to avoid the kind of congestion that marred the Vire River attack), and precise execution from the three assault divisions, which would have to rush forward quickly enough to prevent the Germans from repairing the gaps torn by the aerial bombardment. The American commander had fresh infantry divisions available to spearhead the attack, but he elected to call on three proven divisions instead. Manton Eddy's 9th, Ray Barton's 4th, and Leland Hobbs's weary, understrength 30th Division moved into position at the designated jump-off point just north of the St.-Lô–Périers highway.

The men of Old Hickory didn't know it, but the terrible war in the hedgerows was just a preview of the nightmare they were about to face.

CHAPTER 3: COBRA

The morning of July 25, 1944, dawned bright and clear over the Normandy countryside. The previous day's overcast, the cause of so much misery and delay, was gone, replaced by an impossibly blue sky, broken only by a few scattered clouds.

Cobra, postponed three times for bad weather, was on again. The aerial bombardment was to begin at 0930 with an attack by 350 fighter-bombers. That would be just a minor prelude to the symphony of destruction. More than 1,500 heavy bombers (B-17s and B-24s) would follow, dropping four thousand tons of bombs on a target just six thousand yards wide and twenty-five hundred yards deep. Another 350 dive-bombers would hit any specific targets that survived in the zone of destruction, followed by a final blow delivered by almost 400 medium bombers (B-25s and B-26s) on the enemy's rear areas, where most of his artillery was thought to be. The three infantry divisions lined up opposite the target area—the 30th on the left, closest to St.-Lô; the 4th in the middle; and the 9th on the right—would jump off at 1100, as soon as possible after the bombers were finished.

Sergeant Hubert Pennington was trying to put the last hour before the attack to good use. He and the men of his platoon were calmly brewing coffee, oblivious to their proximity to the front line. "We were about a short city block away from the front," Pennington recalled. "Our guns [two self-propelled, short-barreled, 105mm howitzers] were buttoned up, ready to move out. We were about to have a cup of coffee when a jeep pulled up and a three-star general hopped out."

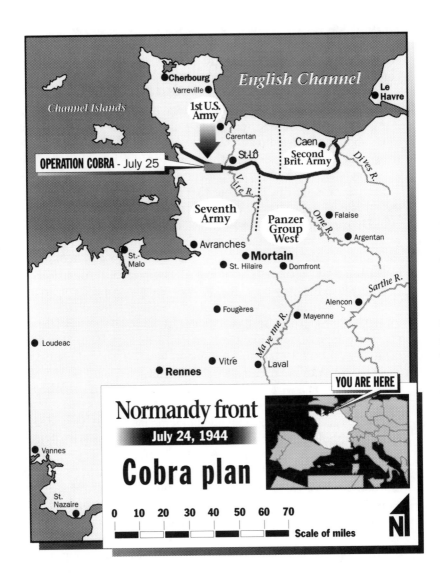

Cherbourg
Varreville
English Channel
Le Havre
Channel Islands
1st U.S. Army
Carentan
Caen
Second Brit. Army
St-Lô
Dives R.
OPERATION COBRA - July 25
V ire R.
Seventh Army
Panzer Group West
Orne R.
Falaise
Avranches
Argentan
Mortain
St.-Malo
St. Hilaire
Domfront
Sarthe R.
Fougères
Alencon
Ma ye nne R.
Mayenne
Loudeac
Vitré
Laval
Rennes

YOU ARE HERE

Normandy front
July 24, 1944
Cobra plan

Vannes
St. Nazaire

0 10 20 30 40 50 60 70
Scale of miles

N

Pennington didn't recognize Lt. Gen. Lesley J. McNair. Officially, the former commander of Army Ground Forces now commanded the 1st Army Group, a formation that existed only on paper, solely to decoy German intelligence. The man who did more than any other to shape and train the U.S. Army in World War II was slated for a real field command in the near future.

"General McNair walked up and asked us how we were doing," Pennington recalled. "I offered him a cup of coffee and he said, 'Only if my driver can have one, too.' I liked that. A lot of generals wouldn't think about an enlisted man. We gave him and his driver a cup, then we sat there on the ground with our feet in my foxhole—we didn't have any chairs—drinking coffee and talking."

McNair was touring the front that July morning, trying to gauge the morale of the troops he had trained. He knew that the men of the 30th Division had good reason to suspect the skill of the airmen who were already winging south from their bases in England. Just twenty-four hours earlier, several squadrons had failed to get the word that Cobra had been postponed because of a heavy overcast. Aiming through holes in the clouds, three hundred heavy bombers dropped almost seven hundred tons of high explosives. Unfortunately, one of the bomber formations dropped its load two thousand yards north of the highway that was supposed to define the limits of the target. The salvo fell on the men of the 120th Infantry Regiment, Pennington's old outfit. The accident killed 25 men, wounded 131, and left thousands more shaken.

"I wrote to my wife and told her that if you didn't experience it, there's no way you could know what it was like," said Pvt. John Weekly, one of the survivors. "I spent all night digging men—and parts of men—out of their holes. I don't agree with the numbers they reported. I think I saw more bodies lined up on the edge of the field than the official count. While we were digging, Air Corps officers drove up in their cars and made all kinds of excuses. They said they'd make sure it didn't happen again."

The airmen made all kinds of excuses to Gen. Omar Bradley, too, but the commander of the U.S. First Army wasn't in a forgiving mood. It had been his understanding that the bombers would approach the target parallel to the American front line (which was clearly marked by the St.-Lô–Périers highway), so that any "shorts" or "overs" would land on the enemy. For reasons of its own—and without telling the army—the air force changed the plan and scheduled a vertical approach to the target. Writing almost four decades after the incident, Bradley was still angry about the deception: "I launched an immediate investigation to find out why the airmen had bombed on a perpendicular course, rather than a parallel one as promised. To my astonishment, the Air Force brass simply lied, claiming they had never agreed to bomb parallel to the road. Not only that, they put me over an impossible barrel. They would not mount a second attack, except perpendicularly to the road. Fearing the Germans were on to us, I had no choice but to accept what the airmen offered."

Extraordinary steps were taken to ensure that the tragedy would not be repeated. The ground troops were pulled back 1,200 yards north of the highway, giving up more than a half mile of hard-won territory, and the heavy bombers were instructed not to bomb within 250 yards of the road, which was easily visible even at high altitude. Bright panels and red smoke bombs marked friendly positions for the fighter-bombers. Every Allied vehicle was repainted with a large white star. A special weather plane checked out the target well before the attack to make sure that cloud cover wouldn't interfere again. The air force assured Bradley it would avoid another tragic mistake.

As McNair learned during his frontline tour, the GIs were skeptical of such claims. The men of the 30th Division commonly referred to Maj. Gen. Elwood "Pete" Quesada's IX Tactical Air Command as the "Ninth Luftwaffe." As one company commander later explained, "We used to say the Air Force was only good for two things—destroying enemy buildings and killing friendly troops." Another GI remembered bitterly, "The infantry took 87 percent of the casualties and the Air Force got 89 percent of the decorations."

McNair left Pennington's position just before 0900, heading for the 120th Infantry, which was dug in one field over. The first bombs fell at 0938, a little late but right on target. The riflemen in the front line cheered as if at a football game when the first wave of heavy bombers dropped their loads on the German positions. Pennington's view of the front was blocked by a hedgerow, but his platoon's forward observer provided a running account of the show. The bombardment had been going on for almost half an hour when Pennington heard the shout.

"The fellow next to me pointed up and said, 'Look at that!'" Pennington remembered. "I looked up and saw a B-26 with its bomb bay open. It seemed to be right on top of us. I dove headfirst into a foxhole just as the bombs started to go off. They fell behind us, around us, in front of us. It was a terrifying experience. Some of the guys in my platoon said, 'To hell with this shit,' and decided to run. I didn't blame them. I felt like running, too." Airmen would later blame the disaster on the wind. A gentle northerly breeze blew the dust and smoke of the first wave's attack back toward the American positions. Many bombardiers, unable to see the highway, simply aimed for the huge smoke cloud marking the earlier attacks. As the cloud slowly drifted north, more and more bombs fell on friendly troops.

A few hundred yards to Pennington's right, the 120th Infantry was being hit hard again. Sergeant John Whitsett had just met McNair before the bombs began to fall. "A couple of other generals came by earlier, but they had left," Whitsett said. "General McNair wanted to stay and see the effects of a saturation bombardment. He went into a small building near us with an observer from the Air Corps. It took a direct hit. When that happened, I was afraid nobody knew we were being bombed, so I ran all the way back to battalion headquarters. They were being bombed, too! I jumped in a foxhole on top of a couple of other guys. A bomb hit so close it blew me out of the hole. They pulled me back in, but it happened again. This time it knocked me out cold. When I woke up, I was in a jeep and they were taking me back to an aid station."

All along the American line, similar scenes of terror were repeated. Private Weekly lived through his second bombing in twenty-four hours: "I looked up and saw four hundred, maybe five hundred, B-17s and B-25s with bombs coming out. I saw a P-51 strafe an aid station." Lieutenant Ronal Woody watched with horror as the bomb line gradually crept toward his company: "You could see them coming closer and closer, but all you could do was lie there in your hole. The concussion killed those who ran. The force of the explosions would lift you two feet off the ground. Trees were being blown out of the ground." Correspondent Ernie Pyle, who was visiting the 4th Division command post, remembered "hitting the ground flat, all spread out like the cartoons of people flattened by steamrollers, and then squirming like an eel to get under one of the heavy wagons in the shed . . . There's no description of the sound and fury of those bombs except to say it was chaos."

Bradley waited out the bombing with Maj. Gen. J. Lawton Collins in a small cafe near Groucherie, less than a mile behind the American front line. "Starched lace curtains hung in the open windows," Collins wrote. "The roar of our incoming heavy bombers was terrific as, once again, they passed overhead and the 'carumps' of the bombs shook the cafe as they exploded. The initial loads seemed to land on target, but some loads began to drop short . . . We could tell this because the blast from the short clusters would perceptibly blow in the lace curtains of the windows. We sat helplessly, fearing that these intermittent shorts, which followed no pattern, were landing among our troops."

Lieutenant Murray Pulver was standing in a small apple orchard with two of his sergeants, watching the bombs fall on the German positions when "those whistling bombs suddenly sounded different to me. I looked up to see that a wave of planes had released too soon. My God, those bombs were going to hit us! We dove into our shallow slit trench. I started to pray . . . I knew that we were all going to die. I began reciting the Twenty-third Psalm: 'The Lord is my shepherd. I shall not want . . .' It came so clearly to me, as if I were reading from the Good Book. The earth trembled and shook. We were covered with dirt, and the dust and the acrid smell of burnt powder choked us. The terror seemed to go on for hours, but actually it ended within a few minutes. We dug our way out of our hole to find everything quiet. The planes were gone and no guns were firing. The stillness was weird. There wasn't an apple left among the trees still standing, nor were there many leaves. I could not believe we were still alive."

The bombardment killed 111 American soldiers. Another 490 were wounded. One of the casualties was McNair, who shared the distinction of being the highest-ranking U.S. Army officer killed in combat with Lt. Gen. Simon B. Buckner, Jr. Buckner was killed by Japanese artillery fire on Okinawa while commanding U.S. ground forces on the island. An officer who saw McNair die reported: "A bomb . . . threw his body sixty feet and mangled it beyond recognition, except for the three stars on his collar."

Bradley was furious. Reports reaching his command post indicated that the tragic bombardment had caused considerable destruction and disorder. Both the 119th and 120th regiments—the latter scheduled to spearhead the assault on the 30th Division's front—suffered heavy casualties (later calculated as 64 killed, 374 wounded, 60 missing, and 164 cases of combat fatigue). On the 30th's right flank, the entire command group of the 37th Infantry Regiment's leading battalion was wiped out.

Not far away, all four assault companies of the 8th Infantry Regiment were hard hit. The 9th Division, on the western edge of the assault area, lost communication between its artillery command post and its forward observers. The accumulation of reports flooding Bradley's headquarters was so grim that the general briefly considered canceling Cobra.

He never got the chance. The frontline troops were already moving forward.

"Sometimes you go without thinking," said Pfc. Leo Temkin, in civilian life a grocer from New Haven, Connecticut. "I was buried during the bombing, and when I dug myself out, my rifle and all my equipment were gone. My squad was just moving out. I picked up the things I needed off some dead soldiers and caught up with them."

Sergeant Whitsett, knocked unconscious by the bombardment, woke up just before he was delivered to an aid station. "I suddenly realized the boys up there didn't have an officer," he said. "Our mission was race to an intersection and set up a roadblock. I knew our guns [three 57mm antitank weapons] would be in no condition to fire. I jumped off the jeep and ran back up front as fast as I could. I caught them just as they were moving forward. I stopped those guns and checked them out. I don't remember much after that. We had so many casualties . . . there was just never any place to stop and think clearly."

Along the line, a handful of leaders stepped forward to start the troops moving. Some were very young, like Pulver and Whitsett. Some were older, such as Brig. Gen. William Harrison.

Sergeant Floyd Montgomery had just finished digging out the last of his squad's survivors when he looked up and saw the assistant division commander standing beside him.

"Sergeant, where are your men?" Harrison asked.

"Sir, I've only got five left, counting me," Montgomery answered.

"Well, we've got five hedgerows to take . . . I'll go with you," Harrison said. The brigadier general led the tiny squad forward.

Hopes of finding the German defenses shattered by the bombardment were quickly dashed when the first troops crossed the bomb-cratered highway. Despite the vast destruction—one German observer said the position looked like the landscape on the moon—numerous strongpoints, manned by experienced, determined defenders, remained untouched.

Captain Reynold Erichson, the Iowa farmer, was leading one of the

120th Infantry's assault companies. He watched his attack bog down as "tanks, spearheading with the point elements of the infantry, ran into minefields covered by enemy antitank gunfire, and were knocked out and set afire. Doughboys, forced off the roads by fire, took to the ditches—and ran into antipersonnel mines. A man a few yards in front of me stepped on one and his entire lower legs were blown off. As I passed by him, he asked me for help. An aidman was summoned and everyone kept going."

Just as the attack was getting underway, the American air force made another unfortunate appearance over the battlefield. Lieutenant Woody's company was strafed by a squadron of P-47 Thunderbolts and Captain Erichson's unit was the target of a formation of medium bombers.

"Bombs started falling far in the rear and worked up to where we were," Erichson wrote. "You could see the bombs actually fall through the air; tiny little dots at first, growing and growing as they neared the earth, and then the dull dry thump as they detonated. One particular stick of bombs dropped quite close to where we were lying in a ditch. A rock near my head, the size of a volleyball, actually bounced in the air. This bombing lasted only a short while and again the attack was resumed."

Word of the stiff German resistance deepened the gloom at Bradley's headquarters. General Eisenhower, who had flown to Normandy to oversee the opening of Cobra, returned to England "completely dejected and furious at the Air Force for killing and maiming so many of our own men."

The soldiers who survived those all-too-frequent "accidents" didn't have time to indulge their anger (except for the company commander who told his men that from now on, they would fire on any aircraft in range, whatever the nationality). The assault troops were too busy reducing the German positions that had survived the aerial bombardment.

On the 4th Division front, Ernie Pyle couldn't believe the reports reaching division headquarters. Moments after emerging from beneath his sheltering wagon, he approached a regimental commander, whom he discovered walking around in a daze, repeating the single word "Goddammit!" Pyle asked if the attack would go off as scheduled. Under the circumstances, the colonel told him, an attack was impossible. Yet the 4th Division's lead company advanced on time, and within an hour reported that it had penetrated eight hundred yards into German territory and was still advancing. "Men with stars on their shoulders almost wept when the word came over the portable radio," Pyle wrote. "The American soldier can be magnificent when the need arises."

On the 30th Division's front, Erichson's company advanced three hundred yards past the highway, then ran into a line of dug-in Panthers (forty-five-ton tanks), protected by machine-gun nests. "Each of these tanks seemed to cover the routes of approach and the attack was stalled momentarily," he reported. "Maneuver was extremely difficult. We crawled to within a few yards of one and fired a bazooka into its front, but since the vegetation, used for camouflage, was placed around it, we couldn't get a detonation on the plate itself."

The German roadblock stretched across a narrow, hardtop road running south to St.-Gilles, a small village about four kilometers away. While the 2d Battalion of the 120th Infantry piled up in front of the formidable obstacle, Col. Hammond Birks sent his other two battalions on flanking marches to the east and west. They found only scattered pockets of resistance and began to make good progress. Artillery finally eliminated the roadblock, and Erichson's company was able to advance against nothing more than sniper fire until sundown.

The reports coming from the front posed a dilemma for General Collins. His intelligence officers concluded that penetration had not been achieved. None of the American infantry divisions had reached their first-day objectives. Yet the German defense, although formidable in places, was sporadic and apparently uncoordinated. Had the attack broken the main line of resistance? If that were the case, then it was vital for Collins to commit his armor before the breach could be repaired. But what if the Germans, warned by the premature air attack on the 24th, had withdrawn their main line and escaped the full force of the aerial bombardment? If so, then releasing the armor would lead to the kind of fatal congestion that had spoiled the earlier opportunity after the Vire River crossing.

Joseph Lawton Collins had picked up the nickname Lightning Joe from the code name of the division he had commanded on Guadalcanal. His actions in the next few hours would give that nickname a new meaning.

"The divisions were discouraged that they had not been able to break through the main German defenses. I had not planned to employ the 1st Division and the 2nd and 3rd Armored Divisions until this was done, but noting the lack of coordination in the German reaction, particularly their failure to launch prompt counterattacks, I sensed their communications and command structure had been damaged more than our troops realized. Before the enemy could recover, I decided in the late afternoon of the 25th to throw in the 1st Division on the morning of the 26th . . . with [the 3d Armored Division's] Combat Command B attached and Ted Brooks' 2nd Armored."

Reasoning that any decision he made would be a gamble, Collins had resolved to make the aggressive choice. He phoned 30th Division headquarters at 1745 on the 25th and warned Maj. Gen. Leland Hobbs to clear the St.-Gilles road at dawn: The armor was going to roll.

The frontline troops heard the code word "Bobcat" not long after sunrise the next day. Two columns of tanks from the 2d Armored Division, known as Hell on Wheels, passed through the lines of the 120th, one on the paved road, one on a parallel dirt track. Lieutenant Wilbur Williams and Capt. Ellis Williamson (the former trombone player) each went to the head of one column and guided the tanks through the devastation caused by the previous day's battle. Not an enemy gun sounded as the Shermans rolled past.

By midafternoon, the lead tanks passed through St.-Gilles. Brigadier General Maurice Rose, who had joined the army as a buck private in 1916 and risen through the ranks, was in command of the two columns. Commanding from a jeep near the front of his columns, Rose reported to Collins that opposition in his zone was negligible. Just before sundown, his men took the hamlet of Canisy after a brief engagement. Instead of halting for the night, Rose kept driving south. In the darkness, a half-track and trailer swerved past the lead Sherman. "Hell, I'm supposed to be leading this column," the tank commander complained. Then he realized that the offending vehicles were fleeing Germans. He opened fire and destroyed the half-track. An hour before midnight, after a penetration of more than eight miles, the American spearhead reached St.-Samson-de-Bonfosse. Rose finally halted his tanks three hours later, after seizing a key road junction just north of Le Mesnil-Herman.

"This thing has busted wide open," Hobbs exulted that night in a phone call to Birks. Hobbs' joy was shared by Bradley, who the next day wrote Eisenhower, "To say that the personnel of the First Army Headquarters are riding high is putting it mildly. Things on our front

look really good. I'm sorry you happened to be here on the one day
when the situation was obscure . . . we believe we have the Germans
out of the ditches and in complete demoralization and expect to take
full advantage of them."

Bradley didn't realize how demoralized the Germans actually were.
The weeks of costly resistance in the hedgerows, added to the constant British pressure on the eastern edge of the Normandy perimeter,
had drained the German army in France of almost all its reserves. Field
Marshal Günther von Kluge, the overall commander in France, was
primarily concerned with the condition of Panzer Group West, facing
the British around Caen. The German Seventh Army, opposite the
American First Army, got less attention, perhaps because the terrain
seemed less suitable for an Allied offensive, or perhaps because of
German contempt for the quality of American troops ("The Americans are to us what the Italians are to you," explained a German prisoner captured in North Africa).

The abortive bombing on July 24 only increased the German confidence. From their point of view, the confused action was an inept
American attack, beaten off with ease by the defenders.

The German complacency was shattered by the bombardment of July
25. General Fritz Bayerlein, commander of the Panzer Lehr Division,
saw his powerful unit virtually wiped out in a matter of a few minutes. "It was hell," he said. "The planes kept coming overhead like a
conveyor belt and the bomb carpets came down, now ahead, now on
the right, now on the left. The fields were burning and smoldering . . . At
least 75 percent of my personnel were out of action—dead, wounded,
crazed or numbed. All my frontline tanks were knocked out."

Bayerlein organized a reserve of fifteen tanks, gathered from the
repair shops, to oppose the American infantry advance. Von Kluge sent
word that the St.-Lô–Périers road must be held at all cost, but the defenses
there had already broken. Bayerlein was told that a new SS panzer
battalion was coming in with sixty tanks. Five tanks arrived. By nightfall
of July 25—the same evening that Eisenhower flew back to England
in such dismay—von Kluge conceded that "the front has burst."

There was still some stiff fighting ahead. Collins's western spearhead—led by the 1st Division and a combat command of the 3d Ar-

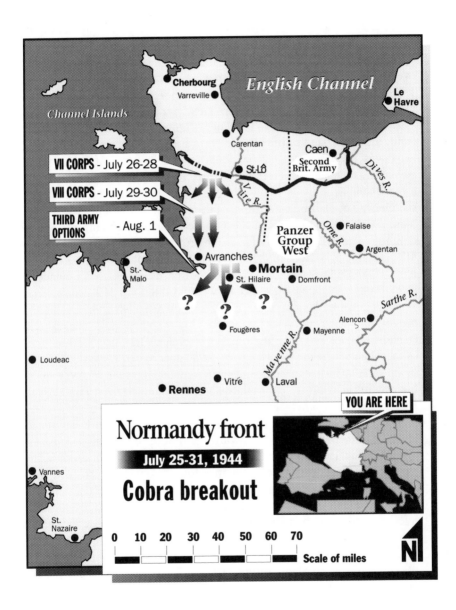

VII CORPS - July 26-28

VIII CORPS - July 29-30

THIRD ARMY
OPTIONS - Aug. 1

Cherbourg
Varreville
English Channel
Le Havre
Channel Islands
Carentan
Caen
St-Lô
Second
Brit. Army
Vire R.
Dives R.
Falaise
Orne R.
Panzer
Group
West
Argentan
Avranches
St.-
Malo
Mortain
St. Hilaire
Domfront
Sarthe R.
?
?
?
Alencon
Fougères
Mayenne R.
Mayenne
Loudeac
Vitré
Laval
Rennes
Vannes
St.
Nazaire

YOU ARE HERE

Normandy front
July 25-31, 1944
Cobra breakout

0 10 20 30 40 50 60 70

Scale of miles

N

mored Division—was temporarily halted outside Marigny by elements of the 2d SS Panzer Division and survivors of the 5th Parachute Division. However, on the German right, where the 30th Division had opened the door for the 2d Armored, there was a vacuum. Bradley poured every unit he could find into the breach. Within forty-eight hours, the 1st Division had smashed through on the western flank and pushed the door wide open.

On the morning of July 28, a new figure appeared on the battlefield, a general as familiar to the troops as McNair was obscure.

"I was back at battalion headquarters," one sergeant said, "when one of my men came in and said, 'Sarge, you've got to see this. There's a three-star general out there directing traffic.'" He raced outside to see George S. Patton, wearing his famous polished helmet and ivory-handled pistols, standing on the hood of his jeep, waving through a column of tanks. The vehicles belonged to Maj. Gen. John Wood's 4th Armored Division, the lead unit of what would become the Third Army. By nightfall of July 28, Wood's spearheads had reached Coutances. The offensive had become a race between Middleton's VIII Corps (with Wood's tanks in the van) and Collins's VII Corps, which had achieved the original breakout. With Patton cracking the whip in the background (technically, he was only an observer until the VIII Corps became part of the Third Army on August 1), Wood's tanks roared forward at speeds of up to fifty miles an hour, not only winning the race to Avranches, but continuing four miles south to capture intact the vital Pontaubault Bridge over the Selune River.

The genie was out of the bottle. The road network at Pontaubault led west into Brittany, south toward the mouth of the Loire, and east toward the interior of France. Less than a week after Cobra's unpromising beginning, General Bradley suddenly found himself confronted with a glittering array of opportunities.

"It's one hell of a mess," von Kluge told Gen. Günther Blumentritt over the phone on the morning of July 31. "It's a madhouse here. You can't imagine what it's like. So far, it appears only the spearheads of various mobile units are through to Avranches. But it's perfectly clear that everything else will follow. Unless I can get infantry and anti-tank weapons there, the [left] wing cannot hold. Someone has to tell the führer that if the Americans get through at Avranches, they'll be able to do what they want."

*   *   *

The 30th Division was not given a rest following its vital work in the first days of the offensive. Instead, the weary division had to wheel to its left and protect the eastern flank of the breakout. In order to widen the breach, the 30th was ordered to drive southeast toward the Vire River. The ultimate objective was the town of Tessy-sur-Vire. The division's first attempt to reach Tessy was stopped with heavy losses on July 28, a bitter disappointment to General Hobbs, who didn't learn until much later that his assault had in fact collided head-on with the relatively fresh 2d Panzer Division, which was trying to mount a counterattack westward to cut off the American breakthrough.

Hobbs launched another assault on Tessy the morning of August 1. Lieutenant Pulver's platoon, spearheading the drive, brushed aside a strongpoint outside the town, then moved across several fields without opposition before an unfamiliar officer appeared and ordered Pulver to stop and let the rest of the 1st Battalion catch up. "We sat down on a log to check the map and determine our location," Pulver said. "As it was getting warm, the officer took off his jacket. There must have been a surprised look on my face when I saw a star on his shoulder. I jumped to my feet and said, 'Sir, I'm sorry, I didn't recognize you.' He replied, 'Sit down, Lieutenant. I should have introduced myself. I'm General Harrison, your division executive officer.' "

Harrison directed Pulver's platoon down a secondary road about a mile outside of Tessy. The Germans opened up with heavy and accurate artillery fire. Pulver was knocked down by the concussion of one blast and the man in front of him was killed. His soldiers raced down the road, soon reaching a German strongpoint built around an anti-tank gun. Private Lenny Groves got close enough to knock out the position with a rifle grenade. Private Francis Kimmel ran down the street with his BAR and blasted an 88mm gun position with armor-piercing bullets, killing the gunners. Pulver's platoon advanced slowly, fighting house-to-house. By midafternoon, they had reached a hospital near the center of Tessy when Pulver got a call from his company commander. Mines had been cleared from the main roads outside of town, and four tanks were en route to assist his platoon.

"We soon heard them coming," Pulver said. "They were buttoned up and were firing their cannons and machine guns in all directions. We took cover in two air raid shelters next to the hospital. When the tanks got abreast of us, they fired into the entrances of our shelters. They must have seen us and thought we were enemy soldiers! Fortunately, the shelter entrances had right angle turns so the shells and bullets could not reach us, but the dust, dirt and smoke [were] nearly snuffing us out. [One of my men] had a white undershirt which I tied to my rifle. I went to the rear entrance and waved it aloft. The tankers saw the white flag and stopped firing."

Pulver chewed out the tank commander, who had been told there were no friendly troops in that part of town. Fortunately, none of Pulver's men were killed by the tankers' mistake. By the next morning, the town was secure, except for an occasional artillery barrage fired by the Germans from positions on the other side of the Vire River and yet another accidental (and fortunately ineffective) attack by American fighter-bombers.

With Tessy firmly in American hands, the 30th Division, which had been in continuous contact with the enemy for forty-nine days, was finally given a break for rest and reorganization. There were showers and clean uniforms and hot food. Red Cross clubmobiles visited each battalion, and attractive American girls passed out coffee and doughnuts to the troops. A barn was converted into a movie theater where GIs watched Lucille Ball and June Allyson in *Best Foot Forward*. A United Service Organizations (USO) troop performed for a larger crowd in a makeshift outdoor arena. The headliner was Edward G. Robinson, who did his tough-guy act for the soldiers. Afterward, the famous actor wanted to meet a German prisoner of war. Since all POWs had been evacuated the day before, a German-speaking sergeant from division headquarters was dressed in an enemy uniform. Guarded by two MPs with tommy guns, he was presented to Robinson. The sergeant clicked his heels, gave a Nazi salute, and assumed an arrogant attitude during the interview. The professional actor never realized he was being conned by an amateur.

During the break at Tessy, more than 1,200 replacements joined the 30th, bringing two of the division's three infantry regiments close to authorized manpower (each was supposed to consist of 157 officers and 3,049 men). Only the 119th, which remained some 800 men short of establishment, was seriously understrength.

One of the newcomers was Pvt. George Neidhardt, a factory worker from Chicago, who joined Company F (120th Infantry). He reported to Captain Erichson and was assigned to the 3d Platoon. Neidhardt felt lucky to be assigned to a veteran combat unit but found "there wasn't a lot of companionship." A buddy he had made on the trip over was assigned to another squad in the same platoon, but Neidhardt's friend was killed by German artillery almost the same day, one of the division's few casualties from the sporadic fire from across the river.

During the break at Tessy, there were promotions and transfers for the surviving veterans. The most important change occurred at the top of the 117th Infantry Regiment, where Col. Henry Kelly was replaced by his executive officer, Lt. Col. Walter M. Johnson. Actually, Kelly had been ill for some time, giving Johnson practical command of the regiment for most of the time it had been in Normandy. At first, Hobbs objected to Johnson's promotion to command, complaining that the quiet West Pointer, whose only ostentation was a jaunty mustache, did not "talk a good war" in his reports from the field. Only a strong endorsement by Harrison, who told Hobbs, "Johnson is an A-1 commanding officer, one of our best," convinced the division commander to (reluctantly) approve the promotion.

While Colonel Birks remained in command of the 120th, the regiment underwent several key changes at the company level. Lieutenant Joseph Reaser, who had served as a member of Birks's staff since Camp Blanding, was given command of Company K, in the 3d Battalion. Lieutenant Ralph Kerley, a veteran platoon leader who was wounded just before St.-Lô, returned from the hospital to take command of Company E, in the 2d Battalion. Captain Delmont Byrn, a replacement officer who had trained with the 6th Division in Missouri, took over Company H, the 2d Battalion's heavy-weapons company. Pulver gave up his platoon to take command of Company B in the 1st Battalion.

Pulver's first job as company commander was to distribute the payroll, his men's first payday in almost three months. As the French population of Tessy returned to their homes, a few enterprising GIs found plenty of places to spend their accumulated pay. One sergeant won twenty-eight hundred dollars in a crap game. Pulver visited a barber who gave him a haircut and the use of a bathtub. The grateful Frenchman refused payment, accepting only a couple of packs of cigarettes in return for his services.

The division orders for Thursday, August 3, and Friday, August 4, listed no activities other than "Reorganization and rest. Baths as scheduled." The orders for Saturday were slightly more explicit: "Training in small group tactics . . . Training in use of mortars in battery with particular emphasis on communication from observer to gun . . . Orientation (Materials will be sent down by Regimental Orientation Officer)."

In addition, General Hobbs scheduled talks with all of his units, starting at 0900 and allotting twenty minutes for each speech. Overall, the orders were careful to note: "Training periods will be five hours per day. Hours to be designated by Battalion Commanders."

It looked as though the 30th might stay in Tessy long enough for the mail to catch up. Lieutenant Pulver was desperate for word from home. He still didn't know if he was a father. More than a month had passed since his wife was due to deliver their first child, but Pulver had received no mail since joining Old Hickory. He begged a Red Cross representative to help him contact his wife.

But the division's restful routine ended before Pulver got any news from home. At 2024 hours, August 5, orders were received directing the 30th to return to the front. Trucks were waiting to transport the division south.

The first contingent, an artillery battalion, left Tessy at 0130 on August 6. The 117th Infantry Regiment was driven to the tiny village of St.-Barthelmy. The 119th Regiment was transported to a reserve position two miles west of St.-Barthelmy. The 120th kept going south, past its sister regiments. It was the first time since arriving in France that the regiment's riflemen had been driven anywhere. The GIs were happy to ride, even if one noted sourly that they would have moved faster by walking. It took almost nine hours for most of the trucks to make the forty-six-mile journey. For long stretches, the drive was almost like a parade, as joyous French civilians lined the route and cheered as the trucks rolled past. The regiment finally reached its destination early in the afternoon, where it was met by guides from the 1st Division, who led the men to their assigned defensive positions.

The 120th had arrived in Mortain.

CHAPTER 4: OPERATION LÜTTICH

Adolf Hitler was slow to appreciate the significance of the Normandy invasion. For many weeks—precious weeks for the Allied troops fighting to expand the small bridgehead—the Nazi führer continued to believe that the June 6 landings were merely a diversion, designed to draw defenders from the real invasion target, the Pas de Calais. He held the powerful Fifteenth Army in position to counter the expected thrust long after the commanders on the spot were certain that Normandy was the Allies' main effort.

Distance may have diminished Hitler's appreciation of the situation. He spent most of June at his Berghof estate in the Bavarian Alps, making just one quick trip to Rheims to confer with Field Marshal Erwin Rommel, in command of Army Group B (the forces fighting in Normandy), and Field Marshal Gerd von Rundstedt, the commander-in-chief West. Hitler was shocked by their pessimism. He resolved to replace the aging von Rundstedt, importing Field Marshal Günther von Kluge from the eastern front to take command in Paris. On July 17, as Rommel was returning from an inspection tour of the front, two RAF Typhoons strafed his staff car. The legendary German commander was seriously injured and von Kluge had to assume his duties as well.

By that date, Hitler was far more concerned by the situation on the eastern front. The Russian summer offensive opened on June 22 (the third anniversary of the German attack on the Soviet Union) and achieved breathtaking gains, tearing a huge gap in the Wehrmacht's Army Group Center. The führer flew to Rastenburg, his remote headquarters in East

Prussia, to oversee the situation. From his new vantage point, half-way across Europe, the Normandy front appeared deceptively stable. Although the British capture of Caen on July 19 finally convinced Hitler to authorize the transfer of the 116th Panzer Division from the Fifteenth Army to the Normandy front—his first tacit admission that the Pas de Calais invasion might be a fantasy—even before the powerful armored unit could arrive, the British Goodwood offensive ground to a halt in the face of ferocious resistance by the famed 1st SS Panzer Division, the Liebstandarte Adolf Hitler.

"Hitler's lifeguards" were resting on their laurels the next day, when the führer miraculously survived the explosion of Count Claus Schenk von Stauffenberg's briefcase bomb during the midday conference at Rastenburg. The blast stunned Hitler and damaged his hearing, but the most serious result of the bungled assassination attempt was the magnification of Hitler's previous distrust of the Prussian-dominated Wehrmacht high command. The investigation of the conspiracy implicated dozens of high-ranking officers, feeding the angry führer's growing paranoia.

The July 20 bomb plot was to have repercussions on the western front. Field Marshal von Kluge had been one of Hitler's most trusted commanders. But after the Rastenburg explosion, no German general was to have Hitler's complete trust. Whereas before it had been difficult to argue with the führer, after July 20 it became impossible. Disagreement meant disloyalty, and disloyalty meant death. Von Kluge's position was particularly perilous, since he had had foreknowledge of the conspirators' plot and knew he might be implicated at any time. Thus von Kluge had little flexibility when the Cobra assault cracked his lines west of St.-Lô.

The safest military course would have been to withdraw all German forces west of the Seine to a new defensive line closer to the German border. Von Kluge's staff prepared such a plan and the field marshal tentatively suggested the idea to Col. Gen. Alfred Jodl, Hitler's operations officer, on July 31—the same day von Kluge learned that Avranches had fallen to Maj. Gen. John Wood's tanks.

Hitler's response was deceptively mild. He calmly told von Kluge that the western front commander did not grasp the entire situation. The ex-corporal patiently explained to the field marshal that the battle in Normandy would be the decisive battle of the war. On August 2, he sent von Kluge a specific order: Army Group B would launch a massive counterattack toward Avranches. "We must strike like lightning," he declared. "When we reach the sea, the American spearheads will be cut off. We might even be able to cut off their entire beachhead." Hitler promised reinforcements from the Fifteenth Army and from troops held in southern France. He envisioned a mighty force of eight panzer divisions, smashing the twenty kilometers west to the coast highway at Avranches, then turning north to roll up the entire Allied position in Normandy.

The plan was designated Operation Lüttich. Lüttich is the German name for the Belgian city of Liège, where, almost exactly thirty years earlier, the kaiser's army had scored its first great victory in World War I.

On paper, Hitler's scheme was not illogical. The corridor supplying Patton's Third Army was extremely narrow opposite Avranches, so narrow that Collins's VII Corps was even then pushing hard to widen it. A surprise attack by eight full-strength panzer divisions might very well have succeeded in cutting off the American forces in Brittany and restoring the static front in Normandy. However, von Kluge knew just how unrealistic Hitler's plan actually was. There simply wasn't time to assemble such a massive striking force. Not only was one American corps already tentatively thrusting out of Brittany toward the heart of France, but the units manning the eastern end of the Normandy front— a line that appeared stable on Hitler's situation maps—were barely holding on against constant pressure from the British and Canadians. Hitler's entire front might collapse at any moment.

Von Kluge could not oppose Hitler's order. Instead, he determined to alter it into something workable. On August 3, he told Gen. Adolf Kuntzen the counterattack would not fundamentally change the situation in Normandy, but it might facilitate a general withdrawal to a new line of defense. Von Kluge's concept of a limited offensive was sound; a successful stab at the vulnerable American lifeline could indeed force Bradley to call back units of the rampaging Third Army to reinforce his flank. That would give von Kluge time to disengage in Normandy and fall back behind the Seine.

The difference between von Kluge's modest tactical goals and Hitler's grand strategic design would come back to haunt Army Group B.

Von Kluge dutifully began working to assemble a striking force in the area of Sourdeval, a small town on the banks of the Sée River, just over thirty kilometers from Avranches. Hitler had promised the 9th Panzer Division from the south of France and the LXXXI Corps (with three panzer divisions) from the Fifteenth Army, but von Kluge wasn't counting on their arrival. Because of Allied air power and its successful campaign to interdict German transportation, it was impossible to shift major units quickly. Most movement had to be made during the brief summer nights, over roads and bridges and railroads that were bombed in the daylight.

Instead of waiting for reinforcements, von Kluge began to pull armored units out of the line facing the British and Canadian armies, replacing them with arriving infantry divisions. These armored units would join two divisions re-forming after failing to halt the Cobra avalanche. First to reach the assembly area near Sourdeval were the 2d Panzer Division, whose counterattack had been blocked by the 30th Division near Tessy, and the 2d SS Panzer Division, which had barely escaped envelopment after engaging the 1st Division at Marigny. The 116th Panzer Division, thrown into the line opposite Collins's VII Corps after its arrival from the Channel coast, was still locked in combat west of Vire and was having difficulty disengaging. The 1st SS Panzer Division would leave its position southeast of Caen as soon as it was relieved by an infantry division provided by the Fifteenth Army.

The four panzer divisions were organized as the XLVII Panzer Corps, commanded by Gen. Hans Freiherr Funck. None of the divisions was at full strength, which in 1944 would have been 66 tanks per division. Instead, the entire corps included less than 190 tanks. Half were twenty-three-ton Mark IVs, an improved 75mm-gun version of the medium tank that overran France in 1940. It was still a good match for the Sherman, the main Allied battle tank. Almost all the remaining German tanks were forty-five-ton Mark V Panthers, also armed with a 75mm gun. These were the finest all-around battle tanks produced during the war, far more mobile and reliable than the heavier Tiger. Although almost every American infantryman to see a tank during the coming battle was to identify it as a Tiger, Funck's corps actually possessed only a handful of the slow but terrifying fifty-five-ton giants. In addition to the panzers, the four divisions included approximately five hundred other armored vehicles: half-tracks, assault guns, armored cars, flak guns, and the like.

Yet, as General George Marshall pointed out in 1940, machines themselves were useless. The training and discipline of a unit were at least as important as its material strength. And, clearly, if von Kluge had any concerns about the material strength of his striking force, he could have no doubts about its quality. General Major Freidherr von Gersdorff, the chief of staff of the Seventh Army, later called the assaulting divisions "[among] the best German armored divisions."

Funck's corps would include two of the most famous divisions in the German army, the 1st and 2d SS Panzer Divisions. The 1st SS Panzers, the Liebstandarte Adolf Hitler, first tasted blood against the Poles in 1939, when the American army was still drilling with wooden rifles. It played a key role in the capture of the Crimea in 1942 and teamed with the 2d SS Panzer Division, known as Das Reich, to spearhead the drive on Rostov later that year. In two years of battle against the Russians, both divisions compiled a record of unbroken success. On the Dnieper River, the Liebstandarte led a counterattack that produced ten thousand Russian casualties and yielded five thousand prisoners. Even when worn out and understrength in November 1943, Das Reich struck like a thunderbolt at Zhitomir, providing the spearhead as the XLVIII Corps scored a crushing victory, killing more than twenty thousand Russians and capturing five thousand men, six hundred tanks, three hundred artillery pieces, and twelve hundred antitank guns.

Both SS panzer divisions were transferred to the western front in the spring of 1944, where they were given a chance to rest and refit. Das Reich was in the south of France when the Allies landed in Normandy. Rushed to the front, Das Reich was slowed by Allied air attacks and by repeated acts of sabotage. Frustrated by the delays, Gen. Heinz Lammerding, the division commander, ordered a brutal reprisal at the village of Oradour-sur-Glâne. The Germans shot all the males in the town, then burned the women and children alive in a church. More than a thousand civilians perished.

Das Reich had suffered heavily in the Normandy fighting. To strengthen the understrength division, von Kluge attached to it a regiment-sized battle group from the 17th SS Panzergrenadier Division, famous in its own right as the Goetz von Berlichingen Division. The 1st SS Panzer was in better shape, despite its long fight with the British around Caen. It was, in fact, the strongest of the divisions committed to Operation Lüttich.

Of Funck's two Wehrmacht divisions, the veteran 2d Panzer Division had also proved itself a quality formation under a superb commander, Maj. Gen. Heinrich von Lüttwitz, a rotund, monocled native of Silesia. His division had a proud record. Four years earlier, the 2d Panzer Division had smashed through the French defensive line at Sedan and raced all the way to the English Channel. If not for an ill-timed stop order from Hitler, the division would have turned north and captured Dunkirk, long before the British Expeditionary Force began its miraculous evacuation.

The 116th Panzer Division was rated only an average division by Allied intelligence. What the Allies didn't know was that the 116th was a new designation for an old and very successful unit, the 16th Panzergrenadier Division. Its commander, Count Gerhard von Schwerin, was only the third Wehrmacht general to receive the Knight's Cross of the Iron Cross with oak leaves and swords. His division had performed with such dash and speed on the Russian front in 1943 that it picked up the nickname The Greyhound Division. Within a month of its arrival in Normandy, the 116th would have its rating upgraded from average to superior by Allied intelligence.

Tactical planning for the attack proved difficult in view of the rapidly changing situation at the front. General Collins's effort to widen the coastal corridor achieved a measure of success, especially at Mortain, where, on the afternoon of August 3, the 1st Infantry Division seized the high ground south of the Sée River. In just forty-eight hours, the distance the Germans would have to travel to reach Avranches had increased from twenty-two to almost thirty kilometers.

Von Kluge's plan, as it finally evolved, called for the four panzer divisions to strike on a ten-kilometer front. The 2d Panzer Division, reinforced by elements of the 1st SS Panzers and the 116th Panzer Division, was to attack in the center, driving along the south bank of the Sée River, clearing the St.-Barthelmy–Juvigny road, the shortest route to Avranches. One wing of the 2d Panzers and the bulk of the 116th would attack north of the river to protect the right flank of the advance. The southern thrust would be headed by the 2d SS Panzer Division, which would strike on both sides of Mortain, recapture the vital high ground east of the town, and drive southwest to St.-Hilaire to protect the left flank of the attack.

The powerful 1st SS Panzer Division would follow the 2d Panzer thrust along the St.-Barthelmy–Juvigny highway to exploit the breakthrough and would spearhead the final dash to Avranches. Because the terrain south of the Sée River was broken by hedgerows, the panzers would be restricted to the area's limited road net. Consequently, the Germans planned to use surprise and speed to prevent the Americans from erecting defenses at key intersections. The decision was made to attack without benefit of a preliminary artillery barrage. The first warning the defenders would have would be the sound of panzers rolling toward their positions.

Von Kluge set H hour for 2200 hours, Sunday, August 6. As the time for that assault approached, von Kluge and his top commanders began to view the enterprise with growing optimism. The attacking force had been assembled without fatally weakening the rest of the front. The bulk of Patton's Third Army was wasting its strength in attacks on the Breton ports, thus reducing the threat of encirclement from the south. Best of all, the weather forecasters predicted that fog would cover the battlefield area through most of August 7, protecting the panzers from Allied air power.

"The headquarters of the [Seventh] Army estimated the situation as quite favorable," General von Gersdorff said. "This was particularly true because we still had the impression that south of the Sée sector, the enemy forces were still weak."

Von Gersdorff's superior, Gen. Paul Hausser, commander of the German Seventh Army, felt that the attacking force would have no trouble regaining Avranches. He was less certain of holding the port once it was taken. He had no hope of turning north and destroying the entire Allied beachhead, as Hitler envisioned. Still, Hausser believed the recapture of Avranches would put Patton's Third Army in considerable jeopardy and give von Kluge a chance to restabilize the front in France.

Von Kluge's optimism was such that he arranged a forward command post west of Alençon so he could supervise the counterattack personally. However, a few hours before he was to leave his headquarters at the Chateau la Roche Guyon (near Paris), the German commander received a disturbing phone call from Hitler's headquarters. General Jodl demanded a report on the progress of the planning. The führer wasn't convinced that von Kluge's attack would be strong enough—

English Channel

Channel Islands

Cherbourg
Varreville
Le Havre

Carentan
St-Lô
Caen
Second Brit. Army

First U.S. Army

V
ire R.

Panzer Group West

Dives R.

Orne R.

Falaise

OPERATION LUTTICH - Aug. 6

XLVII Panzer Corps

Argentan

Avranches

St.-Malo

Mortain

St. Hilaire
Domfront

Seventh Army

Third U.S. Army

Sarthe R.

Alencon

Fougères

Mayenne R.

Mayenne

Loudeac

Vitré
Laval

Rennes

YOU ARE HERE

Normandy front

Aug. 6, 1944

Operation Luttich

Vannes

St. Nazaire

0   10   20   30   40   50   60   70

Scale of miles

N

or would be executed aggressively enough—to accomplish his ambitious goals. The extent of Hitler's ambition was revealed by the message he issued the next day: "The decision in the Battle of France depends on the success of the attack. The C-in-C West has a unique opportunity, which will never return, to drive into an exposed enemy area and thereby to change the situation entirely."

In order to assure the success of the attack, Hitler offered to release sixty Panther tanks being held in reserve east of Paris, plus the 11th Panzer Division with another eighty Mark IV tanks. The reinforcements would virtually double the armored strength of the attacking force. But when von Kluge asked when he could expect these forces to reach the Mortain area, he was told, "at least twenty-four hours, maybe longer." Less than nine hours remained until von Kluge's original H hour.

General Jodl had one more piece of disturbing news. Hitler wanted a change in commanders. He didn't think General Funck was aggressive enough. The führer ordered Gen. Heinrich Eberbach, commander of the Fifth Panzer Army, to assume tactical control of the attack. Von Kluge argued against any major changes in his plan at this late date. He explained to Jodl why it was impossible to delay the attack for twenty-four hours. Not only was his front crumbling, but his intelligence officer was reporting that the Allies had detected the German preparations for Operation Lüttich. Surprise was more important than an additional 140 tanks. Given time to prepare for the German counterattack, the Americans could amass more than enough strength to stop it short of Avranches.

It was an unusual situation for Hitler. Usually, he advocated the swift, bold stroke, whereas his field commanders counseled caution and delay. Now, confronted with a commander urging an immediate attack, Hitler reluctantly gave in. Von Kluge would be permitted to launch Operation Lüttich as planned. However, the führer did not abandon his dreams for a grand strategic success. He secured a promise from von Kluge that the offensive would be vigorously pursued. Hitler directed Eberbach to assume command from Funck at Avranches and swing northeast to attack the flank of the U.S. First Army. To make sure his plans were followed, Hitler dispatched Gen. Walter Buhle from his headquarters to oversee the operation.

Von Kluge did not receive final approval for the attack from Hitler until 1905 hours, less than three hours before H hour. The spearheads of the 2d Panzer and the 2d SS Panzer divisions were already rolling toward their start points. The ultimate purposes of Operation Lüttich might be confused, but the immediate objective of the attack was clear. Four of Germany's finest panzer divisions were pointed toward Avranches. The only thing standing in their way was the 30th Infantry Division, which was just arriving in Mortain after its long drive from Tessy. As the weary GIs took up their defensive positions in the failing light, they had no idea of the tidal wave poised to engulf them.

CHAPTER 5: MORTAIN

Mortain, a picturesque little town of some sixteen hundred inhabitants, nestles in a valley alongside the Cance River. Just southwest of town, the shallow stream cascades through a deep gorge, then winds its way seven kilometers south to a confluence with the Selune.

Rising from the eastern edge of the town is a high hill, a spur of the wooded plateau known locally as La Suisse Normande (Norman Switzerland). Identified on U.S. Army maps as Hill 314 (the number being the number of meters above sea level of the crest), the rocky height rises gently from the north, more steeply on the eastern and southern faces. The hill's western edge, behind the town, is a sheer drop, known as the Cliffs of Montjoie. A well-maintained dirt road transverses the height from east to west, curving south at the last moment to avoid the cliffs. Cultivated fields—surrounded by the inevitable hedgerows—cover the northern half of the hill. The Forêt de Mortain climbs the southern slope, thinning out into an apple orchard as it reaches the twin summits.

Near the southwestern summit stands a tiny church, La Petite Chapelle, overlooking a small cemetery. A crag of bare rock rises from the slightly higher southwestern summit. The latter position offers the best view in Normandy. On a clear day, an observer can see parts of three provinces: Normandy, Brittany, and Maine. Avranches and the Bay of Mont-St.-Michel are visible to the west, the lush Bourberouge Forest spreads to the south beyond the flat plain of the Selune River, and the twisted gorge of the Sée River outlines the northern horizon.

Also visible from Hill 314 were the key roads that in 1944 connected Mortain to the coast. A wide, hard-surfaced highway—Route Nationale 177—emerged from the southern edge of town and ran straight as an arrow to the southwest. The 2d SS Panzer Division was to follow this route the sixteen kilometers to St.-Hilaire on the Selune River. There the road curved to the northwest and ran directly to the coast highway at Pontaubault. Hill 314 also overlooked the road junction just north of Mortain, near L'Abbaye Blanche. One highway ran east to Ger (still held by the Germans). Another (the northern leg of Route 177) ran a kilometer north to the hamlet of La Dainie, where it forked, the eastern branch running north to Sourdeval, the western branch leading to the little village of St.-Barthelmy (sometimes spelled St.-Barthélemy), where the highway forked again. The main road—the designated route of the 2d Panzer Division—curved due west and ran along the crest of a high ridge that pointed like a finger toward Avranches. The secondary road out of St.-Barthelmy curved down the ridge to the lowlands bordering the Sée River. It crossed the river and followed the north bank to Avranches. A dirt road ran parallel along the Sée's south bank. Shielded by the high east-west ridge, the two river roads were in one of the few spots hidden from observers on Hill 314. Unfortunately, the high ground to the northeast—around Sourdeval, where the German counterattack was assembling—was another blind spot.

Mortain was liberated on the afternoon of August 3 by the 1st Division's 18th Infantry Regiment. As the GIs approached the town along the St.-Hilaire road, a recon company of the 2d Panzer Division retreated toward Ger without a fight. Two officers in the French resistance met the 18th's commander and urged him to occupy Hill 314 without delay. A platoon was dispatched. Two hours later, when the VII Corps commander, Maj. Gen. J. Lawton Collins, arrived to inspect Mortain, the first thing he did was point to the high ground.

"Ralph," he told the 1st Division commander, Maj. Gen. Clarence R. Huebner, "be sure to get Hill 314."

"Joe," a smug Huebner replied, "I got it."

The capture of Mortain came as welcome news to General Bradley, now commanding the 12th Army Group (which included General Patton's Third Army and Bradley's old First Army command, now headed by Lt. Gen. Courtney Hodges). Bradley could read a map at least as

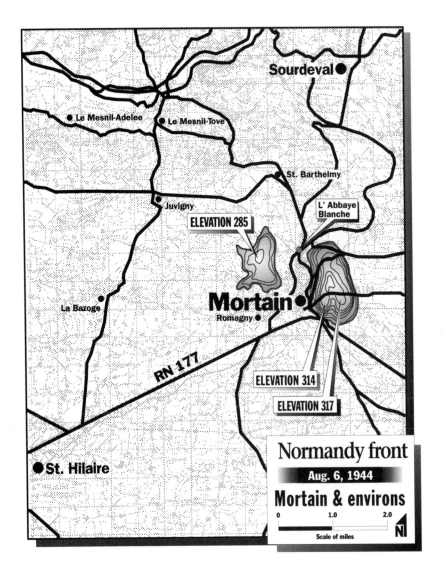

Sourdeval

Le Mesnil-Adelee

Le Mesnil-Tove

St. Barthelmy

Juvigny

L' Abbaye Blanche

ELEVATION 285

Mortain

La Bazoge

Romagny

RN 177

ELEVATION 314

ELEVATION 317

St. Hilaire

Normandy front

Aug. 6, 1944

Mortain & environs

0   1.0   2.0

Scale of miles

N

well as the former Bavarian corporal. The narrow corridor opposite Avranches was clearly the most vulnerable spot in his sector, the obvious target for a German counterattack. The acquisition of the high ground that dominated the region greatly increased the security of Patton's supply lines.

However, Bradley was not thinking defensively. Instead, he was trying to devise a plan to capitalize on the inexplicable enemy failure to withdraw from his tenuous position in Normandy. After the American breakout at St.-Lô, Bradley expected the Germans to pull back to prepared defensive positions along the Seine River. Instead, the divisions confronting the First Army and the British continued to stand firm, even as the Third Army was slicing through Brittany. Intelligence confirmed that new units were reinforcing the enemy's line. Bradley confessed his confusion to his aide, Chet Hansen: "They tell me he's fighting for time, but I'll be damned if I know how time can help him, except to enable him to live a little longer. He'd better straighten out on our front or he'll be terribly embarrassed one day."

The stubborn German defense suggested a great opportunity: a vast encirclement of the two German armies in Normandy. Bradley envisioned a wide sweep by Patton's Third Army. Six armored divisions would race from Le Mans toward Paris, preceded by an airdrop of three airborne divisions. Patton's spearhead would bypass Paris to the southeast, then drive north up the east bank of the Seine to Dieppe on the English Channel. Bradley's enthusiasm for the plan was evident when he unveiled the outline to his staff: "Let's talk big turkey," he said. "I'm ready to eat meat all the way."

Bradley spent the first week of August at his new headquarters in Coutances refining his grand scheme. The 1st Division's capture of Mortain opened another road south (through St.-Hilaire), which allowed him to feed another corps to Patton's burgeoning Third Army. Instead of adding Maj. Gen. Wade Hampton Haislip's XV Corps to the force occupying Brittany, Bradley pointed it to the southeast—toward Le Mans, which would be the starting point of his projected "vast encirclement." By nightfall of August 5, Haislip's lead division, the 90th, ably commanded by former 30th Division artillery commander Maj. Gen. Raymond McLain, had reached the Mayenne River, just twenty miles from Le Mans, meeting only light resistance. But the advance was opening a gap between the First and Third armies. To fill the gap and protect

Haislip's left flank, Bradley ordered the 1st Division to leave Mortain and move southeast through Fougères to Mayenne.

To help cover the vital hinge at Mortain, Bradley temporarily assigned the 30th Division to Collins's VII Corps. Old Hickory was ordered to leave Tessy and take over the 1st Division's positions in and around Mortain.

The 117th Infantry Regiment relieved the 1st Division's 26th Regiment's defensive positions near the picture-postcard village of St.-Barthelmy. "There's nothing to speak of in the front," a 1st Division officer told Lt. Robert Murray. "We had no trouble taking the place. You're lucky to be sent up just to hold a position already taken."

All along the line on that warm Saturday afternoon, the same sentiment was being repeated.

"We thought we'd be getting a rest," reported Pfc. George Neidhardt. "They told us we'd be holding a quiet area."

Mortain certainly looked quiet when Col. Hammond Birks, the commander of the 120th Infantry Regiment, arrived on the evening of August 5. The shops were open and the hotels were full. "It seemed like an excellent place for a little rest and recreation," one member of his staff recorded.

The commander of the 1st Division's 18th Infantry Regiment pointed out the significance of Hill 314, adding the prophetic warning that in case of emergency, the hill would have to be held at all costs. The next day, Birks assigned the first of his units to complete the long, dusty ride from Tessy to occupy the hill. As fate would have it, the job went to the 2d Battalion of the 120th.

"We arrived about 1:30 in the afternoon," recalled Lt. Guy Hagen, the 2d Battalion's communications officer. "We were told to take over the positions the 18th Infantry had prepared. There was only one indication something was up. Just as we reached the outskirts of town, we were strafed by German planes. They came right over Hill 314, so close they almost scraped it. That was a little bit of a surprise—usually when we were strafed, it was by our own air force."

The battalion commander, Lt. Col. Eads Hardaway, had an extra company at his disposal, Company K of the 3d Battalion. However, he had duties other than the occupation of Hill 314. His battalion had to occupy the town itself and establish roadblocks on the routes running just north and south of Mortain. Only Lt. Ralph Kerley's E Company,

Lt. Joe Reaser's K Company, two platoons of Lt. Ronal Woody's G Company, and a part of Capt. Delmont Byrn's H (heavy weapons) Company were assigned to Hill 314. About six hundred men, armed with rifles, machine guns, and a few mortars, walked up the hill on the afternoon of August 6.

"We had to carry everything up that damn hill—guns, tripods, ammo, everything!" said Pvt. John Weekly of H Company. "We didn't have a jeep or an ammo carrier. I was carrying the tripod for our .50-caliber machine gun. We set up in an orchard. It was a machine gunner's paradise. You could see for miles and miles. The problem was we only had minimal ammunition. We brought all we could carry, but that wasn't much."

Preceding the riflemen up the hill were two observers from the 230th Field Artillery Battalion: 1st Lt. Charles Bartz of Lincoln, Nebraska, and 2d Lt. Robert Weiss of Valparaiso, Indiana.

"On arriving at the hill, we contacted Lt. Walsh," Weiss wrote. "He was the forward observer of the artillery battalion we were relieving. He pointed out possible observation points and in particular showed us one which gave a view straight down the east-west road which ran over our hill and into Mortain. This road paralleled another [one] fifteen hundred yards to the north which was a main highway and was the principal avenue of escape for the German units we believed were trapped in front of us. It was pointed out to us that shooting the retreating Germans on these roads was a regular picnic as enemy movement was always revealed by a cloud of dust. It must be noted our hill was one of the highest points in Normandy and dominated the land to our front, to the northeast and in the north and to the south."

When the riflemen reached the top of the hill, they took over 1st Division positions almost foxhole for foxhole.

"The positions prepared by the 18th Infantry were for a hasty defense only and never intended to contain a strong counterattack," Lieutenant Kerley later wrote. "We were aware of this and planned to improve the positions with fortifications, mines, etc., as soon as they became available. Unfortunately, these intended improvements never came to pass."

The officers of the 120th were not too concerned about the inadequate defensive preparations.

"Perhaps the battalion was suffering a false sense of security," Kerley said. "There was no concrete information about the enemy. We had just driven to Mortain with French civilians lining the roads, cheering, throwing bouquets and offering drinks at every halt. One could easily feel the Germans would not stop short of the Rhine." That optimistic view was not restricted to the officers and men of the 120th. "The captain of the company we were relieving told me not to worry, there was nothing to our front," Lieutenant Reaser said. The 30th Division's own intelligence summary came to the same conclusion, rating enemy capabilities with the following estimate: "To withdraw to the east, fighting a delaying action, accompanied by local counterattacks."

Reaser's company was placed on the northern edge of the knoll that caps Hill 314. The new company commander was nicknamed Indian Joe for an incident that occurred during the hedgerow fighting. A group of Germans were discovered holed up on the second floor of a building. Reaser suggested setting fire to the first floor of the building "to smoke them out." A newspaperman who heard the story said that it sounded like an old Indian trick. The nickname stuck. Actually, Reaser was a native of Gettysburg, Pennsylvania, where as a boy he had played on the famous Civil War battlefield. He was working for a furniture company in his hometown when drafted in July 1941. He trained as a ranger before attending officer candidate school and joining the 30th Division at Camp Blanding.

Kerley's company and the squad from H Company occupied the center of the position, facing east, astride the dirt trail that ran over the hill into Mortain. Most of Woody's men took over foxholes overlooking the southern face. One platoon was deployed on the western slope, below the cliff, just above the town. The positions were not connected and the three lieutenants on the hill, all newcomers to company command, found orientation difficult.

"The movement was executed so rapidly, it was impossible to secure maps of the area," Lieutenant Kerley complained. "The 2d Battalion S-2 secured a few large-scale maps, scarcely enough for a company. In addition, the company commanders of 1st Battalion, 18th Infantry, turned their maps over to the relieving companies. These had been in use for several days and were crumpled and badly marked."

Colonel Hardaway, who established his headquarters in the Grande Hotel on Mortain's main street, was trying to sort out the confusion. The 1st Battalion of the 18th Infantry had set up its switchboard in the Church of St. Evroult across the street, but Hardaway's communications staff found the phone net unusable.

"It was a mess," said Robert Bondurant, the 2d Battalion's communications sergeant. "The only thing to do was replace it. That's what I did—I started stringing new wire to all our positions."

Captain Reynold Erichson's F Company was split up to man the roadblocks in the battalion's sector. Private Neidhardt's squad was assigned to cover two 57mm antitank guns blocking a dirt road at the foot of Hill 314. He inherited a foxhole from a 1st Division private. "He had only dug down about eighteen inches," Neidhardt recalled. The squad reached the position early in the afternoon. "It was a bright, sunny day. There were a lot of German planes flying overhead. Most of them weren't dropping anything. I thought they must be taking pictures. That's when I decided to dig deeper. I went down four feet, deep enough to stand in up to my armpits." Neidhardt didn't know it at the time, but his spadework that afternoon was to save his life the next morning.

Erichson's 1st Platoon, under Lt. Tom Andrews, was assigned to the key crossroad at L'Abbaye Blanche (named for the large white abbey that sits just across the Cance River). Two 57mm guns from the regiment's antitank platoon initially provided the roadblock's main firepower, supported by Andrews's rifle squads and a small section from H Company with machine guns and mortars.

The roadblock received an important reinforcement when Lt. Thomas Springfield arrived at 1700 to scout positions for his tank-destroyer platoon. Springfield's four guns belonged to Company A of the 823d Tank-Destroyer (TD) Battalion. The 3-inch rifles of the 823d were far more effective antitank weapons than the 57mm popguns issued to the infantry. Springfield's guns fired a fifteen-pound shell that could penetrate three inches of armor at two thousand yards. The rifle's high muzzle velocity and flat trajectory made it extremely accurate.

Springfield was not thrilled by his rapid survey of the position. The 634th TD Battalion, attached to the 1st Division, was equipped with the self-propelled M10 (the same 3-inch rifles but mounted on a tank chassis). The 823d TD Battalion's guns were M6s, mounted on an artillery carriage and towed into position by half-tracks. The positions used by the 634th would not do for his guns. Instead, Springfield picked out new emplacements at the northern end of the roadblock. Two guns were located behind a hedgerow, facing east, where they could cover the northern exit from Mortain. The other two guns were placed in shallow ditches on either side of Route 177, covering the highway north to St.-Barthelmy. Lieutenant Andrews's platoon was positioned to defend the southern approach to the roadblock. Two bridges over the shallow Cance River were mined and covered by 57mm guns and machine-gun positions.

The defensive preparations at L'Abbaye Blanche were not completed until just before sundown. Luckily, the long summer day didn't end until an hour before midnight. The 30th Division needed the extra daylight to complete its occupation of the front around Mortain. Some units were still moving into position as twilight turned into darkness.

One of those late-arriving units was Lt. George Greene's 3d Platoon, B Company, 823d TD Battalion. Assigned to defend the road junction at St.-Barthelmy, Greene headed north from Mortain in a jeep to scout the position. At the crossroads at La Dainie, just north of L'Abbaye Blanche, he was stopped at an infantry checkpoint, where he was warned that the enemy had mortars zeroed in on the flat stretch of highway ahead. Greene and his platoon sergeant left their jeep at the checkpoint and used a deep ditch alongside the highway to approach St.-Barthelmy unobserved. Once in the town, Greene contacted the infantry units detailed to guard the town, A and C companies of the 117th Infantry. He was shown the gun positions vacated by the 634th TD Battalion.

"They were terrible [positions]," Greene said. "Some of them were in gardens where the ground was real soft. I later found out they were for self-propelled guns." The young lieutenant, a newcomer to the 823d, had trained on the M10. He wasn't pleased with the towed weapons of his new unit. "Our guns were the biggest pieces of junk . . . they had no flexibility in combat. You could hardly move them." Each gun weighed almost three tons; before firing, the crews would dig the wheels into the ground. "To move one," Greene explained, "one guy would have to hang on to the barrel and pull it down, then it would take four or five guys pushing the wheels. You can imagine doing all that under fire."

Greene didn't have time to scout new positions for his guns, but he resolved to find better locations the next day. He did get lucky in one respect, discovering a sunken road parallel to the exposed highway. He moved his guns forward on the hidden road just as night was falling. His platoon didn't finish emplacing its last gun until 0200 the next morning.

*   *   *

General Leland Hobbs established his command post in a beautiful chateau near La Bazoge, ten kilometers west of Mortain. His divisional front extended from just north of St.-Barthelmy, where the 117th Infantry Regiment was curved along the ridgeline overlooking the Sée River, to just south of Mortain, where the 120th Infantry was replacing the 18th Infantry—Colonel Birks establishing his 2d Battalion on Hill 314 and in the town, and his 1st Battalion on Hill 285 west of the Cance River. The 119th Regiment, minus the 2d Battalion (which was on detached duty with the 2d Armored Division near Vire), was in reserve just north of the ridge road to Avranches, about twelve kilometers west of St.-Barthelmy.

The division artillery was spread on a rough line stretching from the ridge road five kilometers west of St.-Barthelmy to the tiny village of Romagny. Brigadier General James Lewis, the 30th's new artillery commander, wanted to set up his headquarters near the division command post (CP) at La Bazoge. However, in order to use the wire communications net left by the 1st Division artillery, Lewis was forced to occupy the existing artillery CP at Les Monts, about four kilometers from La Bazoge. Lewis was also unhappy with the placement of his batteries. The sites his gunners inherited from the 1st Division were too far forward. They had been established in the expectation that the division would continue its advance. In a defensive situation, his batteries would be dangerously exposed.

Hobbs was not thinking defensively on the evening of August 6. His orders were to continue the VII Corps's drive toward the southeast. He was busy preparing a movement in that direction for the next morning. The 119th Infantry was alerted to spearhead an advance toward Domfront, twenty kilometers southeast of Mortain. The shorthanded regiment was to be accompanied by two companies of Sherman tanks from the 743d Tank Battalion. It was obvious Hobbs had no intimation that the Germans might beat him to the punch. If there had been any hint that the 30th would soon be attacked, Hobbs would have paid less attention to his own advance and more attention to his flanks, both of which were dangling in thin air.

Elements of the 4th and 9th divisions were supposed to be north of the 117th Regiment on Old Hickory's left flank. The 4th Division was in reserve to the northwest. The 39th Regiment of the 9th Division

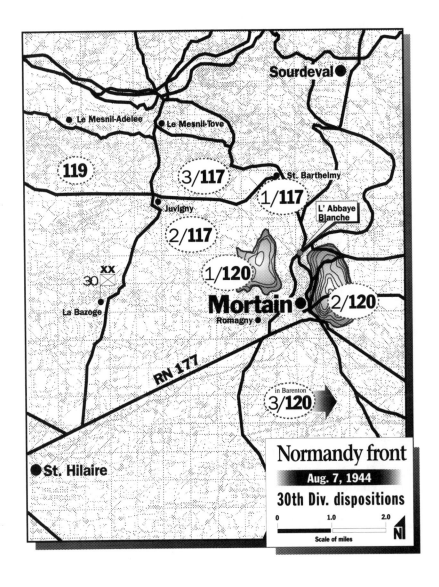

Normandy front
Aug. 7, 1944
30th Div. dispositions

was forward but facing north toward a German pocket on the Vire River. Patrols sent to locate the friendly units did not succeed in making contact. The situation on the right flank was even more unclear. VII Corps cavalry (motorized recon units) was operating to the south. A task force of the 3d Armored Division was reportedly in Barenton, a small town about ten kilometers southeast of Mortain, halfway along the road to Domfront that the 119th would be taking the next morning.

Assuming that Barenton was in American hands, Hobbs ordered Colonel Birks to send his 3d Battalion (minus Company K) to help hold the town. The riflemen were loaded into trucks and were accompanied by a company of Shermans from the 743d, the 30th Division's recon troop, and the 120th's recon platoon. The convoy moved out at 2030 hours. Less than a mile beyond Mortain, the head of the column was strafed by nine FW-190s armed with rockets. The German attack inflicted forty-seven casualties and delayed the convoy for almost an hour. That delay was to have unfortunate consequences. When the 3d Battalion finally reached Barenton at 2300 (after following a circuitous course to avoid German artillery fire), the survivors of the 3d Armored's Task Force X, reduced to only ten tanks and eighty men, were discovered outside town, digging defensive positions. They had been forced out of Barenton less than half an hour earlier by arriving troops of the German 275th Division. Lieutenant Colonel Paul McCollum, commanding the 3d Battalion, decided to dig in for the night and retake the town the next morning.

In the hills around Mortain, men were also digging in for the night. However, in the town itself, GIs and townspeople were celebrating Mortain's liberation. The small city was remarkably fortunate, suffering almost no damage during the German withdrawal. The retreating Nazis had fired a single artillery shell into Mortain on August 3, but it exploded in the public gardens, doing no real harm. The town fathers offered thanks to God for sparing their homes the desolation that had visited nearby cities such as Vire, Tessy, and St.-Lô.

The offerings were premature.

CHAPTER 6: COUNTDOWN TO H HOUR

B letchley Park, tucked away in a quiet, pastoral corner of Buckinghamshire, England, was in 1944 the home of the British Government Code and Cipher School. The innocent name and the rural setting were deliberately misleading. Bletchley Park was the home of the war's most important secret weapon—Ultra.

Ultra was the code name that British cryptographers assigned to the process of intercepting and deciphering German communications. Thanks to a gift from the doomed Polish government, which in July 1939 turned over a copy of the German Enigma machine to the code and cipher school, and to the genius of a handful of mathematicians led by Alan Turing, the British were able to manage a significant and sustained penetration of the "unbreakable" German ciphers. Ultra first proved its value during the Battle of Britain, and it played a vital role in Great Britain's survival during the 1940–41 crisis in the Battle of the Atlantic.

Unfortunately, possession of such sensitive intelligence made distribution difficult. Had Ultra reports been widely distributed, it would have been only a matter of time until the secret was compromised. Instead, the British elected to keep knowledge of Ultra extremely limited, a decision supported by Gen. George C. Marshall, the U.S. Army chief of staff, when the American high command was informed of the British miracle. Under Marshall's instructions, American armies and army groups were accompanied by special liaison units, which handled all Ultra intelligence. No Ultra information was distributed at corps or division level. The system proved highly effective in protecting the Ultra secret (it was not in fact revealed until 1974) but occasionally prevented the rapid dissemination of vital intelligence.

That was not Ultra's sole limitation. Only German radio traffic was intercepted. The enemy's phone and teletype lines remained secure. Hitler's August 2 attack order to Field Marshal von Kluge was undetected, since it was delivered by teletype. Von Kluge's subsequent orders to his subordinate commanders, delivered in every case by messenger, phone, or teletype, were also undetected.

Allegations that Ultra provided an early warning of these plans stem from F. W. Winterbotham's 1974 book, *The Ultra Secret,* in which he writes, "On August the second, in a long signal which I remember covered two whole sheets of my Ultra paper, Hitler told Kluge . . . to collect together four of the armored divisions from the Caen front with sufficient infantry divisions to make a decisive counter-attack to retake Avranches." In response to this intercept, "Bradley was told to make the necessary preparations to meet the attack with defense in depth in the Avranches area."

Winterbotham's book was based on memory, not on documents. Despite the convincing detail he provides ("This highly-important signal arrived just as I was preparing to go back to my club for some food."), his memory is clearly faulty. No evidence of his "long signal" exists, either in German radio logs or in the Ultra logs at Bletchley Park. In addition, the idea of withdrawing four armored divisions from the Caen front came from von Kluge. Hitler's original idea was to assemble eight divisions, drawing on forces from the Fifteenth Army and the south of France.

In fact, Ralph Bennett in his 1979 book *Ultra in the West,* based on the official Ultra logs, writes of Hitler's August 2 attack order: "Hotter news there could hardly be, yet no unwise use of the information was made and the secret was safely kept . . . There was no evidence of this in Ultra."

Bennett addressed the question of Winterbotham's claims: "There appears to be no Ultra warrant for a number of his statements, in spite of the circumstantial detail with which he surrounds some of them. Several can, however, be approximately reconciled with the signals by a change in the dating. There are three stages in the Mortain attack: (1) Hitler's order of 2 August, of which Ultra knew nothing, (2) the attack order of 6 August, and (3) von Kluge's renewal order of 9

August, both of which Ultra reported in time. It seems possible that Group Captain Winterbotham's memory confused stages (2) and (3) with (1)."

General Bradley hotly disputed the claim that he had five days' warning to prepare for the Mortain counterattack. "My recollection is in sharp variance," he wrote in 1983. "In this instance, Ultra was of little or no value. Ultra alerted us to the attack only a few hours before it came, and that was too late to make any major defensive preparations." Indeed, Bradley's memory is not only supported by the historical record, but by his actions in the days leading up to the attack. Had he known that a major counterattack was coming at Mortain, it is most unlikely he would have pulled the 1st Division out of line at the point of attack, exposing the newly arrived 30th Division to destruction before it was firmly established.

In truth, even without Ultra, Bradley suspected the Germans were planning a counterattack. His own intelligence sources picked up evidence that von Kluge was pulling armored divisions out of the line and replacing them with infantry, obvious signs that the Germans were preparing a counterstroke. On August 6, Allied aircraft detected and attacked concentrations of armor in the Sourdeval area. Even without Ultra, Bradley knew that the narrow corridor between the Sée and the Selune rivers would be the likely target of a counterattack. However, he believed that by continuing to push eastward toward Domfront and Le Mans, he could keep the Germans off balance and force the enemy to commit his armor in those sectors.

The first real clue provided by Ultra that the Germans were mounting a counterattack at Mortain was not intercepted until the afternoon of August 6. A message from the Seventh Army to the Luftwaffe in Paris, requesting night fighter protection for the 2d SS Panzer Division in an attack through Mortain to St.-Hilaire, was received at Bletchley Park at 1400 hours and decoded five hours later. An earlier message, intercepted at 1300 hours, but not decoded until 1948 hours, identified all four attacking divisions. A third message, the most explicit of all, was intercepted at 1700 hours and decoded at eleven minutes after midnight. It gave the start line of the attack as Sourdeval-Mortain, identified the first objective as the Brécey-Montigny road, and set H hour at 1830, which was actually three and a half hours before the scheduled start of the attack.

Since reports by the special liaison units were not recorded in G-2 or G-3 diaries, it is impossible to determine exactly when Bletchley's warnings reached Bradley and his army commanders. However, Maj. Melvin Helfers, a British officer serving as head of the Third Army's special liaison unit, remembers receiving word of the German armored buildup east of Mortain sometime around 2000 hours. Helfers first took the news to Col. Oscar Koch, General Patton's G-2; then the two officers rushed to Patton's command trailer, located in the woods near Beauchamps on the Villedieu-Granville road. Because of the tight Ultra security, Patton did not know who Helfers was or what his information represented. However, Patton immediately recognized the importance of the intercepts he was shown.

"How much of this have we been getting?" Patton asked. "How long has this officer been with us?"

Patton would record the incident in his diary, using somewhat guarded language: "We got a rumor last night from a secret source that several Panzer divisions would attack west from Mortain to Avranches. Personally, I think it is a German bluff to cover a withdrawal, but I stopped the 80th, French 2nd Armored and the 35th in the vicinity of St. Hilaire just in case something might happen."

Actually, Patton had received a phone call from General Bradley, ordering the halt of the three divisions, two of which were slated to join the XV Corps advancing on Le Mans. The 35th Division, a veteran infantry unit commanded by Maj. Gen. Paul Baade, was on its way to join Maj. Gen. Walton Walker's XX Corps. It was, however, transferred to General Collins's VII Corps that evening, in anticipation of its commitment to the battle Ultra had just revealed. Bradley took one other important step, asking the Allied air forces to provide all-out air support as soon as it was light. That was all Bradley could do on such short notice, other than rush a warning down through the chain of command to General Hobbs at Mortain. The warning arrived at thirty-eight minutes past midnight on teletype from the VII Corps:

> Enemy counterattack expected vicinity Mortain from East and slant or North within the next 12 hours. 1st Division protect lines of communication south of Le Tellevil. 30th Division suspend movement of RCT [Regimental Combat Team] to Domfront until 1000 7 August. RCT 119 remain division reserve, moving one battalion vicinity of Le Tellevil to protect lines of communica-

tion there and to the North. 30th Division also reinforce battalion on Hill (314). Acknowledge receipt of this message without delay.

This warning arrived two hours and thirty-eight minutes *after* the German attack should have begun. However, General Funck was having trouble getting Operation Lüttich rolling. The 1st SS Panzer Division, which had the longest way to go to reach the assembly area, was late getting started because the 89th Infantry Division had been slow in relieving the panzer division near Caen. Traffic congestion and Allied air attacks had further delayed its progress. The tank battalion sent to assist the 2d Panzer Division was slowed by an incredible piece of bad luck. A British Typhoon was shot down by a German antiaircraft unit and it crashed into the lead Panther, blocking the column in a narrow defile. Less excusable was the attitude of Lt. Gen. Count Gerhard von Schwerin, the commander of the 116th Panzer Division. His command was not in position to support the attack, nor had he dispatched the tank battalion he was supposed to furnish to the 2d Panzer Division.

Funck telephoned Gen. Paul Hausser, the Seventh Army commander, at 2200 hours and requested a delay. He also demanded the relief of von Schwerin, whose division, he complained, "practically always mucks up the situation." Hausser was sympathetic to Funck's problems but, under pressure from von Kluge, was able to grant only a two-hour postponement of H hour. "This does not alter the fact," he told Funck, "that Lüttich will be executed as ordered."

Inevitably, the last-minute delay led to confusion and resulted in some lack of coordination among German units. At La Fantay, a roadblock seven hundred meters north of St.-Barthelmy, German vehicles had been sighted as early as 2030 hours, but both sides withheld their fire until just after midnight, when a force of two to four panzers, accompanied by infantry, approached the roadblock. The defenders—two squads of Company B, 117th Infantry—fired fifteen rounds from their two 57mm antitank guns, scoring one hit on the lead Panther. Not surprisingly, the shell failed to penetrate the tank's frontal armor. A shot from the Panther killed two men and destroyed one of the antitank guns. Judging the position untenable, the lieutenant in command ordered his men to retire. The German force did not follow.

Lieutenant Colonel R. Ernest Frankland, commanding the 117th's 1st Battalion, ordered Lt. Robert Cushman to take a squad forward and reestablish the roadblock. As Cushman's small force approached the road junction, he could hear the Germans talking and milling around, almost in their original position. American artillery began to fall on the road junction, several rounds falling short and wounding three of Cushman's men.

The brief action at La Fantay didn't cause an alarm. It was typical of the confused, close-quarters skirmishes that occurred frequently in the hedgerow country. It was not a particularly quiet night anywhere along the 30th Division's front. Beginning soon after sundown, German artillery fire began to fall around St.-Barthelmy and Mortain. This wasn't the kind of concentrated barrage that normally presaged an attack, but harassing fire, designed to keep the weary Americans awake and cover the noise of the approaching panzers. Inside Mortain itself, the incoming artillery, supplemented by an air raid, started several fires. Around midnight, civilians began evacuating the town, many taking refuge in a large cave located near the roadblock at L'Abbaye Blanche.

It was a bright, moonlit night. Adding the light of the fires made Mortain as bright as Manhattan on New Year's Eve. For Sgt. Robert Bondurant, busy stringing telephone wire through the streets, the enhanced visibility was a great convenience. "That's how I saw them," he said. "I was in the street, checking lines when I looked up and there they were at the other end of the street—German soldiers. Maybe thirty or more. All with burp guns. The town was full of them."

Sergeant Bondurant, a grocery-store clerk from Reidsville, North Carolina, had joined the National Guard in 1938 and stayed in the 120th Regiment when most of his buddies left in 1941 and 1942. Although he claimed, "I wasn't no hero," he had been decorated with the Bronze Star with oak-leaf clusters.

In Mortain, Bondurant's moment of shock didn't last long. Within seconds of spotting the German soldiers, he ran to the battalion headquarters and warned Lieutenant Colonel Hardaway that the enemy was in the town.

"He called Regiment right away," Bondurant reported. "Colonel Birks got on the phone and said, 'Hold the town at all costs.' I can still hear those words: 'Hold the town at all costs.' I went back to my switchboard. We were told to stay, so I was going to stay."

It was just a few minutes after one o'clock in the morning on August 7. The Battle of Mortain had begun.

CHAPTER 7: OUT OF THE FOG

T*he fog of battle* is a term that military professionals use to describe the confusion normal to combat. As the Battle of Mortain began, the words were both literally and figuratively true.

Confusion reigned on both sides. The Americans, just settling into their new and unfamiliar defensive positions, were surprised by the first sharp encounters with the enemy. They did not know what to make of the unexpected attacks, which appeared to be widely scattered and uncoordinated. In truth, the first attacks *were* widely scattered and uncoordinated as the Germans labored to launch Operation Lüttich without proper preparation. Units attacked as they reached their starting points, often while supporting units were still struggling to reach the front. Adding to the night's confusion was a real fog, thick and seemingly impenetrable, which rolled into the area at about 0300 hours, turning the clear, moonlit night into a soupy blackness.

The first German advances came on the flanks. The Recon Battalion of the 2d Panzer Division, probing along the north bank of the Sée River, found no resistance and pushed across the river, then west along the narrow valley road. At 0100 hours, Lt. Anthony Ponticello, an observer for the 26th Field Artillery Battalion (supporting the 9th Division's 39th Infantry Regiment), heard the tanks moving west, but when he phoned in to report the noise, he was told the sound was coming from friendly vehicles. However, someone at battalion headquarters must have had second thoughts, because a few minutes later, the order to fire was given and the 26th opened up with its twelve 105mm guns at a range of five thousand yards. Because of the fog, Ponticello had to adjust fire entirely by sound. Even though 535 high-explosive (HE) rounds were directed at the advancing armored column, it is unlikely that much damage was done in the fog and darkness.

The 39th Regiment's Cannon Company, manning a roadblock in Le Mesnil-Tove (three miles behind where the front lines were supposed to be) was attacked at about 0200 by approximately twenty tanks supported by dismounted infantry. The roadblock's defenders were forced to abandon their equipment and withdraw to the south. They pulled out the electrical wires on their vehicles and the breech blocks from their guns to prevent the Germans from using the equipment. The technique worked: they recovered everything intact several days later.

At about the same moment that the 39th Regiment's Cannon Company was pulling out of Le Mesnil-Tove, a force of between two hundred and three hundred German infantrymen made an infiltration attack north of the Sée River, penetrating to positions held by the 4th Division near Lingeard. Company F of the 22d Infantry Regiment, holding the Lingeard Chateau, detected the Germans advancing up a narrow defile toward their position. The American soldiers withheld rifle fire while Sgt. John Pettyman's mortar squad dropped some 370 rounds on the defile, blocking four distinct attempts to advance up the hill toward the chateau. The next morning, the advancing riflemen captured sixty prisoners and counted ninety dead Germans in the defile.

Members of the 39th Regiment later complained of difficulty convincing the 30th Division that a German attack was in progress. It was not until 0300 hours that the 119th Infantry was ordered to send a task force consisting of an infantry company and an antitank platoon to try to set up a roadblock at Le Mesnil-Adelée (three miles west of Le Mesnil-Tove). The regiment's 3d Battalion was to move north from its position near Juvigny and cut off the German penetration from behind, near the vicinity of Le Mesnil-Tove. The 39th Regiment, which was split by the German drive (its headquarters and artillery south of the penetration, its infantry to the north), ordered its K Company to drive on Le Mesnil-Tove from the north. Artillery on the heights bordering both sides of the river valley maintained sporadic fire in the darkness. Once daylight arrived, the guns of three American divisions, the 30th, the 9th, and the 4th, would be able to pour a devastating fire on the exposed German tank battalion.

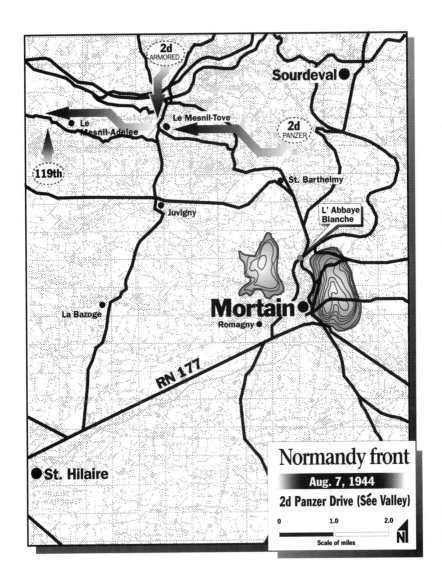

Normandy front

Aug. 7, 1944

2d Panzer Drive (Sée Valley)

0   1.0   2.0

Scale of miles

The situation on the 30th Division's southern flank was potentially more serious. At the same time as the right wing of the 2d Panzer Division was moving west along the Sée River, the Deutschland Regiment of the 2d SS Panzer Division swept out of the Forêt de Mortain, around the southern edge of Hill 314, and into the town along the rue de Fleurs and the rue du Rochers. The roadblocks south of Mortain were overrun before the Americans knew what was happening.

"I was sleeping in a slit trench, when a boy came over and shook me awake," said Sgt. John Whitsett of the 120th Regiment's Headquarters Company. His unit's three 57mm antitank guns were entrenched alongside the well-maintained dirt road that ran beneath the southern bluffs of Hill 314. "The boy said the lieutenant wanted to see me. He said, 'The Germans are coming.' I told him the Germans don't attack at night."

Whitsett didn't have a lot of faith in his new platoon leader, a raw second lieutenant who had only joined the company at Tessy.

"Everything was quiet," Sergeant Whitsett said. "I started to walk up the road a little ways, smoking a cigarette. I could hear men moving. I wondered where the infantry was going. I hopped up on a hedgerow so I could see better. I caught a glimpse of a German helmet. A guy saw me and started firing. I jumped down and ran back toward the gun, yelling at them to get back."

Whitsett's warning came too late. The German troops, moving on the fields as well as the road, were already behind the roadblock. The sergeant, cut off from the rest of his platoon, hid at the base of the hedgerow, counting on the darkness to conceal him. "I laid there listening, waiting for our guns to open up," he said. "But they didn't. Some German soldiers found our jeep and I could hear them messing with it. Apparently, they couldn't figure out the gears because all they did was run it around in low gear. I figured I better get away from there, so when they drove the jeep past where I was hiding, I used the noise as cover. I must have startled them, because I ran right past a group of soldiers and they didn't fire a shot."

The infiltration tactics of the Deutschland Regiment were quite successful in the darkness. The scattered roadblocks south of Mortain and Hill 314, unwarned either by high command or by the noisy approach of German armor, were swept up one by one by the SS

Panzergrenadiers. A roadblock manned by a platoon of the 823d TD Battalion would have been formidable against an armored assault, but Lt. Elmer Miller didn't have the manpower to hold off the advancing infantry. Concentrated small-arms fire made it impossible to use the platoon's four 3-inch guns, so Lieutenant Miller and his men fought as infantry. The majority, including Miller, were quickly captured. One group of sixteen men fought alone for five days, eventually rejoining another platoon of the 823d north of Mortain.

Sergeant Whitsett and the survivors of Miller's platoon weren't the only GIs at large behind the fast-moving German spearhead. Private First Class Lloyd Briese, a member of a roadblock set up by the 2d Battalion's antitank platoon, got separated from his unit as the German soldiers swept out of the fog. Armed with only a .45-caliber pistol and three clips of ammunition, Briese used two of the clips in the action before deciding to save the last clip, "for fear [I'd get] into a tight spot."

If the 2d Battalion of the 120th Regiment wasn't in a tight spot in the predawn hours of August 7, 1944, it is hard to imagine what a tight spot would have been. Panzergrenadiers were pouring into Mortain from the south with armored columns not far behind them. Squad-sized units were beginning to infiltrate Hill 314, threatening the three unconnected companies defending the heights. "They were screaming at the top of their voices, 'Heil Hitler!'" Lt. Ralph Kerley reported. "They made enough noise that one could easily believe an entire battalion was attacking." Adding to the perilous position of the three isolated companies was the Der Führer Regiment of the 2d SS Panzers, which was belatedly making its push north of Hill 314 toward the roadblock at L'Abbaye Blanche.

The sudden arrival of the panzergrenadiers caught Lt. Ronal Woody in a dangerous spot. He was visiting G Company's kitchen area, below the Cliffs of Montjoie, when he spotted the enemy troops. "When the firing started, I knew I had to get up to where my men were, up on top of the hill, so I went up the cliff," Woody said. "They were shooting all around me as I climbed. Somehow I made it up there. When I looked back and saw the way I'd come, I couldn't believe I'd climbed it."

For Col. Hammond Birks at his headquarters in a stone farmhouse near the tiny village of Le Neufbourg, just west of Mortain, the situation was turning into a nightmare. His first warning of trouble had come at 0125 hours, when the 2d Battalion reported hearing small-arms fire to the east. Just minutes later, Lt. Col. Eads Hardaway reported that enemy troops were entering Mortain in force. There was little Birks could do to help. The 3d Battalion had been his regimental reserve. When that unit was ordered to Barenton, Birks pulled C Company off Hill 285 and designated that small unit as his reserve. At 0250 hours, he ordered Lt. Albert Smith, C Company's commander, to lead his men into Mortain, clean out the town, and reestablish the roadblock south of Hill 314.

It was a formidable task for less than two hundred riflemen.

Lieutenant Smith led his company into Mortain from the southwest. His small relief force was soon scattered and fighting for its life. Most of the 1st Platoon was driven from the middle of town and forced to establish a defensive position on a small hill west of town. Part of the 3d Platoon was driven in the other direction, eventually seeking refuge on Hill 314 to the east. The bulk of C Company, augmented by refugees from the 2d Battalion, was fighting grimly in the center of town but was gradually being pushed north. Lieutenant Smith was killed by the concussion of an 88mm shell and Lt. R. H. White assumed command of the remnants of the company. The battle in the town was bloody and confused, waged in fog and darkness, with visibility provided only by the light of burning buildings.

"A lot of the town was on fire," said Cpl. Dudley Wilkerson, who moved into Mortain with C Company. "All hell was breaking loose with severe shelling, tanks moving in and German SS troops. A lieutenant asked me if I could load a bazooka. We went to the corner of a building and I put a shell in the bazooka. He fired and knocked out a German tank. Then he said, 'Run!' I saw why. A shell from an 88 hit the corner of the building where we had been. It knocked me down. When I got up, I didn't see the lieutenant again. I don't know whether he was killed or not."

Wilkerson, now alone, tried to return to his squad. "I heard a guy yell for help. He wanted somebody to cover him. He had a machine gun set up in a building that the front had been blown out of. He had a crossroad covered, and he was piling them up as they tried to cross the street. I stayed with him for some time, shooting at Germans who were throwing grenades from the windows of the building above us. A concussion grenade finally rolled down near us. I was in a crouched position and it ended up right between my legs. I tried to grab it, but it went off and picked me up off the ground. That's the last I remember, until a medic stopped by and helped me up. The machine gunner was dead. I never knew his name. I could walk, but I kept passing out. The blast had broken my rifle and my watch and had blown the setting right out of my ring. The medic helped me to a building, down into the basement, and I blacked out again. When I woke up, there was a cage of rabbits right in front of me. I thought I was in heaven."

But Wilkerson was still in the hell of Mortain. As the darkness gave way to dawn, the situation continued to deteriorate. At 0345 hours, Hardaway reported to Colonel Birks that the Germans were in possession of a portion of Hill 314. The harried regimental commander had no more reinforcements to send; he ordered Hardaway to use his own Company G to retake the ground. Woody coolly organized his men and prepared to sweep the enemy off the hill.

The 2d Battalion was rapidly losing touch with the outside world. The phone net, most of it inherited from the 1st Division, some of it hastily laid the night before, had broken down. Hardaway's only contact with regimental headquarters was via radio. The lines to his rifle companies on Hill 314 had been cut. Captain Reynold Erichson, commander of Company F, had lost contact with his scattered roadblocks. As a result, many men not actually involved in combat slept through the first hours of the attack. Sergeant Luther Myers, with E Company atop Hill 314, dozed in his foxhole, unaware that less than a kilometer away, his comrades were fighting for their lives. Lieutenant Joe Reaser, commanding K Company on the hill, knew that German soldiers were infiltrating between his position and Company E but judged that "they were just combat patrols. Maybe fifteen, twenty men probing our positions." At L'Abbaye Blanche, Lt. Thomas Springfield had no idea that the noise coming from his right was anything other than normal harassing fire from a distant enemy.

The confusion was such that at 0315, an observer from the VII Corps noted, "Division G-3 states Division not yet greatly concerned," even as Hobbs was telling VII Corps headquarters: "We are getting an attack all along the front. They have penetrated through the town of Mortain;

however, we still hold the high ground. There is also a penetration between the 39th Infantry and the 117th, vicinity of Mes Niltove [Le Mesnil-Tove]. We are moving in to counterattack."

Hobbs might have been more concerned if he had known that the Germans had so far managed to strike with just one tank battalion in the north and one panzergrenadier regiment in the south. The remainder of General Funck's forces—the mass of the 2d Panzer Division, the entire 1st SS Panzer Division, and the remainder of the 2d SS Panzers—were, however, on the move. The 30th Division was to feel the full weight of the German attack at dawn.

CHAPTER 8: DAWN

It's a fact of military life—the new guy always gets the cruddy detail. As a replacement with less than five days' duty with the 3d Platoon, F Company, Pvt. George Neidhardt wasn't surprised or offended when Tex, his squad sergeant, ordered him to leave his foxhole and find the company kitchen to bring back breakfast for the rest of the squad. "A runner was supposed to bring our breakfast at 5:00 A.M., but he was late," Neidhardt said. "Tex asked me to run back and find out what happened to our chow."

Neidhardt's squad was dug in alongside a dirt road that ran just below Hill 314. The worried GIs had just spent a long night listening to the sounds of battle going on around them. The sergeant kept his squad on alert all night, but no Germans tried to pass down the narrow road in the darkness. Now it was dawn, but the faint light of the rising sun barely made a dent in the thick fog that had rolled in overnight.

"I was walking towards the hill, maybe 150 yards away," Neidhardt said, "when I ran into another GI. I said hello, but he kept walking toward the hill. I'm sure now that he had to be a German soldier in an American uniform. I didn't realize that at the time. I was just puzzled. I was still thinking about it when I got to where the first and second squads were dug in. Nobody was in the foxholes. Now I was *really* puzzled. I decided to walk on up the hill."

Neidhardt, his rifle slung over his shoulder, reached the top of a small knoll and suddenly found himself face to face with a German soldier holding *his* rifle at the ready. "He told me to halt. I froze. He asked me something in German. Maybe he thought I was one of theirs, I don't know. He was upset for a second by a motion behind him. When he turned, I got my rifle off the strap, emptied all eight shells in the clip in his direction, then turned and ran like a bat out of hell."

Neidhardt reached his squad and told them that the first and second squads were gone and German troops were between them and the hill. As the breathless private was telling his story, German tanks started to move up the dirt road from the south. It didn't take the enemy long to knock out the roadblock's two antitank guns. However, the squad's machine gun withheld its fire for the first few minutes of the action, and the Germans didn't spot it in the fog. Soldiers confidently moved forward with the tanks. When the .30-caliber gun finally did open up, it took a fearful toll on the panzergrenadiers.

But a machine gun can't stop a tank. Neidhardt watched in terror as a panzer clanked to a halt near his foxhole and swung its turret in his direction. Just a few feet away, the squad leader was crouching in another foxhole. "They leveled the 88 right at our holes," he said. "Then he fired—but we were too close. The shell went over our heads and hit a stone wall right behind us. We knew we had to get out of there."

The survivors of Neidhardt's squad took advantage of the temporary absence of enemy infantry to escape through the hole in the wall so conveniently provided by the German tank. The thick fog helped cover their escape, but another road to Mortain was open and German armor was starting to move forward.

The Germans failed to use the first hours of the attack, the hours when darkness and surprise were on their side, to seize the high ground overlooking Mortain. That would prove to be a fatal mistake.

A few squads of panzergrenadiers did infiltrate the southern and western slopes of the hill, but a dawn counterattack by Lt. Ronal Woody's G Company cleared the heights, overwhelming the Germans in a brief, bitter battle. "We ran into hand-to-hand combat," Woody said. He had no idea what strength his men were facing. "All I knew was they were there and we had to fight like hell."

Other small groups tried to penetrate between the positions held by E and K on the eastern slope, but fire from the two companies discouraged the probing. In fact, the "attack" from the east was so feeble, many GIs on the hill didn't realize that a major German counteroffensive was in progress. "The first we heard about it was when our jeep brought us up supplies just about dawn," said Sgt. Luther Myers of E Company. "The driver begged us to unload fast. He said he wanted to get back, and if he didn't leave right away, he'd never make it."

Not far away, another E Company soldier learned of the German attack from another source. Private Paul Nethery was on a roadblock at the base of the hill, just below Myers's position. At dawn, "tanks came up to where the road went around the hill and rolled past so close I could have reached out and touched them." Nethery's squad wisely kept their heads down and let the tanks roll past. Following the tanks was a German officer in a small open car. He stopped opposite Nethery's position and stood up in the car, apparently studying a map. "He saw somebody's head move and pulled out a pistol. He fired and shot me in the head." The bullet penetrated Nethery's helmet and grazed his skull. The private was still able to aim and fire at the officer, hitting him in the leg. "He wouldn't drop his gun," said Nethery, who was shot again, this time in the thigh.

Both the wounded GI and the wounded German officer were evacuated back up the hill by other members of the squad. Nethery was laid on a rocky ledge near the top of the hill. The German he had shot, who turned out to be an SS artillery observer, was laid alongside him. To Nethery's surprise, the German spoke excellent English. "He told me Hitler was a great man, but he admitted we were going to win the war." The SS officer was killed later in the day by a German mortar shell.

The situation in G Company's sector remained tense, even after the dawn elimination of the Germans on the hilltop. Panzergrenadiers, supported by armor, began to pour out of Mortain and up the western face of the hill. Private Grady Deal's squad was dug in to the south of the cliffs, guarding the dirt road leading from the town up the hill. Deal watched the German tanks roll toward his position. "They came partway up, almost to our foxholes," Deal said. "Then our artillery started to fall right on 'em. Their tanks turned around and went back down the hill. I never understood it. I believe they could have come right up the hill. We couldn't have stopped them."

Woody's riflemen, supported by his company's two 60mm mortars, easily beat off the infantry attack. The artillery support had been furnished by the 230th Field Artillery Battalion, called in by Lt. Robert Weiss. It was too foggy for Weiss to direct the fire visually, but the area was registered and he was able to assign fire missions on the basis of reports from infantry listening posts. "Some artillery fire hit a trifle close, but injured none of our own troops and probably beat off the German menace," Weiss wrote.

Although Hill 314 remained in American hands, the position was becoming increasingly isolated. Phone communications with battalion headquarters in Mortain had broken down. Radio communications with regimental headquarters were possible, but Colonel Birks could offer nothing but encouragement. Company C, his last reserve, was fighting for its life in the town. Although 30th Division Headquarters had assigned the 2d Battalion of the 117th Infantry (minus Company G) to assist Birks, this new unit would not be in position to counterattack until late in the day.

The 120th's 1st Battalion would not be able to provide any immediate help. The troops on Hill 285—a gently sloping, round-topped hill known locally as Roche Grise—had spent a peaceful night, oblivious to the sporadic shellfire and bombing going on to the east and north.

That peace was shattered just before dawn, when gunfire erupted at the northern base of the hill, at the roadblock established on the dirt road running toward St.-Barthelmy. The noise woke Lt. Murray Pulver, commanding B Company. His 1st Platoon was covering the roadblock. The early morning fog made it impossible to see what was happening, but a few minutes after the firing stopped, Pvt. Harold Chocklett and two other men rushed toward Pulver's command post, yelling that the roadblock had been overrun.

Chocklett reported that a Sherman tank had come up the road, accompanied by a French man and girl. When challenged, the Frenchman explained in broken English that the tank had gotten lost and they were trying to direct it back to the American lines. When the curious men manning the roadblock climbed out of their foxholes to see what was going on, German soldiers suddenly appeared, like apparitions in the fog, shooting three GIs and capturing the rest, including Chocklett's twin brother. Only Harold Chocklett and his two companions, who had stayed in their foxholes, escaped capture. They fired a few shots at the Germans but hightailed it back to the CP when they heard more tanks approaching.

"They had no more finished their story when Lester Carbonneau, the company jeep driver, came running over to tell me there were German tanks and foot soldiers coming into the farmyard," Pulver said. "I sent men to warn the 2d and 3d platoons. Just then we heard firing from the 2d and 3d platoon areas. I can't help but believe that the Germans must have observed us setting up our defenses the day before. They knew right where to hit us!" Pulver immediately telephoned battalion headquarters to report his company was under attack. The reply was simple: "Hold at all costs."

Private Ken Parker, manning a machine-gun position near the crest of the hill, could see nothing in the fog except a stream of red tracers fired from a nearby German tank. The enemy vehicle was so close that Parker could hear the commander shout orders at the accompanying infantry. One of the men in Parker's squad was German-born, and he whispered a translation: "He's telling his men to move forward again."

Pulver's company was in a perilous position, its perimeter split by the advancing Germans. Platoons and even squads were forced to fight alone. Pulver found himself isolated with his tiny headquarters group—just five men.

"It was beginning to get light, but it was still very foggy," Pulver recalled. "Suddenly I heard a tank come rumbling our way. It was coming down a lane in an orchard, directly towards our front. My first sergeant grabbed a bazooka and loaded it. Since my first attack in combat, when I knocked out two Jerry tanks, that great weapon was never more than an arm's length from me. The sergeant handed me the bazooka and I aimed it over a stone wall. That monster came out of the fog not more than ten yards away. I fired, hitting it right under the turret. The tank came to a stop. I swear I could have reached out and touched the muzzle of the cannon if I had been tall enough. The concussion of the bazooka blast killed all the occupants of the tank, but the tank's motor continued to run and did so for most of the day."

Pulver's face was a bloody mess. The blast was so close that the exploding bazooka rocket sprayed tiny particles into his face, just breaking the skin. The lieutenant was not seriously hurt. He barely had time to wipe off the blood when one of his men shouted a warning: German soldiers were advancing across a field on the right. "They were shooting and hollering 'Americans, *kamerad!*'" Pulver said. "The Jerries were in the open and we were behind a hedge. We got them all without any of the five of us getting a scratch. It was like an old Western with the Indians attacking a circled wagon train."

Carried away by his two successful actions, Pulver got, as he later admitted, "a little gung-ho." He decided to crawl up a ditch to a nearby barn, where the company ammunition carrier was hidden. He was going

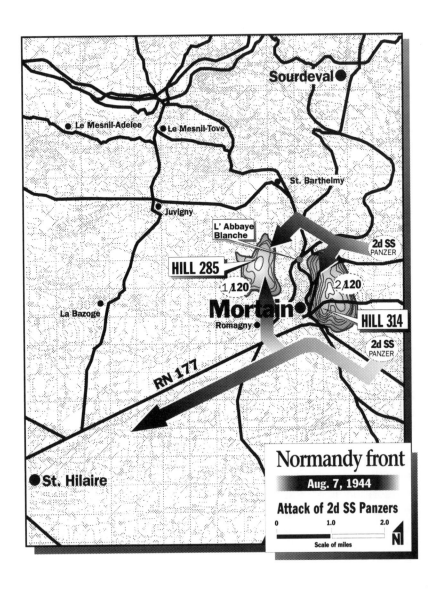

Sourdeval

Le Mesnil-Adelee   Le Mesnil-Tove

St. Barthelmy

Juvigny

L' Abbaye Blanche

HILL 285   2d SS PANZER

1/120   2/120

Mortain   HILL 314

La Bazoge   Romagny   2d SS PANZER

RN 177

St. Hilaire

Normandy front

Aug. 7, 1944

Attack of 2d SS Panzers

0   1.0   2.0

Scale of miles

to blow up the vehicle so the Germans wouldn't get it. "I put a rifle grenade on my rifle and quickly crawled the forty yards to the barn. I peeked through a small window. It was still quite dark inside, but by the light of the open door at the other end, I saw four Jerries around the jeep. I didn't dare break the window for fear of alerting them. I found a small door ajar next to the window. I eased it open carefully, stepped in, took aim and pulled the trigger.

"The damn gun misfired! The Jerries heard the click and spotted me. I dropped the gun and dove for the ditch as a hail of bullets ripped through the door. It seemed like an hour before I made the forty yards back to my hole. I could almost feel the bullets ripping into my back. If the Jerries had run the thirty feet to my end of the barn, I would have been a dead duck. Maybe they were as scared as I was."

To Pulver's left, a platoon from the 823d TD Battalion was covering a gap between Pulver's company and A Company on the left flank of the hill. About the time the Germans overran Pulver's roadblock, the men manning the TD guns detected tanks moving in the fog. Sergeant Ames Broussard went forward with a bazooka and succeeded in knocking out a Mark IV. He was trapped behind the infiltrating panzergrenadiers and wasn't able to rejoin his unit until after dark. The platoon's No. 2 gun managed to knock out two Mark IV tanks at about 0900 hours. Another Mark IV crept to within fifty yards of the defenders before the No. 1 gun, hidden in the fog, succeeded in hitting the tank. It retreated slowly, trailing smoke. It was later found abandoned near the Le Neufbourg road. The TD platoon also succeeded in destroying two self-propelled guns and an armored car.

The battle on Hill 285 settled down into an extended firefight. German mortars knocked out Pulver's phone lines to battalion and another shell blew up his radio, leaving the company without communications of any kind. However, the 1st Battalion's nearby Cannon Company, firing its three short-barreled 105s so fast that they burned out three gun barrels, knocked out three more German tanks and forced the enemy infantry to dig in. A mortar squad from D Company (heavy weapons) fired almost three thousand rounds in support of B Company's position.

Pulver's men tenaciously held their ground, sharing the hilltop with the enemy but blocking the Germans from approaching the roadblock at L'Abbaye Blanche from the rear. As the day wore on and the fog burned off, that was to become a most important accomplishment.

CHAPTER 9: L'ABBAYE BLANCHE

Lieutenant Tom Springfield had been in combat long enough to learn not to pay too much attention to intelligence reports. When told that his position at the roadblock above L'Abbaye Blanche was a safe one because there weren't any Germans around, Springfield said, "We listened, but we also stayed on our feet."

His platoon spent a relatively quiet night, undisturbed by the artillery fire falling on Mortain, a little more than a kilometer to the south. Just before dawn, however, the sound of rifle fire to the southeast alerted Springfield that something was up. Soon a handful of refugees from other platoons reached the roadblock and informed the young officer that the Germans were attacking.

"We were ready for them," Springfield said. The fact is, he had boundless confidence in the men of his platoon. Back in the States, the 1st Platoon of A Company had outshot every other unit in the 823d TD Battalion. "We won all the marksmanship awards. We had the best platoon over there."

Springfield was working in a chain store in Wichita, Kansas, when the war began. He decided to enlist before he was drafted, joining the army in April 1942. He first tried to join the air corps. "I couldn't get in," he said. "I was color-blind. As it turned out, that was an advantage since I could pick out camouflage better." Springfield attended tank destroyer school at Fort Hood, then joined the 823d in Louisiana. He was with the TD battalion when it was attached to the 30th Division in England. He survived the brutal combat in the hedgerows, the St.-Lô bloodbath, and the chaos of the Cobra bombing. Along the way, he watched a curious love-hate relationship develop between the 30th's riflemen and the 823d's gunners. "The infantry didn't like us to get too close, because they said we drew fire. Until they got hit, then they wanted us right there."

Springfield and Lt. Tom Andrews, commanding the 1st Platoon of F Company, 120th Infantry, worked well together at L'Abbaye Blanche. Because Springfield was senior, he was in overall command of the roadblock. His four 3-inch guns, mounted atop the crest of a low, humpbacked ridge (about seventy-five feet above the nearby Cance River), commanded the northern end of the position. Andrews's riflemen, augmented by two 57mm guns from the 120th's Antitank Platoon, guarded the southern end of the position. The railroad ran alongside the eastern edge of the roadblock, the small station just a few hundred feet south of the orchard where Springfield's first two guns were located.

"My guns lucked out," Springfield said of his position. "We sited my No. 1 and No. 2 guns behind a hedgerow, then dug them in to lower the silhouette even further. I think the Germans had a hard time spotting them." Both guns had a clear shot at the highway running north to St.-Barthelmy as it crossed the Cance four hundred meters away. His other two guns were also well sited, on either side of Route 177. The Cance River paralleled the railroad to the east, but provided only scant protection. "It was more like a creek than a river," Springfield observed. "It was shallow, maybe eight to ten feet wide. It did have steep banks on each side, but a tank with a bulldozer could have knocked them down and cleared a path." Two bridges near the abbey crossed the stream, but Andrews's men covered both with a combination of minefields, machine-gun positions, and bazooka teams. One 57mm gun covered each crossing. In addition, Springfield prepared alternate positions for his No. 3 and No. 4 guns in case they were needed to repel an attack from the south.

It was a formidable position, made more formidable by the fact that the Germans apparently had no idea it was in their path.

The Der Führer Regiment of the 2d SS Panzer Division didn't clear its assembly area around Le Petit Fieffe (three kilometers east of Mortain) until almost 0430, but once the column started moving, it didn't take long for the lead elements to drive west along the wide, hard-surfaced highway from Ger into the northern outskirts of Mortain. There, the German spearhead turned right to follow the highway north, over the

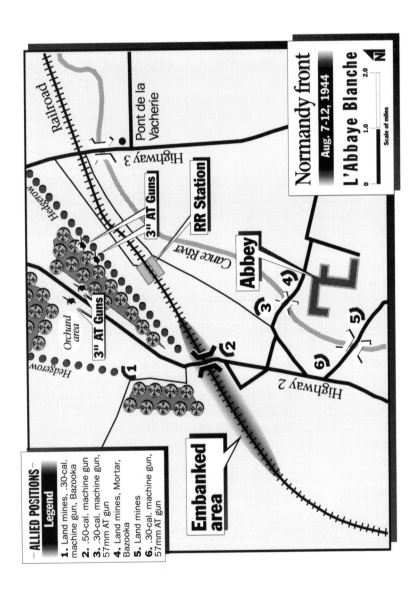

Normandy front
Aug. 7-12, 1944
L'Abbaye Blanche

N

Scale of miles
0   1.0   2.0

Railroad

Pont de la Vacherie

Highway 3

Hedgerow

3" AT Guns

RR Station

Cane River

Abbey

3" AT Guns

Orchard area

3) 4)

5)

Hedgerow

1) 2)

6)

Highway 2

Embanked area

─ALLIED POSITIONS─
Legend

1. Land mines, .30-cal. machine gun, Bazooka

2. .50-cal. machine gun

3. .30-cal. machine gun, 57mm AT gun

4. Land mines, Mortar, Bazooka

5. Land mines

6. .30-cal. machine gun, 57mm AT gun

Cance River at the Pont de la Vacherie (the Bridge of the Dairy), to La Dainie, where it merged with Route 177 out of L'Abbaye Blanche. The column planned to sweep into St.-Barthelmy from the south, turn left, and support the 1st SS Panzer Division's drive west along Route 177 toward Avranches.

The fog was patchy at L'Abbaye Blanche when the advancing Germans first made contact at about 0500 hours. A German recon unit crossed the river without being spotted and advanced south from the railroad station along a trail running between the railroad and the riverbank. A motorcycle with a sidecar led the small force, which also included a four-wheeled armored car, a Kübelwagen (a small car similar to a Volkswagen), and an officer's limousine. As the Germans approached the antitank position covering the northern bridge over the Cance, a .30-caliber machine gun opened up, destroying the motorcycle and the Kuebelwagen. The 57mm gun, commanded by Sgt. Jacob Rhyne, fired two rounds, blasting the armored car and the limousine. As survivors tried to escape the burning vehicles, they were cut down by the American machine guns. The Germans never succeeded in returning fire. The brief, one-sided action effectively blocked the narrow river trail, preventing the Germans from using it again.

Almost as soon as the firing died down along the trail, the main body of the German column attempted to cross the Cance at Pont de la Vacherie. Two of Springfield's guns had an unobstructed view of the German traffic as it slowly climbed the steep hill just north of the river, approximately four hundred yards away. "The road was so steep, they had to shift into low gear to climb it," Springfield said. "That's when we hit them."

His gun crews performed as coolly as if on the firing range back in Louisiana. The two 3-inch guns expended five armor-piercing shells and destroyed five vehicles—three half-tracks, one ammo truck (which exploded in a spectacular fireball), and a Mark IV tank. Command troops following closely behind the head of the column found the road blocked and had to scramble for cover. The regimental commander of Der Führer and his entire staff took refuge in the dairy barn just south of the bridge. "We could see the building through the trees," Springfield said. "If we had known they were in it, we'd have blasted it." Instead, the German officers remained trapped in the barn for the next eight hours, perhaps explaining the regiment's failure to coordinate a strong attack on the American roadblock.

German artillery began to fall on Springfield's position, but the high-velocity shells from the 88s, so deadly in most situations, were ineffective when fired upward toward the narrow ridge. The shells either hit the face of the ridge below the American positions or passed over the crest of the ridge and exploded well beyond. More dangerous was the German *Nebelwerfer*, a six-barreled rocket launcher that fired high-explosive projectiles, christened screaming meemies by the GIs.

"I remember walking back to the infantry CP when they started to fall," Springfield said. "The explosions bounced me up and down. They could shake the whole street." The first German salvos were uncannily accurate, but after a shell from one of the 3-inch guns knocked the steeple off a church overlooking the position, the fire became much less effective.

A more direct threat materialized at about 0600 hours, when a German attack developed from a new direction. Two German half-tracks, mounting 75mm guns and accompanied by at least a company of infantry, moved south down Route 177, apparently in an attempt to outflank the two guns that had done so much damage to the column trying to cross the river. Instead, the attack ran head-on into Springfield's No. 3 and No. 4 guns, defended by his heavily armed security squad. "We had a lot of firepower," Springfield said. "As we'd moved through France, we'd picked up a lot of weapons abandoned by the infantry. We had .50-caliber machine guns mounted on all our half-tracks and jeeps. We had several .30-caliber machine guns and most of our squad leaders carried BARs. We might have carried too much ammo, but we didn't think so. We wanted to be ready."

Springfield's men were ready and waiting when the Germans rounded a bend in the road and emerged from behind an orchard. The two 3-inch guns fired from a range of thirty meters, quickly destroying the two lightly armored German vehicles. The accompanying panzer-grenadiers, advancing along both sides of the highway, found themselves trapped in a minefield Andrews's men had laid the night before. Raked by machine-gun fire, the Germans tried to fight back, but after a fifteen-minute firefight, the few survivors pulled back, having failed to inflict a single casualty on the defenders.

It would be four more hours before the Germans would attempt another assault on the defenders at L'Abbaye Blanche. Until then, the only north-south roads connecting the two wings of the German offensive would remain firmly in American hands.

CHAPTER 10: ST.-BARTHELMY

The morning fog was very thick around St.-Barthelmy, the tiny crossroads village where Route 177 curved east toward Avranches. Lieutenant George Greene, commanding the 3d Platoon of B Company, 823d TD Battalion, estimated that the visibility of his gunners was limited to fifteen to twenty yards. For the riflemen of the 117th Infantry Regiment's 1st Battalion, crouching in their foxholes just outside the town, the thick fog created an eerie feeling of isolation and disorientation.

Private First Class Alfred Overbeck must have been less than half a mile from St.-Barthelmy. His squad, part of the 1st Battalion's C Company, had moved into position late the day before without passing through the town. Only the officers and sergeants knew exactly where they were. As for Overbeck, all he could see was part of the boxed-in field where his foxhole was located, just at the base of a thick hedgerow.

"I was awake most of the night on guard duty," said Overbeck, a native of Jersey City, New Jersey, who had enlisted in the army out of high school. "My post was at the corner of the field, where there was a gap in the hedgerows, an opening where the farmers could drive their equipment in and out. It was a cool, damp night. It was quite discernible when the fog rolled in. It was like a wall. You could barely see eight or nine feet away."

When Overbeck came off guard just before dawn, he drew a new duty. He and another private were detailed to return to the company kitchen and pick up the squad's hot breakfast. "The fog was so thick we had to follow the telephone wires back to the crossroads, where the kitchen jeep was waiting," he said. "Just as we got there, mortar rounds began falling around us. There was no cover, so we got the hell out of there. On the way back, we got off the beaten track. We were trying to figure out how to get back to our squad when we reached this highway. As we crossed, we drew small-arms fire. We could see German troops just a little ways off, removing mines from the road."

Overbeck made it back to his squad position just as the first German tanks appeared. "They came out of a wall of fog," he recalled. "I don't know what kind they were. They were so big, they looked like battleships. They were bumper to bumper. The attack was altogether unexpected. They took us entirely by surprise."

The squad leader was in phone communication with the company commander, who was set up in a nearby field. The squad was ordered to hold its position. However, without antitank weapons, there was little the outnumbered riflemen could do. Overbeck was carrying a bag of rifle grenades. He began to aim and fire them at the passing tanks. "A rifle grenade won't stop a tank," he admitted. "Not unless you drop it down the turret. But I got some foot soldiers walking alongside the tanks. And I'm sure I hit a tank commander. He was standing up in his turret when my grenade went off right beside him."

Overbeck moved from foxhole to foxhole, trying to keep the German from getting a fix on his position. He described a nightmarish scene: "Tracers were crisscrossing the field from above the hedgerows, artillery was falling all around, and tanks were everywhere. They would fire at anything. They'd see one guy running and fire an 88 at him, just like it was a rifle." Overbeck had just landed in a new position when he heard "a heavy explosion to the rear. Maybe a hundred yards back. I turned and there was a huge fireball in the air. I heard shrapnel bounce all around me."

The explosion could have been the ammunition truck blown up by Lieutenant Springfield's gunners about that time on the road just above Pont de la Vacherie. However, that was considerably more than a hundred yards away from Overbeck's probable location. More likely, the fireball was either a tank hit by one of Lieutenant Greene's 3-inch guns just south of St.-Barthelmy or one of three tanks destroyed farther south by Sgt. Samuel Hardy's four-man bazooka patrol.

The German attack was not a total surprise to St.-Barthelmy's defenders. Civilians sneaked through the American lines, warning that the Boche were massing for an attack. The night was punctuated by intermittent artillery fire, annoying, but not enough to disturb the sleep of the hardened veterans of the hedgerow fighting. However, a heavier barrage just before daybreak confirmed to the GIs that an attack was imminent. Only the strength and the direction of the attack turned out to be a surprise.

When Lt. Col. Robert E. Frankland's 1st Battalion replaced the 1st Division's 26th Regiment in and around St.-Barthelmy the previous afternoon, he was told that the only German troops in the area were located to the northeast, where, in fact, the 2d Panzer Division was assembling for its attack. Consequently, Frankland shaped his defense to provide the most cover in the northeast quadrant.

Frankland had served in the 117th Infantry for almost twenty years, entering the Tennessee National Guard unit as a private and rising through the ranks to battalion command. He was a member of a prominent Jackson, Tennessee, family. His father had emigrated from Canada in 1904 and founded the Frankland Carriage Company. He brought each of his five sons into the carriage-making business, which eventually made a very successful switch into auto parts; he also added a hotel, a furniture business, and other ventures. The two oldest sons, Leonard and Walter, served in World War I. The fourth son, Ernest (as Robert E. was generally known), joined the National Guard along with his older brother, Walter, in the 1920s.

Both were first lieutenants when the 117th was called into federal service on September 16, 1940. Lieutenant Colonel Walter Frankland became the 30th Division's supply officer (G-4) and was with General Hobbs at La Bazoge when the German counterattack hit his brother's battalion.

The 1st Battalion of the 117th Infantry *belonged* to Ernest Frankland, much like the medieval military formations that were the personal property of the barons who raised, trained, and commanded them. The small, handsome National Guard officer was to lead his battalion every step of the way from Omaha Beach to the Elbe River. Although Frankland's unit was diluted by replacements, like all combat-tested rifle battalions, it never lost that hard core of men he had known and trained with back in Tennessee.

"He was the finest soldier I ever served with," said Sgt. James Waldrop, a neighbor from Jackson who would later win a battlefield commission. "He just couldn't be beat. The day he died, it almost felt like I'd lost my own father."

Ben Emerson, a veteran of the China-Burma-India theater who served with Frankland in the Tennessee National Guard after the war, said, "He and Joe Stilwell were the two finest soldiers I ever saw. He was a fun-loving man. He was the drummer in a swing band when he was younger. He used to say, 'I believe in working hard, then playing hard.'"

The morning of August 7, 1944, was a time to work hard. Frankland's battalion was facing annihilation.

Frankland, acting on intelligence information that put the prime threat to the northeast, had deployed his B Company several hundred yards north and east of St.-Barthelmy; A Company was placed on the northern edge of the tiny crossroads village. C Company alone covered the southern approach to the town. The midnight skirmish at La Fantay, eight hundred meters north of the battalion's main defenses, only reinforced the perception that the German threat lay to the north.

However, the 1st SS Panzer Division was approaching from the south. The Liebstandarte Adolf Hitler was the strongest of the four panzer divisions assigned to Operation Lüttich. Its role was to follow the 2d Panzer Division's lead, presumably to Juvigny (seven kilometers west of St.-Barthelmy), where it would spearhead a drive the remaining eighteen kilometers to Avranches. The left wing of the 2d Panzer Division was supposed to strike St.-Barthelmy soon after H hour, but the attacking units—the 2d Panzergrenadier Regiment, supported by the tanks of the 3d Panzer Regiment (mostly Mark IVs) and the tank destroyers of the 38th Panzerjaeger Battalion—were late getting started and had still not arrived at dawn. Expecting the area around St.-Barthelmy to be cleared by the 2d Panzer Division, the 1st SS Panzer advanced along the best highway in the area, driving southwest on the wide road from La Tournerie to the intersection of La Dainie, where it turned north to approach St.-Barthelmy from the south.

The lack of coordination between the two divisions would cost the Germans dearly, but the initial consequence of the confusion was to

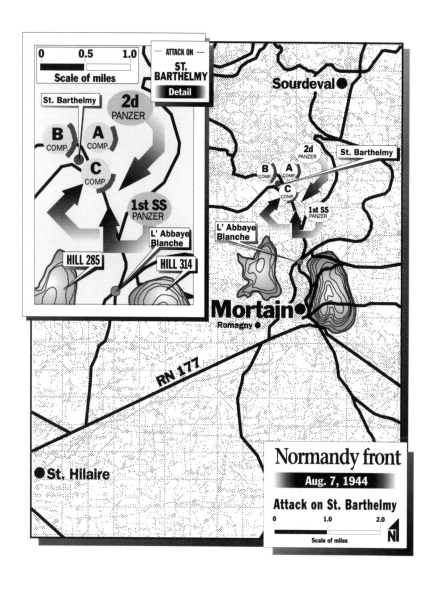

provide a nasty shock for the defenders in St.-Barthelmy. A light roadblock below the town was rapidly overrun, and the German spearhead approached St.-Barthelmy in the thick fog, just as the covering barrage lifted at about 0615 hours.

"Suddenly it was so quiet we could not only hear the tanks moving, we could also hear the Jerries shouting orders," Greene said. Visibility was so poor that it was impossible to call in artillery, since observers would be unable to adjust fire onto the target. However, the lead German tank began firing its hull-mounted machine gun at the C Company riflemen dug in south of town. The tank itself was still invisible to Greene's antitank guns, but the flashes from the machine gun gave Cpl. Walter Christianson, the gunner on the No. 1 gun, a target to aim for. His 3-inch rifle spit out an eighteen-foot spurt of flame, hurling the armor-piercing (AP) projectile at the approaching tank, perhaps fifty meters away. The shell penetrated the tank's frontal armor, setting the vehicle afire. The burning Panther stopped in the middle of the road, blocking the narrow lane, which was bordered on both sides by thick hedgerows. The long column of tanks ground to a halt.

"A little while later, we heard a recovery vehicle come up to drag that one out of the way," Greene said. He could again make out the Germans shouting commands in the fog. Sergeant Charles Martin, the gun captain, ordered Christianson to fire two HE rounds blindly into the fog, hoping to disrupt the enemy activity. It is unlikely that the two shots did any damage, but the destruction of the lead tank had halted the attack by the 1st SS Panzer Division. For the next forty-five minutes, the St.-Barthelmy defenders had to fight off only a series of infantry probes.

During the delay, Sergeant Hardy's patrol discovered the stationary line of armored vehicles. The four GIs had helped emplace a roadblock on the sunken road south of St.-Barthelmy before first light. At about 0600 hours, Hardy and three privates left the position to scout southward, armed with a bazooka and small arms. Apparently, the noise from the artillery barrage falling on St.-Barthelmy covered the sound of the approaching German tanks. They passed east of the advancing column without detecting it and continued south for approximately three hundred yards. Upon hearing tank sounds to their right (after the barrage lifted), Hardy cautiously crawled atop a hedgerow to see what was going on. Across a field, approximately seventy meters away, he saw another hedgerow and beyond that, on the raised main highway, he saw three German tanks pointing north. The tanks were stopped, their crews standing together beside their vehicles, talking noisily.

Hardy's view was obscured by the patchy fog. For five minutes he watched and listened, hearing the idling engines of the tanks and the surprisingly loud conversation of the tankers. Finally, he ordered Pvt. Alfred Ericcson, a native of Norway who had fled his country when the Germans invaded in 1940, to mount the hedgerow with his bazooka. Ericcson's first rocket exploded among the talking soldiers. The survivors scattered, none of them manning their tanks. With no enemy fire to worry about, Ericcson took careful aim and fired five more rockets. He hit two of the tanks in the engine compartment, setting them afire. He also hit the third tank, although smoke from the two burning vehicles, mixed with the thickening fog, prevented him from seeing just what damage he had done to it.

Hardy, knowing the tanks would be accompanied by infantry, led the small patrol back north toward the roadblock. When they reached the position, the 57mm gun and the gun crew had disappeared. Hardy led his men west and soon found the abandoned gun, still attached to its tow truck, stuck in a muddy field. The gun crew had removed the gun's firing pin and disabled the truck. Two days would pass before Hardy's patrol was able to rejoin the Antitank Company.

The Germans were not about to repeat their initial mistake at St.-Barthelmy. Clearly, the 1st SS Panzer Division had not expected to find a major roadblock in the town. The veteran German tankers would never intentionally have approached a defended position in a single column, along a narrow, easily blocked road.

The delay occasioned by Christianson's kill allowed the German infantry to scout alternate approaches into the town. When the attack was resumed around 0700, one column began a cautious approach up the main highway, while seven Panthers, accompanied by a strong panzergrenadier force, swung left and approached the town from the southwest. C Company was dug in along the high ground to the south of town, the 1st Platoon to the west of the highway, the 2d and 3d platoons to the east. Frankland ordered his riflemen to stay in their foxholes, let the armor pass over them, then get the infantry that followed. "If I'd realized the strength of the attack, I'd have withdrawn and fought a delaying action," Frankland later wrote. "It was a mistake to try and hold [St.-Barthelmy] with two companies."

Indeed, Frankland's two infantry companies and the 823d's TD platoon, augmented only by B Company north of town and his small headquarters staff, were being attacked from two directions by an entire regiment of the 1st SS Panzer Division from the south. Within a few minutes, the late-arriving left wing of the 2d Panzer Division finally made its appearance on the battlefield, striking with a hammer blow from the northeast, overrunning B Company's roadblocks, and catching A Company's GIs—already engaged with the 1st SS Panzer from the south—by surprise.

The embattled Able Company was soon in desperate condition. The company commander, Lt. Myrl MacArthur, had joined the regiment only the week before. His men had no bazookas, and the attached artillery observers could not register their fire in the fog. Of MacArthur's 135 men (77 under establishment), 55 were green replacements who had joined the battalion at Tessy.

"Those replacements were straight from the States," said Maj. Warren Giles, a National Guard veteran from Athens, Tennessee, who was serving as the 117th's intelligence officer. "When the Germans hit us, hell, they tried to run."

Not all of them ran. A few veteran soldiers were able to organize an orderly retreat.

A column of Mark IV tanks struck A Company's 1st Platoon, slicing between the 1st and 3d squads. One tank blew a gap in the hedgerow directly in front of Sgt. Abbie Reviere, the 1st Squad leader, who was sharing a foxhole with Sgt. Grover Wright.

"Should we shoot him, Abbie, should we shoot him?" Wright asked excitedly.

Reviere had no bazooka to shoot the tank with. Instead, he ordered his squad to withdraw, using the thick fog as cover. Wright wanted to retreat through the gap blown in the hedgerow, but Reviere thought it better to climb the hedgerow to their rear. It proved a wise decision. Sergeant Francis Vadrine and three other men used the gap and were cut down. Vadrine was wounded and his companions were killed. Reviere extricated the rest of the squad.

The 3d Squad also pulled back but the men found their retreat blocked by a line of tanks. Most of the squad members tried to reach friendly territory by going uphill toward St.-Barthelmy. They were all killed or captured. Two privates, Byrne Jones and Raymond Cizmowski, took a longer route. They found a narrow draw and hid there until dark. At one point, they were attacked by a British Typhoon, the near miss blowing Cizmowski's BAR out of his hands. Jones noted philosophically, "It's better than being captured." The two men circled the Germans and reached the regimental command post by the next morning.

They made out far better than Lieutenant MacArthur and his headquarters group, all of whom were captured in the first hour of fighting. The 2d and 3d platoons, hit from the rear by tanks, were almost wiped out—only six men, all from the 1st Squad of the 3d Platoon, escaped. The day after the attack, A Company consisted of one officer and twenty-seven men.

The miracle was that the destruction of A Company wasn't repeated everywhere on the St.-Barthelmy battlefield. The 1st Battalion was engaged with the equivalent of an entire panzer division. To add to the problem, the presence of the thick morning fog kept Allied air power from intervening during the morning hours. It also prevented the powerful American artillery from providing more than token support.

Frankland's defenses should have disintegrated under the three-pronged assault. Instead, the outnumbered GIs fought back with incredible tenacity and resourcefulness. Although many men were killed and captured in the first few minutes of the assault, the survivors exacted a terrible toll on the attackers.

Lieutenant Greene's four 3-inch guns were the most effective antitank weapons available to St.-Barthelmy's defenders. His No. 1 and No. 2 guns were well sited to cover the approach from the south, and his No. 3 gun had a good field of fire toward the northwest. Unfortunately, none of his weapons was positioned to defend the southwestern quadrant.

Martin's gun claimed its second victim just after 0700. A Panther, attempting a cautious approach from the south, got to within thirty yards of the No. 1 gun before Christianson, again aiming at the German's gun flashes, opened fire and scored a direct hit with his first shot, setting the tank afire. Most of the panzergrenadiers following the tank were locked in close-quarters battle with the 2d and 3d platoons of C Company east of the road. However, an increasing number of German riflemen turned their attention on Greene's two antitank guns, pinging bullets off the armored shields protecting the gun crews. For the time being, Greene's security squad, heavily armed with machine guns and BARs, was sufficient to keep the German troops at bay, but as the pressure mounted, his gunners became increasingly vulnerable.

Heavily outnumbered, C Company's two platoons east of the road were soon overwhelmed. Many GIs were killed or captured. However, a group of thirteen 2d Platoon men under Sgt. Irving Katzman and Sgt. Roy Arthur managed to escape encirclement and make their way south.

Another refugee, Pvt. Pete Preslipsky of the 3d Platoon, was driven from his foxhole by the enemy attack. Armed with a bazooka, Preslipsky crawled close enough in the fog to get off a shot at a German tank. This was old hat for the private from the small Pennsylvania community of Leechburg. On July 12, he earned the Distinguished Service Cross for single-handedly destroying a dug-in enemy tank. Unfortunately, his trusty bazooka wouldn't fire this time. No matter what he did, Preslipsky couldn't make it work.

Frustrated but undeterred, the solitary private threw away the useless weapon and began to work his way back toward town. He came across an abandoned bazooka and two rockets. Preslipsky decided to try again. He used the cover of the fog to approach another tank. This time the weapon worked perfectly, and Preslipsky had the satisfaction of seeing a Mark IV go up in flames. Encouraged by his success, he loaded the other rocket and began stalking another tank. Again he fired at close range and again watched as the rocket streaked toward the target and exploded. With two more tank kills to his credit, Preslipsky discarded the empty weapon and made his way back to the American lines.

West of the highway, Charlie Company's 1st Platoon was hanging on against overwhelming odds. An outpost manned by the 3d Squad was attacked by two tanks and about sixteen riflemen. Sergeant Norman Willis shot one panzergrenadier who charged him with a bayonet. Willis pulled his squad back a few hedges, where they were joined by the 2d Squad. Meanwhile, 2d Lt. Quentin Robb, the platoon's executive officer, made his way back to Frankland's command post in St.-Barthelmy and asked for reinforcements. The battalion commander assigned the

1st Platoon of B Company to bolster the defenses southwest of the town. Robb returned to the dugout serving as C Company's command post just in time to count sixteen German tanks roll past. Finally, one tank turned to fire into the dugout.

"About that time," Robb reported, "I took a bite out of Mother Earth." When German riflemen began to fire into the dugout, Robb decided it was time to leave. He hopped a couple of hedgerows, made contact with the advancing platoon from B Company, and led them into position across a sunken road that approached St.-Barthelmy from the southwest. The survivors of the 1st Platoon fell back to join Robb's makeshift line. A few minutes after Robb escaped the dugout, the C Company's command group, including Capt. Walter Schoener, the company commander, was captured.

Frankland almost met the same fate. Despite the best efforts of Greene's guns and the numerous bazooka teams stalking German tanks in the fog, it didn't take long for the attackers to penetrate the small village. The battalion commander was trying to raise some of his dispersed units on the shattered phone net when Capt. David Easlik, the battalion's S-3 (operations officer), looked out the window of the CP and saw a Panther parked right outside the front door. Frankland heard noises in the rear of the house and went to investigate. He reached the kitchen just as two of his radiomen were being marched out the back door with their hands up. Frankland, armed with his .45 automatic, followed them out the door and shot the two Germans guarding them.

The battalion command group hastily escaped out a window and headed for A Company's CP to try and find some men with bazookas. As they left the building, the German tank commander was standing in his turret, his back to the escaping Americans. Two other tanks were to the rear.

There are several versions of what happened next. Frankland reported that he and his staff merely slipped away to safety. However, several veterans of the battle claim that Frankland shot the tank commander before leaving. Sergeant James Waldrop heard it differently.

"I know this is true," he insisted. "I got this from a fellow I knew who saw it all. The tank was attacking the headquarters and Colonel Frankland not only shot the tank commander, he jumped up on the tank and started blasting away down the hatch with his .45. He got the whole crew. If it had been written up, he'd have gotten the Congressional Medal of Honor. But the colonel never reported it. He wouldn't brag on himself. No way, no shape, no form or fashion."

Frankland certainly had the skill to make effective use of his .45. During prewar summer National Guard encampments at Camp Perry, Indiana, he was a member of the 117th's target-pistol team. Veterans remember him as a deadly shot.

Whatever really happened outside the battalion headquarters, Frankland's command group made its way back to B Company's command post—all except Frankland, who headed alone toward A Company's position and made contact with Lt. Robert Murray, the shattered company's only surviving officer. Together, they got several men who had evaded capture to the rear. Frankland then joined his staff at B Company's CP, where he contacted Col. Walter Johnson at the regimental command post at La Rossaye (about a thousand meters west of St.-Barthelmy) to explain the situation and ask for help. While there, he also arranged for the battalion's trucks and jeeps to withdraw, just in time for all but two of the vehicles to escape safely.

That might have been the last moment when Lieutenant Greene could have gotten his guns away, but the young officer never considered withdrawal. He sent his support vehicles to safety early in the action but decided his guns would stay. Greene felt a responsibility to the outnumbered GIs. He wanted to give them as much protection as possible. "Those guys were taking a beating," he said. "We were doing the best we could to keep the armor off them."

Greene was a newcomer to his command. The twenty-two-year-old second lieutenant was a 1943 ROTC graduate of South Dakota State College. He attended the TD school at Fort Hood, reached England three days before D day, and was dumped in the replacement pool. He joined the 823d at Tessy, just days before going into action at St.-Barthelmy. "I didn't even know the names of the men under me," he said. He found himself in a hopeless, confused struggle against impossible odds. All he could do was what so many others did that terrible morning. He kept fighting.

"The whole thing was a mess," he said. "The only thing was, they were just as confused as we were."

Confused or not, Greene's gunners were scoring against the two famous panzer divisions. Moments after Christianson got his second kill, the fog parted enough for the No. 2 gun to see a German tank moving across a field one hundred meters to the southeast. The first shot struck the Panther's sponson above the right tread, stopping it in its tracks. A second AP shell set the tank afire. About the same time, the No. 3 gun hit and killed a Mark IV at a range of fifty meters as it was trying to enter the village from the north.

Frankland, who reached his rear command post near La Rossaye around 0930, tried to send Greene some help. He ordered Lt. Lawson Neel, commanding the 1st Platoon of B Company, to reinforce the roadblock in St.-Barthelmy. Neel's four guns were dug in two kilometers west of the town on Route 177.

"It was general practice for the platoon leader to go forward and scout out positions for his guns, then go back and bring his guns up," Neel explained. "But we had this thing called rapid deployment we'd practiced back in the States. It was just like something you'd see in an old-time Civil War movie, where the gunners ride up, turn the gun around, and start firing. Like I said, we practiced it, but I never expected to do it in combat."

The thirty-two-year-old Neel was one of the 823d's most experienced officers. He was a self-described ribbon clerk in a Thomasville, Georgia, department store before he enlisted in 1942. Neel was assigned to the 823d when it was formed at Camp Carson and led his platoon from Omaha Beach, through the hedgerows, and during the breakout at St.-Lô. "Neel was a fantastic fighter," said Capt. Frank Wilts, who was the commander of B Company during the same period. "He had great instincts and a great rapport with his men."

August 7 was a special day for Neel. "It was my thirteenth wedding anniversary," he said. "All I could think of was, my wife was going to be a beautiful widow."

Ordered to support the beleaguered 3d Platoon, Neel and a driver raced toward St.-Barthelmy to pick out positions for his guns. Fire coming from the town convinced the veteran officer that there was no time to lose. He drove back to his platoon and immediately brought up a single 3-inch gun, towed by a half-track. The gun crew stopped at a fork where two roads emerged from St.-Barthelmy and backed the gun through a gate into a small field. "We had to park the half-track across the road and carry the ammunition back to the gun," Neel said. "We hadn't been there three or four minutes before a German tank came down the road."

A Panther, supported by a large infantry formation, emerged from behind a house on the northern fork of the road. Neel was close enough to hear the German officer shout a command. Before the tank's 75mm gun could traverse far enough to fire, Neel's 3-inch gun got in the first shot at a range of less than twenty yards. The shell hit the Panther in the left sponson, forcing the crew to abandon the tank. However, the accompanying panzergrenadiers opened up heavy small-arms fire on the American position. Without infantry support, Neel's gunners couldn't man the gun.

"I could hear bullets bouncing off our gun shield," he said. "I took the firing pin and we took off across the field. Private [Milton] Daly asked, 'Sir, we're not running away, are we?' I told him, 'Hell, no. This is a strategic retreat.'"

Neel believed St.-Barthelmy had fallen when he ran into Germans emerging from the town. However, Greene's gunners were still in action, protected by their own security squads and a handful of stubborn 1st Battalion riflemen. In fact, a few minutes after Neel's "strategic retreat," Greene's No. 3 gun scored its second kill, twice hitting a Mark IV near the burned-out shell of its first victim. However, visibility was improving, and the smoke and flame of the gun's muzzle blast began to attract an increasing volume of small-arms fire.

Greene was trying to move his No. 4 gun, which had been unable to find a target all morning because of its poor field of fire, to cover the southwestern approach to the town. His No. 1 gun had been knocked out a few minutes earlier, the explosion wounding Martin and Christianson, who were taken to the aid station set up in the wine cellar of the small town's only hotel. The new location for the No. 4 gun was supposed to cover the sunken trail where the hasty defensive line organized by Lieutenant Robb had held up the advancing Germans for almost forty-five minutes. After killing at least thirty-five panzergrenadiers and destroying two tanks with bazooka fire, Robb executed a masterful withdrawal, saving his small force but leaving the antitank gunners on their own. Greene's unlucky No. 4 gun would not depress far enough to prevent a half-track from advancing up the lane and unloading a squad of panzergrenadiers. Without infantry support, the sergeant commanding the gun had to pull the firing pin from his weapon and withdraw.

Greene's No. 2 gun was in similar trouble. Not only were German troops close enough to wound several of the gunners and the accompanying security squad, at least one panzergrenadier got close enough to try and roll grenades under the protective gun shield. However, the 3-inch gun stayed in action. Just before 1100 hours, it scored another kill, hitting a Panther as it rolled up the highway. The AP shell struck the tank's frontal armor, but the Panther continued its advance past the No. 2 gun and on into town. It came to a halt just outside Greene's CP, where it began to burn. That was the last hurrah for Greene's platoon. An HE round from another tank wrecked the No. 2 gun and wounded several of its gunners. The fate of the No. 3 gun is not certain, although several days after the battle, one 1st Battalion soldier reported watching a TD gun engage the three tanks that had reached Frankland's CP. The TD gun destroyed the lead tank, he reported, before being blasted by the other two Panthers.

With all his guns gone, Greene was finally ready to pull the remnants of his platoon out of St.-Barthelmy. Before he could act on that decision, an infantry sergeant rushed into Greene's CP and asked for help, explaining that his squad's machine gun had malfunctioned and his position was about to be overrun. Greene led the unknown sergeant to one of his half-tracks, parked nearby; then the two of them detached the vehicle's .30-caliber machine gun from its ring mount. As they were carrying the weapon forward, a Panther fired an HE round, which exploded in a hedgerow next to the two men. Fragments ripped open the sergeant's body. Greene, who took a piece of shrapnel in his arm, grabbed the bloody GI.

"He died in my arms," Greene said. "It's pretty damn rough to have a guy blow up all over you. I must have lost my head for a moment. The guys claim I grabbed the machine gun and started firing. I don't really remember."

A member of Greene's security squad reported seeing the young officer pick up the heavy machine gun and begin firing it from the hip, as it was so often done in the movies (and so rarely in actual combat). His action allowed several of his men, including the soldier who reported the incident, to disengage and retreat safely out of town. Greene fired an entire belt of ammunition before he came to his senses. He dropped the empty weapon and found himself confronted by a German soldier holding a submachine gun.

George Greene's battle was over. Resistance in St.-Barthelmy was ending. Frankland's battalion and the supporting TD platoon had suffered heavy casualties: more than 350 killed, wounded, and missing.

The losses looked even worse that morning, with many of the battalion's men scattered over the French countryside, many still behind German lines. Some, like Private First Class Overbeck, would end up as German prisoners. Others, like Private Preslipsky and Sergeant Hardy, would filter back with their patrols in the next few days.

Still, Frankland's battalion would survive. Despite the heavy losses, it had inflicted far heavier casualties on the two attacking panzer divisions. Much more importantly, it had delayed what was supposed to be the main thrust of the German attack for six precious hours. Surprised, outnumbered, and largely unsupported, the defenders of St.-Barthelmy turned the tide of the Battle of Mortain in a forgotten struggle that ranks as one of the epic engagements in World War II.

It was almost noon when the last American gun in St.-Barthelmy fell silent. The 1st SS Panzer Division was still twenty-seven kilometers from Avranches. Just as importantly, the hot August sun had burned off the heavy morning fog.

CHAPTER 11: DAYLIGHT AT MORTAIN

The fog lifted somewhat earlier in Mortain than at St.-Barthelmy, a few kilometers to the north. The improved visibility was a blessing at L'Abbaye Blanche, where Lt. Tom Springfield's TD gunners continued their morning "turkey shoot" at German vehicles trying to climb the hill beyond Pont de la Vacherie.

"That first day was just run, run, run," Springfield said. The roadblock accounted for seventeen German vehicles before noon, including five Mark IV tanks, a half-track, three full-track personnel carriers, two two-and-a-half-ton trucks, and an ammo carrier.

After the early-morning assault from the north was beaten off, the Germans made no further attempts to dislodge Springfield's force. The defenders were reinforced around 1000 hours, when 2d Lt. George Stewart of F Company arrived with two squads, the survivors of a platoon-sized roadblock overrun by the Germans to the south. Lieutenant Tom Andrews assigned Stewart to command the southern end of the roadblock, facing Mortain.

Stewart's group was among the few refugees of the 120th's overrun roadblocks to reach safety that morning. Many more refugees were still at large behind German lines. Some were in hiding, like Sgt. John Whitsett, who was lying underneath a large bush, listening to Germans pass a few yards away. Others were trying to find their way back to the fight, like Pvt. George Neidhardt's decimated squad.

"We were trying to reach Mortain," Neidhardt said. "We hadn't gone very far when we got strafed by British planes and a couple of guys in our squad were killed. We reached a farmhouse. It was empty. We were only there a few minutes when one of the guys standing in the front door got blasted at point-blank range by a German tank. We ran out the back door, then took off towards the left. As we crossed the fields, we ran into artillery fire—I don't know if it was German or American—and we lost a few more guys."

The tiny group reached a patch of woods where Tex, the squad leader, took stock of the situation. Neidhardt found himself promoted to BAR gunner. Only four unwounded men were left. The sergeant led the survivors west, where they passed south of Mortain and reached another farmhouse alongside a good secondary road. "Four tanks came down from the north," Neidhardt said. "U.S. tanks. Their commander said they were going to scout down the road and asked if we'd go with them to protect them from infantry. Tex told them to pick us up on the way back."

Neidhardt's squad retired to the courtyard of the farmhouse as the tanks headed south. "They hadn't gone half a block when the first tank was blasted. Then a round of German artillery hit the top of the farmhouse and set it on fire. The second tank was hit when he tried to turn around. The last two tanks turned west. Most of the squad was able to pile on. I was left in the courtyard with the BAR to cover their withdrawal. Then I heard Tex yelling for me. The tank slowed down just long enough for me to hop on. Everybody else was packed inside and there wasn't room for me to do more than stick my head and shoulders down the hatch. That's how we drove away, with my butt sticking in the air."

Lieutenant Colonel Hardaway was also caught in an embarrassing position. The commander of the 120th Regiment's 2d Battalion was in the process of abandoning his command post in Mortain. He notified Colonel Birks, the 120th's commander, of his intention, then gathered his command group together.

"We were going to try and reach our rifle companies on Hill 314," said Lt. Guy Hagen, the battalion communications officer. "There were twenty-seven of us. We had rifles, but we were out of ammo. All our ammo was on a communications jeep that got hit trying to reach our pioneer platoon on a roadblock. All we could do was try to sneak out of town between the buildings. We didn't get very far before we saw Germans between us and the hill. We finally snuck in a building. It was about four blocks from the CP, near the hospital."

Sergeant Robert Bondurant didn't join the exodus. He stayed at his switchboard to the end. He was captured soon after dawn and forced to huddle in the middle of the main street with several other prisoners. "I thought they were going to shoot us," he said. "Instead, they walked us back. Maybe five or six miles. They had an aid station set up. Wounded were lying around everywhere, both German and American."

Birks received a radio message from Hardaway reporting his situation. Fearing that the Germans were monitoring the frequency, Hardaway would not reveal where he was in hiding. He was out of touch with his companies on the hill and had to use his radio sparingly to save its batteries. Major Gardner Simes, Hardaway's executive officer, was stuck in hiding with the rest of the command group, so command of the 2d Battalion fell upon Capt. Reynold Erichson, the senior company commander.

Erichson, the tall, blond farmer from Iowa, was just twenty-four years old at the time of Mortain, but there wasn't a more respected officer in the regiment. "Captain Erichson was very stable, calm and cooperative," said the H Company commander, Delmont Byrn. "He inspired confidence."

Erichson, commanding the widely scattered Company F, almost ended up stuck in hiding with Hardaway and Simes. When communications broke down with his roadblocks at 0300 hours, he reported to the battalion CP in town. Hardaway gave him one platoon from Company C, which was at that time fighting its losing battle to keep the Germans out of Mortain, and ordered him to establish contact with the companies on Hill 314. Leaving in the predawn fog and darkness, Erichson led approximately forty riflemen up a steep trail toward K Company.

"We walked right up on thirty Germans before we could see them," he wrote. "My scouts were so near to the enemy they could have shaken hands with them." Erichson managed to set up a hasty defense as the Germans opened up with automatic weapons. Finding his route to the crest of the hill blocked, he contacted Hardaway, who ordered him to return to town. Disengaging in the fog, the platoon pulled back and established a defensive position at the base of the hill. Erichson braved machine-gun fire to report to the battalion CP. Hardaway issued new orders, sending Erichson to link up with the rest of C Company, which was being driven north out of town. However, when Erichson attempted to move the platoon, he discovered that his position was surrounded on three sides. The only avenue of escape was to the east, back toward the hill. This time Erichson was able to find an unguarded trail and reach Lt. Ronal Woody's G Company on the crest overlooking Mortain.

Another refugee reached the hill that morning, but he was looking for trouble, not running away from it. Captain Byrn was at 2d Battalion headquarters in Mortain when the Germans attacked before dawn. "It was apparent things were going to be pretty wild," he said. "The enemy was running around, shooting up the town. It was bedlam." When Byrn lost phone contact with his scattered heavy-weapons squads, he decided to pull his command group out of trouble. He led his small party west to safety, escaping the town before it was cut off. It was just after dawn when he decided he could be more useful on Hill 314 than anywhere else. Byrn headed toward the hill alone, circling around the German troops swarming through Mortain.

Byrn, a native of South Dakota, grew up in the little town of Redfield, where his father sold Raleigh products. Like George Greene, at that moment fighting for his life on the roadblock at St.-Barthelmy, Byrn attended South Dakota State College. He graduated in June 1941. "As soon as the ceremony was over, we threw off our gowns," he said. "I had my ROTC uniform on underneath. We then marched right out on stage again and were sworn into the army." Byrn was assigned to the 6th Division, a regular army formation training at Fort Leonard Wood in Missouri. He expected to get out after a one-year hitch, but Pearl Harbor changed his plans—and forced him to seek emergency leave to get married when his fiancée graduated from South Dakota State in the spring of 1942. She followed him from post to post until 1944, when Byrn was ordered to England as a replacement officer. He was sent to France soon after D day, but waited weeks for a combat assignment. "I laid around on the beach, censoring the mail. I was bored to tears."

Byrn wasn't bored as he cautiously made his way up Hill 314 on the morning of August 7. He was one of the last outsiders to reach the position, although he remembers hitching a jeep ride partway up the hill. He found Lieutenant Kerley's company and was stunned by the sight of wounded men lying around the CP. "It was my first week of combat," he said. "I was kind of shocked to see injured men lying there in the open, being hit again by shrapnel."

The sun was beginning to burn through the fog by the time Erichson reached G Company on the cliffs overlooking Mortain. The position offered a spectacular view of the conflict below. "We were high enough to see German and American units come together in the town," Woody said. "Every time the Germans would come out of the houses, we'd shoot 'em." However, heavy artillery and mortar fire began to fall on Woody's men. He and Erichson pulled the exposed GIs higher up the hill, eventually linking up with K Company to form a consolidated defense facing north and west on the southwestern nose of Hill 314's crest. Lieutenant Joe Reaser, commanding K Company, reported that E Company was to his right, facing east, but he wasn't in contact with his neighbor.

Lieutenant Ralph Kerley watched the fog burn off with relief. The sounds of German activity were ominous, but until the mist cleared, there was little that E Company's commander could do about it. However, the improving view revealed a chilling sight: "Columns of enemy armor and foot troops streaming [towards us] from the east and northeast," he reported. The armor belonged to the Der Führer Regiment of the 2d SS Panzer Division. The foot soldiers were panzergrenadiers of the Goetz von Berlichingen Division. Kerley's company had no antitank guns and only a handful of bazookas, mortars, and machine guns. What it did have was far more deadly: a forward observer from the 230th Field Artillery Battalion.

"Whether the enemy was unaware of the fact the hill was occupied or had simply chosen to ignore it, is not known and really doesn't matter," Kerley wrote. "His closed formations made a beautiful target for our artillery. Corps artillery was called and the casualties and damage to vehicles was incredible. The undamaged vehicles quickly dispersed and withdrew. The artillery and cannon observers registered additional concentrations and now a solid ring of artillery fire could be fired on call."

Actually, Kerley overestimated the volume of fire. The men on Hill 314 were being supported by the 230th Field Artillery Battalion alone. The rest of the VII Corps artillery was occupied with other missions. Two batteries of the 197th Field Artillery Battalion were unable to fire their 105mm guns at all. German infantry suddenly approached their location just west of the small town of Romagny. An urgent message from the 30th Division Artillery CP reached division headquarters at

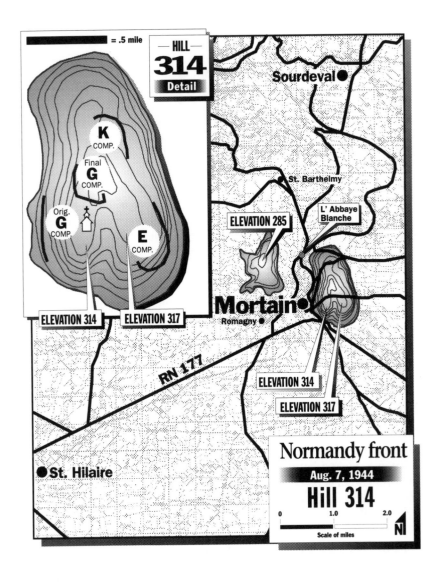

= .5 mile

— HILL —
314
Detail

K
COMP.

Final
G
COMP.

Orig.
G
COMP.

E
COMP.

ELEVATION 314

ELEVATION 317

Sourdeval●

St. Barthelmy

L' Abbaye
Blanche

ELEVATION 285

Mortain●

Romagny ●

ELEVATION 314

ELEVATION 317

RN 177

●St. Hilaire

Normandy front
Aug. 7, 1944
Hill 314

0   1.0   2.0

Scale of miles

N

0735 hours: "C Battery of Crunch [the battalion's code name] is being attacked and request[s] immediate aid. Is there something you can send down there to help them out?" Hobbs's operations officer replied: "You will have to tell them to fight as infantry. We don't have anything we can send them." For the next two hours, every man in the two batteries (B was also hit) fought as a rifleman until the Germans were driven back. The 197th lost one man killed and one jeep and one truck destroyed, but it destroyed two German tanks and saved its guns.

The Germans roaming through the American rear belonged to the Deutschland Regiment of the 2d SS Panzers. While part of the unit was engaged in Mortain itself, the rest of the regiment was pushing to the southwest, toward St.-Hilaire. One column found no opposition along Route 177 and advanced more than five kilometers to a position halfway between Mortain and St.-Hilaire. The drive would have continued the rest of the way to the Selune River, except the failure to capture Hill 314 meant that as soon as the fog burned off at midmorning, American artillery fire, directed by observers on the hill, began to fall with dismaying accuracy on the column. Pinned down by the artillery and fearing the appearance of Allied aircraft, von Kluge ordered the column to pull off the road, dig in, and erect camouflage.

A more serious threat to the 120th Regiment was another German probe, along a secondary road just north of Route 177. This column pushed three kilometers west of Mortain, just past the village of Romagny. The 120th's Intelligence and Recon Platoon blundered into an ambush there just after dawn. Only two vehicles and a handful of men escaped the trap, but those who remained held off the enemy for two hours before surrendering. The radioman, who kept the regimental CP informed even after his comrades had surrendered, later succeeded in escaping.

The road from Mortain to Romagny led west to the division headquarters at La Bazoge, but instead of driving west from Romagny, the Germans turned north to menace Hill 285 from the south and east. The stone farmhouse that served as Colonel Birks's command post was in the way.

Early in the afternoon, two German tanks worked their way to within 250 yards of the regimental CP. A switchboard operator, Pfc. Joe Shipley, left his post and knocked out one of the tanks with a bazooka. The other German tank pulled back. Shipley had never before fired a bazooka, not even in training.

*   *   *

As desperate as things were for the 120th in and around Mortain, twelve kilometers to the southeast, one portion of the regiment was enjoying considerable success. Lieutenant Colonel Paul McCollum launched a predawn attack to capture Barenton.

The assault was executed with textbook precision. At 0300 hours, Lt. Harold Kothenbeuthe led the 134 men of L Company around the town to set a roadblock on the highway just west of Barenton. Lieutenant Charles Shaw led the depleted I Company (just 79 men) east to set up a roadblock on the other side of town. Both companies drew small-arms fire as they worked their way into the outskirts of Barenton, but each reached its assigned position before dawn.

The rest of the battalion jumped off at 0600, accompanied by the Shermans of the 743d Battalion. With the 230th Field Artillery (FA) Battalion committed to the support of Hill 314, the 3d Battalion's only fire support came from its own heavy-weapons company, which covered the attack with a battery of 81mm mortars. The remnants of Task Force X remained outside the town during the attack, except for some of its antitank guns, which were used to bolster the roadblocks.

A platoon from Company L, supported by a platoon of tanks, swept through the town, driving the enemy—estimated as three hundred men and eight tanks from the 2d Battalion of the 985th Regiment (275th Division)—out of the north end of town.

By 0940 hours, the 3d Battalion was in possession of Barenton, although large groups of Germans remained in hiding. A member of the Barenton police force, a man named Barthoneuf, who claimed to be a former member of the French foreign legion, helped track town the hidden enemy. He reported a large group of Germans hiding in a house on the outskirts of town. Captain Howard Greer, Lieutenant Colonel McCollum's exec, took two jeeps loaded with members of the battalion staff to try and round them up. Unable to find the Germans, Greer and his group returned empty-handed and had the unusual experience of seeing Barthoneuf literally tear his hair out in frustration. Later, the policeman led a squad from the Reconnaissance Troop to the Germans' hiding place, where 180 of them were captured without a fight. They reported seeing Greer's two-jeep expedition drive past their hiding place without spotting them.

The success of the 3d Battalion provided little comfort to the rest of the 120th Regiment. The Germans were in firm control of the highway between Mortain and Barenton. An ambulance loaded with the 3d Battalion's wounded tried to reach the regimental aid station but was halted by a German roadblock. Two slightly wounded men were taken prisoner; the medics and two more seriously wounded GIs were allowed to return to Barenton. The 3d Battalion was isolated, at least temporarily.

It was a lonely position for McCollum's men. But they were far better off than the rest of the regiment.

CHAPTER 12: CHATEAU NEBELWERFER

Lieutenant Lawson Neel wasn't kidding when he told Pvt. Milton Daly that their headlong flight was a strategic retreat. Less than an hour after being chased away from his No. 1 gun just outside St.-Barthelmy, Neel was back in action, having rushed his No. 2 gun forward to set up a new roadblock about eight hundred meters west of the town. His 3-inch gun was hidden about twenty yards off the highway, alongside a hedgerow growing perpendicular to the road.

"We hadn't been there very long when a tank came along the road," Neel said. "We fired before they saw us." The AP shell hit the side of the Panther. No damage was visible, but the tank stopped in the middle of the road and the crew immediately evacuated, probably expecting to be hit again. Instead, Neel fired an HE shell, which caused the crewmen to scatter. "The tank's engine was still running," Neel reported. "We thought about trying to capture it, but just about this time the air force arrived and started to strafe everything that moved. We were as worried about them as we were of the Germans."

Neel didn't have much time to worry about the air force. Two more German tanks approached, much more cautiously this time. "We played a cat-and-mouse game for about forty-five minutes, waiting to get the second tank while sweating out the third." The second tank finally came into range, and the aimer, Pvt. Raymond Dautrieve, killed it with an AP shell, blocking the road. However, the shot revealed the gun's position to the third tank, which aimed an HE shell at Neel's position. The round exploded near enough to the gun to wound Dautrieve and the gun commander, Sgt. Joseph Pesak.

"We had to leave the gun," Neel said. "We pulled the pin and fell back. We hadn't gone very far until we ran into our infantry, digging in along a footpath."

The GIs Neel encountered were preparing a defensive line on a low hill about a kilometer west of St.-Barthelmy. Manning the position were the survivors of the 1st Battalion—now down to little more than the strength of a company—plus the regimental Headquarters Company and every other live body Lt. Col. Walter Johnson could get his hands on. Cooks, clerks, messengers, and truck drivers were thrown into the line, located just a few hundred yards in front of the small stone farmhouse that served as the regimental command post. The remainder of Johnson's regiment was busy elsewhere. His 2d Battalion (minus G Company) was en route to reinforce the 120th at Mortain. His 3d Battalion (plus Company G) was north of the highway, holding the ridgeline against the German penetration in the Sée Valley.

"It was our SOP [standard operating procedure] to dig in every time we set up a new CP," said S. Sgt. W. M. Killingsworth, a member of the 117th's Intelligence and Recon Platoon. "We were stationed around the farmhouse where Colonel Johnson set up, [serving] as a security squad. The Frenchman who lived there had this stack of cordwood we used to roof our foxholes. We logged them over, then put dirt on top."

Killingsworth, a National Guard veteran from Athens, Tennessee, was with Col. Henry Kelly when the former regimental commander was wounded by a shell fragment at St.-Lô. "I carried him back to the aid station. He told me to go back and tell Colonel Johnson to take command of the regiment." The sergeant had come to admire the new commander of the 117th. "He was the nicest, most soldierly gentleman I have ever known. He was West Point. Strictly soldier all the way."

Johnson, a native of Missoula, Montana, graduated from the U.S. Military Academy in 1927. He was married to a remarkable woman, the author Virginia Weisel Johnson. They had an infant daughter, born while the 30th Division was at Camp Atterbury.

Sergeant James Waldrop, who had seen Johnson run the regiment in combat for two months while the physically incapacitated Col. Henry Kelly held titular command, also admired the regiment's commander. "Sometimes we called him 'Little Hitler' because he had this little mustache and because he was so small, his .45 hung around his knees. But that was just a joke. We respected the hell out of him."

But there were others who still had to be convinced. Hobbs's dislike for the 117th's new commander went back to the division's days at Fort Jackson, when Johnson served as the 30th's intelligence officer (G-2). "He and Hobbs didn't get along at all," Major Giles said. "Hobbs got him off the staff as fast as he could. Then he didn't want to promote him [from temporary to permanent command of the 117th], but General Harrison insisted Johnson stay where he was."

Harrison arrived at the height of the crisis to check on the man he had talked General Hobbs into appointing as regimental commander. When Harrison's jeep pulled up to the farmhouse, German troops were less than 250 yards away and artillery fire was falling all around the position.

"Johnson told me, first thing, that he had no intention of moving back," Harrison reported. "He was determined to fight it out right there. That convinced me he was my kind of regimental commander."

Johnson deployed the remnants of B Company north of the highway, while the survivors from A and C companies, supported by the headquarters company, were bent in an arc, facing east to cover the area south of the highway and curving south to prevent German infiltration from that direction. After Johnson made his arrangements, Harrison took a few moments to address the assembled unit commanders. According to Capt. Bill Ziegler, who attended the briefing, Harrison told them their mission was not defense.

"We were to organize a movement forward," Ziegler reported. "Hopefully, we'd soon have the support of another infantry division. Until then, we were to go forward. As we listened and took notes, a few artillery shells landed outside the building. The house shuddered; we were coated with plaster and dust. General Harrison paused a moment, smiled at us and said, 'Gentlemen, perhaps we'd best put on our helmets.' How cool and courageous he was! The confidence he radiated drove away our fear."

Johnson's refusal to move his CP had a similar effect on the GIs of the 117th. German artillery hammered the position with so much fire that the cool regimental commander dubbed the position "Chateau Nebelwerfer." He clung to it with the same grim tenacity he was asking of his men.

*   *   *

Conditions at La Bazoge were somewhat less frantic than at Chateau Nebelwerfer. General Hobbs spent most of the morning on the telephone, trying to come to grips with the battle engulfing his division.

"With a heavy onion breath that day, the Germans would have achieved their objective," Hobbs wrote long after the battle. He didn't sound that concerned at the time. For instance, at 1550 hours, Jayhawk 6 (code name for VII Corps commander J. Lawton Collins) phoned to offer Custom 6 (Hobbs) the use of the 12th Regimental Combat Team from the 4th Division. Hobbs's response was recorded as "he didn't know if we would need it." Collins told him to "play it safe and take it anyway."

Plenty of help for the 30th Division was on the way, but only a handful of reinforcements would be in place to help the battered division on August 7. It's easy, in retrospect, to understand Hobbs's lack of enthusiasm for troops who couldn't help solve his immediate problems.

The northern threat attracted most of Hobbs's attention in the early hours of the morning. Oddly, the north was where he had the most help. Major General Raymond Barton, commanding the 4th Division north of the river, massed his artillery to fire on the German penetration. A patrol from one of his companies was directed to proceed to Le Mesnil-Adelée to contact friendly troops. Instead, the five-man patrol ran into strong German forces, the spearhead of the 2d Panzer Division's penetration eastward down the Sée Valley. The lieutenant commanding the patrol was killed and four men were captured, but Barton's artillery immediately targeted Le Mesnil-Adelée and the road from Le Mesnil-Tove. His guns began to rain "tremendous concentrations" of fire on the enemy. One mixed convoy of twenty-three vehicles was caught on the road and completely destroyed. The 20th FA Battalion alone fired more than six hundred 155mm shells at the road during the barrage.

Private First Class John Cole, one of the four patrol members captured early in the morning, escaped later that day and returned to the 4th Division's lines. He gave a vivid account of the artillery's effect on the veteran German soldiers. "They were drinking cognac heavily. The officers had bottles of cognac in the house and during the barrage, they would take several swallows before going outside. Then when the next concentration came in, they would dash back in, shaking their heads violently and taking another pull. The soldiers were also drinking heavily, but it seemed like the officers were deliberately doping themselves." The Germans holding Cole shifted positions three times in an attempt to escape the American fire. During the third move, Cole was left with a single guard. The GI overpowered the German soldier and brought him back to the American lines as a prisoner.

Just south of Le Mesnil-Adelée, the 26th FA Battalion, which had fired the first shots of the battle hours earlier, was fighting for its life. The thrust by the 2d Panzer Division had penetrated between the gunners and riflemen of the 39th Infantry Regiment. The artillerymen were forced to defend their own guns from attacking tanks and armored personnel carriers.

"If they had exploited their attack with accompanying infantry, we would have been goners," reported Maj. Carl M. Johnson, the battalion's exec. "We could keep on firing our artillery on their tanks and worry them; likewise, we knew by observation that our artillery caused many casualties among the enemy who were riding in personnel carriers. But if he had used a great many foot infantry, he could have assaulted and over-run our positions with ease. We can't fire 105s and beat off enemy infantry at the same time. We can take care of tanks, but not both tanks and infantry."

Lieutenant Colonel Evert E. Stong, who commanded the 26th FA Battalion, made the easiest decision of the day. When told that his unit had fired its daily quota of four hundred rounds, but had its basic load (three thousand rounds) on hand, he calmly ordered, "Shoot it."

"Throughout the operation, Colonel Stong was cool, and moved his batteries at the height of the counterattack to more effective firing positions closer to the infantry battalions," noted Col. William C. Westmoreland, the executive officer of the 9th Division's artillery (and the future commander of American forces in Vietnam). "We only had occasional communication with the 26th by SCR 608 [radio]. The 26th called for reinforcing fire from the other battalions, but the mediums [155mm] of the 34th Battalion were the only guns able to reach that distance."

Stong was afraid that the German spearheads would try to push south from Le Mesnil-Tove along the paved road connecting Chèrence-le-Roussel on the Sée River with Juvigny atop the high ridge overlooking the river valley. To protect against such a move, Stong pulled three of his batteries south, halfway up the ridge, leaving A Battery, reinforced by a 40mm Bofors gun and every machine gun and bazooka in the battalion, behind to cover the withdrawal. However, the Germans continued to push west and the "sacrifice battery" was able to pull back to join the rest of the battalion on the ridge.

The 2d Panzer Division's recon battalion, the spearhead for the drive down the Sée River valley, had reached Le Mesnil-Adelée just before dawn. The division's assigned task was to protect the flank of the main German thrust along the ridge road to Juvigny. However, the tenacious defense by the 117th Infantry Regiment had stalled the 1st SS Panzer Division just outside St.-Barthelmy. Thus there were only Americans on the high ground to the south. In addition, the failure of the 116th Panzer Division to attack on time meant that there were only Americans on the high ground to the north.

But the 2d Panzer Division got its worst shock just before dawn, when the recon battalion collided with forward elements of the U.S. 2d Armored Division.

The fortunate appearance of this powerful unit at such a vital spot has long been a source of misunderstanding. The 2d Armored Division's own history states, "For years historians and military officers have argued whether [it] was planned or whether it was one of those successful accidents. We now know it was planned and executed in such a manner [as] to lead the Germans to conclude it was an accidental placement of Allied troops."

Unfortunately, the source for this statement is Winterbotham's flawed *The Ultra Secret*. The truth is, the presence of the 2d Armored Division (minus one of its combat commands) at Chèrènce-le-Roussel *was* an accident, and not an especially unlikely one. The narrow corridor behind Mortain was, after all, the main route of communications for the Third Army. The whole purpose of holding the corridor was to allow General Bradley to feed supplies and fresh formations to the forces driving into the heart of France. An almost continual stream of combat units was passing through the corridor, all of them heading south. The real surprise would have been having no units in the pipeline at the crucial moment.

It was Maj. Gen. J. Lawton Collins, with no knowledge of Ultra (which was not distributed on the corps level), who ordered the 2d Armored Division to leave its positions around Vire and join the 1st Infantry Division near Mayenne. Combat Command A was left behind to help the 28th Division capture Gathemo. Major General Ted Brooks led the rest of his battle-hardened division south. The 82d Reconnaissance Battalion, the advance guard, left the St.-Sever–Calvados area just after midnight, reaching Chèrènce-le-Roussel at almost the same moment that the recon battalion of the 2d Panzer Division was arriving in Le Mesnil-Adelée just two kilometers to the south.

Oddly, considering the myth that the 2d Armored Division was deliberately placed in position to trap the attacking Germans, the collision between the two veteran armored units produced remarkably little combat. Heavy mortar fire hit the 82d Recon Battalion as it tried to move south from Chèrènce-le-Roussel toward Juvigny. Probing around the German units, the battalion turned west—away from the Germans—and led the division along the north bank of the Sée River to Brécey, where it turned south and drove behind the Mortain battlefield to St.-Hilaire. The division then moved southeast by a circuitous route to Barenton, joining the 3d Battalion of the 120th Infantry there late in the afternoon.

The brief, unexpected clash with American armor—reinforced by the increasing volume of artillery fire pouring down on his positions—convinced General Lüttwitz to halt his exposed spearhead at Le Mesnil-Adelée and wait for the flanking units to catch up.

With the 2d Armored Division disengaged and already en route to the other side of the battlefield, the task of reducing the 2d Panzer's penetration would fall on the infantry. Hobbs called on his 119th Infantry Regiment to repair the breach in his northern flank. An earlier probe by B Company, supported by two 57mm guns from the 1st Battalion's Headquarters Company, had struck the head of the German column near Le Mesnil-Adelée at dawn, destroying a Mark V tank before its withdrawal. For the next attack, Col. Edwin Sutherland, the 119th's commander, determined to strike a heavier blow. He ordered his 3d Battalion, along with a company of Shermans from the 743d Tank Battalion, to drive north from Juvigny to Le Mesnil-Tove, where it was expected that they would link up with a similar force from the 8th Infantry Regiment striking south from Chèrènce-le-Roussel and cut off the German spearhead.

Hobbs also planned to use Combat Command B of the 3d Armored Division, which was attached to his division, to strike north toward Le Mesnil-Adelée. Unfortunately, Col. Truman E. Boudinot's tanks were down for maintenance when the attack began and wouldn't be ready to leave their assembly area near Reffuveille until very late in the day.

The Germans launched an all-out assault on the 117th's position in front of Chateau Nebelwerfer early in the afternoon. Many of the enemy soldiers were wearing American uniforms, apparently taken from a 9th Division supply dump captured early in the day. Despite the GI uniforms, there was no attempt at deception: the attack was simply a powerful, well-coordinated assault by infantry and armor.

A battery of 81mm mortars, commanded by Lt. Ray Rose, poured devastating fire on the attackers from a range of less than 175 yards. Two privates used a little individual initiative to help stall the armored column supporting the infantry's advance. Frank Joseph and Clifford Buzzard, a bazooka team from D Company of the 117th Infantry, sneaked forward along a hedgerow and knocked out two Mark IV tanks in such a way that the remainder of the tanks were blocked and became sitting ducks for American artillery.

The German infantry struck the defensive line established by B Company north of the highway, but the GIs dug in along the sunken road refused to budge. After a bitter thirty-minute fight, much of it hand-to-hand, the Germans withdrew.

Forward observers reported that the enemy was regrouping for another attack. Colonel Johnson must have wondered how much longer his fragile line could hold against the powerful assault of two panzer divisions.

George Greene was exhausted. He'd had no sleep the night before. The morning hours had been filled with activity and strain. Now he was a prisoner and drained of the adrenaline that had sustained him in the final moments of the fight in St.-Barthelmy. In addition, his wounded arm hurt like hell.

"Practically everybody they captured took at least one wound," Greene said. "The stretcher cases they left in the wine cellar we'd been using as an aid station. Everybody who could walk was lined up for photographs. The Germans kept questioning us about our numbers and the size of the units they were up against. It didn't do much good. We were all so pooped that every time we'd sit down we'd go to sleep."

Sometime between 1300 and 1400 hours (Greene couldn't be sure of the exact time—a German soldier had stolen his watch), the prisoners at St.-Barthelmy were split into small groups and loaded into trucks packed with German soldiers. Greene couldn't understand the arrangement. As the convoy moved out of town, he learned why. "The Germans used us as decoys," he said. "They were hoping our aircraft wouldn't shoot at trucks carrying American prisoners." Unfortunately, the strategy overlooked the inability of a fighter pilot moving at four hundred miles an hour to distinguish between a GI and a panzergrenadier. The column had barely moved out before it was strafed, putting Greene's life in jeopardy again. The Germans "were able to jump out of the truck and hide in the ditches. We had to stay in the trucks. I tell you, I wouldn't be a prisoner a second time."

The arrival of Allied aircraft over the battlefield was unlucky for Greene and his fellow prisoners. However, it was to be far more unfortunate for the German army.

Mortain before the battle, as seen from the northwest. *U.S. Army Military History Institute*

General William K. Harrison, *left,* with the War Plans staff. *Center,* Brig. Gen. Leonard Gerow; Brig. Gen. Dwight Eisenhower, Gerow's assistant, sits at his right. *U.S. Army Military History Institute*

Major Gen. Lightning Joe Collins decorates a first sergeant. *U.S. Army Military History Institute*

Left to right: XIX Corps commander Maj. Gen. Charles Corlett, Maj. Gen. Leland Hobbs, Brig. Gen. James Lewis, Brig. Gen. William K. Harrison. *U.S. Army Military History Institute*

Major Gen. Wade Hampton Haislip.
U.S. Army Military History Institute

Murray Pulver as a sergeant
in 1941. *Courtesy of Murray
Pulver*

An American truck crosses a bridge over the river Cance at the southern end of the Abbaye Blanche roadblock after the battle. *National Archives*

Looking south at the northern end of the Abbaye Blanche roadblock. *National Archives*

A gun crew fires a towed 3-inch antitank gun during a winter exercise in the United States. *U.S. Army Military History Institute*

A destroyed forty-five-ton Mark V Panther, an example of the finest German battle tank produced during the war. *National Archives*

Hill 314 as seen from the southwest. *National Archives*

American GIs sprint along the base of a hedgerow just outside St.-Barthelmy. *U.S. Military History Institute*

A rifleman from Company A, 119th Infantry, fires through the base of a hedgerow. *U.S. Army Military History Institute*

The defenders of Hill 314. *Left to right:* Lt. Willie Irby, Capt. Delmont Byrn, Capt. Reynold Erichson, Lt. Guy Hagen, and Sgt. Forrest Hodges. *Courtesy of Mrs. Leah Little*

A German half-track, probably destroyed by Allied aircraft. Note the dead panzergrenadier. *U.S. Military History Institute*

A Panther destroyed by 3-inch guns at the Abbaye Blanche roadblock. *National Archives*

A French farmer and his daughter examine the wreckage of a German staff car and its dead driver, victims of the Abbaye Blanche roadblock guns. *U.S. Military History Institute*

Two German tanks and a half-track destroyed by the gunners at L'Abbaye Blanche. *National Archives*

Foreground, a Mark V Panther tank; *background,* a Mark IV. Spare tracks were hung on the Panther turret to provide extra protection against American antitank weapons. *National Archives*

Wrecked vehicles near Le Neufbourg. *Left to right:* a heavy truck, a *Kübelwagen* (jeep), a half-track, and two American jeeps. *U.S. Army Military History Institute*

Soldiers of the 119th Infantry Regiment pick their way through the ruins of Mortain on the morning of August 12, 1944. *Courtesy of North Carolina Military History Museum*

An aerial view of Mortain taken from the west. *U.S. Military History Institute*

Victory: Lt. Col. R. Ernest Frankland, *left,* shakes hands with his brother, Lt. Col. Walter Frankland, in Magdeburg, Germany. *Courtesy of Mrs. Stella Fitts*

CHAPTER 13: DAY OF THE TYPHOON

T he heavy ground fog that caused so much confusion at Mortain and St.-Barthelmy also delayed Charles Green's early morning reconnaissance flight. The small, primitive fighter strip at Le Fresne Camilly, just a few hundred yards behind the beaches where the British had landed in Normandy two months earlier, was chilled by a cool breeze blowing off the water. It was chilly enough that the ground crewmen took turns thawing out in the cockpits of the two Typhoons they were warming up for the recon mission. Warrant Officer Paddy Gray, who would be flying on Green's wing, was having tea and biscuits as he waited for the mist to lift.

Gray suspected that this wasn't going to be an ordinary flight. Wing commanders usually didn't fly recon flights. And Green wasn't just any wing commander. The big, burly South African was a legend in the RAF, as well known for his hatred of the Germans as for the two .38 Smith & Wesson revolvers he habitually wore into combat. Now he was pacing impatiently outside the intelligence tent, anxious to get off the ground. The dirty gray mist was lifting very slowly. Finally, Green decided visibility was good enough for takeoff. The meteorology officer predicted that the fog would be gone in another hour. Gray looked at the low-hanging cloud base and hoped he was right. If not, they might have to divert back across the Channel to England.

Green's Typhoon led the two-plane flight through the overcast. They burst out of fog and into the sunlight just a few hundred feet above the strip, then steered southwest on a heading of 230 degrees. Below,

Gray could see nothing but an undulating blanket of white fog. The two planes continued southwest until Green decided that they had reached Avranches, where they turned east. Gray was beginning to think the mission would be a waste of time when he heard the wing commander's voice on the radio. "There's a hole down there at two o'clock. I thought I saw something moving. Going down in five seconds—now!"

The cloud base was so low that the two pilots had only a few seconds to observe before they had to pull out of their dives. Gray reported seeing some vehicles, but he was unable to identify them. Green ordered another dive. This time Green was able to see tanks. A third dive revealed a long column of German armor.

That was all Green needed to see. He headed straight back to the field at Le Fresne Camilly, where the sun had indeed burned off enough of the mist for the two Typhoons to land. As Green raced to the intelligence tent, Gray observed crewmen stacking rockets and cases of 20mm cannon shells just off the end of the runway.

Ultra's midnight warning caused General Bradley to order "all-out" air support for the morning of August 7. Field Marshal von Kluge was expecting the same from the Luftwaffe. He was promised that three hundred fighters would be in the air over Mortain to protect his armored columns.

Instead, not one German airplane reached the battlefield after daylight on August 7. The reason for the Luftwaffe's dismal showing was the intervention of the United States' Ninth Air Force, which assumed responsibility for erecting an impenetrable barrier between the Luftwaffe airfields around Paris and the fighting around Mortain.

It is unfortunate that the infantry should harbor such dislike for Maj. Gen. Elwood Quesada's IX Tactical Air Command. Of all the high-ranking officers in the U.S. Army Air Forces, none had as much interest in solving the problems of ground support as "Pete" Quesada. During the tragic Cobra bombings, his fighter-bombers were the only planes in the air that day ordered to approach the target parallel to the front line as General Bradley demanded. It was also the boyish-looking general who developed the Air Support Party (ASP), which was to play such a large role in the Allied armored dash across France.

Quesada's simple but brilliant suggestion was to install an air force–style VHF radio in one tank of each armored column, then to provide each column with a continuous cover of fighter-bombers. After a frustrating start (the first two tanks equipped with the special radios were mistakenly dispatched to the front as replacement vehicles before the sets could be tested), the ASP proved its value as General Patton's tanks swept south from St.-Lô into Brittany. Quesada ordered that "each of the rapidly advancing columns will be covered at all times by a four ship flight which will maintain armed recce in advance of the column. They may attack any target which is identified as enemy, directing their attention to the terrain immediately in front of the advancing column. The combat command commander may monitor channel 'C' to receive information transmitted by the fighter-bombers covering him. He may also ask the flight to attack targets immediately in front of him. Targets which require more strength than the four ship flight will be passed back through ASP channels and the mission will be accomplished by fighter-bombers on ground alert."

Quesada's system worked beautifully. In contrast to the riflemen's contempt for the airmen, the tankers developed a close, friendly relationship with their aerial protectors, especially the stubby P-47 Thunderbolts, called "Jugs" by their pilots and "Jabos" (the German word for fighter-bomber) by the tankers.

"If Jerry hated our Jabos because they were deadly, men of the 3d Armored Division loved them well," wrote a spokesman for the Spearhead Division. "These chunky fighters seemed to be a part of the armored striking force. It was a constant source of satisfaction to see them slant down in those long, beautiful dives. You'd see the thin line of smoke which told of the hammering machine guns, and then, while 'Blitz Doughs' held their breath in suspense, the fly boys would release their bombs and slant up into the blue again."

General Quesada could have dispatched his Jabos to Mortain. However, as deadly as his bomb-carrying Thunderbolts were, there was a more potent tank killer in the Allied air arsenal: the rocket-firing Typhoons of the British Second Tactical Air Force. In one of the outstanding instances of Allied cooperation seen during the war, Quesada contacted Air Vice Marshal Sir Harry Broadhurst, who commanded ten squadrons of Typhoons in Normandy, and arranged to share responsibility for the crisis at Mortain. Quesada's fighters would keep the Luftwaffe away from the battlefield, while Broadhurst's Typhoons would take on the German armor at Mortain.

The American airmen did their job well. Most German fighters were engaged as soon as they left the ground. Others were shot up before they could get in the air. The few that managed to even approach the battle area found themselves ambushed by P-51 Mustangs from the XIX Tactical Air Command, which backstopped the P-47 Thunderbolts of the IX Tactical Air Command.

In four aerial engagements, the American pilots claimed fourteen kills for a loss of two of their own. Two squadrons of the 373d Fighter Group encountered more than twenty-five German fighters near Chartres and shot down five without a loss. Another squadron from the same group was vectored to the fight and claimed a sixth kill. Eight Thunderbolts from the 362d Group jumped sixteen Germans near Le Mans, killed three, and drove off the rest. A squadron of Mustangs from the 354th Group tangled with twelve Germans near Mayenne—about as close as the Luftwaffe got to Mortain—and shot down five with a loss of two. Two busy airfields near Chartres were the targets of Mustang raids. Three P-51s fell victim to flak but claimed nineteen planes destroyed on the ground.

In all, the Ninth Air Force flew 429 sorties on August 7. It is impossible to determine the exact number of losses inflicted upon the Luftwaffe that day, but six days later, Luftflotte Three (based in Paris) reported that it had only seventy fighters available for combat. Whatever the actual number of kills, the American fighters succeeded in keeping the sky over Mortain clear for the Typhoons of the British Second Tactical Air Force.

The Typhoon was a powerful single-seat fighter-bomber designed by Sydney Camm and the Hawker Aircraft Company. Camm conceived the plane as a successor to the Hurricane, which he had designed in the early thirties. The first Typhoon test model was flown before the Battle of Britain, but it didn't go into production until 1942. Powered by a twenty-one-hundred horsepower Sabre II engine, the Typhoon had a top speed of 405 miles per hour in level flight, but could dive well in excess of 500 miles per hour. Despite its speed, it was somewhat disappointing as a fighter. However, it proved to be a superb attack aircraft. Broadhurst's Typhoons were armed with four 20mm cannon and up to eight 60-pound rockets. The cannon were effective against light armor and could occasionally penetrate a Mark IV tank. However, the rockets were the real tank busters. A single rocket hit was usually enough to destroy even the best-armored German tank.

Broadhurst's ten Typhoon squadrons were alerted for action before sunup on August 7, but the heavy fog kept the Typhoons grounded throughout the early morning.

In view of the widely held perception that the German counteroffensive at Mortain was stopped by the sudden appearance of rocket-firing Typhoons, it is important to note that the first Typhoon sorties (other than Green's recon flight) did not arrive over the battlefield until 1230 hours. At that time, the German armor columns were no longer advancing at any point. The northern penetration along the Sée Valley was halted just after dawn, when General Lüttwitz ordered the column to halt and dig in just west of Le Mesnil-Adelée. The drive by the 2d SS Panzer down Route 177 to St.-Hilaire was brought to a halt before noon by accurate American artillery fire directed from Hill 314. The main thrust of Operation Lüttich, the drive by the 1st SS Panzer Division west along the ridge highway toward Juvigny, met such fierce resistance from the 1st Battalion of the 117th Infantry at St.-Barthelmy that after the repulse in front of the Chateau Nebelwerfer, General Funck halted the attack and ordered the column to dig in and erect camouflage.

Certainly the threat of attack from the air played a role in Funck's decision. German meteorologists had predicted that the morning fog would persist most of the day, providing protection from Allied air attacks. The clearing weather came as a rude shock to the exposed panzer columns. It also allowed the American defenders at Mortain to make effective use of their superior artillery.

Brigadier General James Lewis, the 30th Division's artillery commander, had control of a massive assembly of twelve and a half field artillery battalions—a total of seventy-eight 105mm guns, forty-eight 155mm guns, twelve 4.5-inch guns, and twelve 8-inch guns. A concentration of fire from Lewis's batteries helped break the last major attack by the 1st SS Panzers in front of Lieutenant Colonel Johnson's command post. The veteran German troops, feeling the weight of the American fire and aware of the threat from the air, were already stopped and trying to get under camouflage when the first Typhoons arrived.

*   *   *

Wing Commander Green conducted the briefing at Le Fresne Camilly, pointing out the armored column he and Paddy Gray had sighted. "They're moving along this road," he said, "from Mortain towards St.-Barthelmy. The job for 245 [Squadron] pilots, who will be first in, is to concentrate on the lead tanks and jam up the road." The squadron was to operate in two-plane formations. Each team would take off together, make the fifteen-minute flight to the target, then return to rearm and attack again. That way, the 121st Wing would maintain a continuous cycle of Typhoon sorties.

Green claimed the honor of leading the first assault. With Gray on his wing again, he led the 245th Squadron toward the target at four thousand feet. Over Mortain, Green dipped his wing, then pushed his stick forward to dive on the target. He raked the column with two of his rockets and a long burst from his cannon, then pulled back on the stick to pull his plane's nose up into a hard climb, just clearing the trees alongside the road.

The column Green's wing attacked was actually halted, backed up behind St.-Barthelmy. Caught on a high, exposed road between lines of hedgerows, there was little the Germans could do to camouflage their presence. A few flak vehicles accompanied the panzer regiments, but their fire was ineffective and quickly suppressed by the Typhoons' deadly cannon. It wasn't long before the greatest threat to the British pilots wasn't the German flak, but the danger of mid-air collisions. Desmond Scott, a New Zealander commanding the 123d Wing, had also arrived over the target with his Typhoon squadrons. The air was filled with diving planes, many taking different approach angles to the target.

Scott left a vivid picture of the scene: "The road was crammed with enemy vehicles—tanks, trucks, half-tracks, even horse-drawn wagons and ambulances, nose to tail, all in a frantic bid to reach cover . . . As I sped to the head of this mile-long column, hundreds of German troops began spilling out into the road to sprint for the open fields and hedgerows. There was no escape. Typhoons were already attacking in deadly swoops at the other end of the column and within seconds the whole stretch of road was bursting and blazing under streams of rocket and cannon fire. Ammunition wagons exploded like multicolored volcanoes. A large long-barreled tank standing in a field just off the road was hit by a rocket and overturned into a ditch. It was an awesome sight: flames, smoke, burning rockets and showers of colored tracer. The once-proud ranks of Hitler's Third Reich were being massacred from the Normandy skies by the relentless and devastating firepower of our rocket-firing Typhoons."

The British Second Tactical Air Force flew 294 sorties between 1230 hours and dusk, expending 2,088 rockets and 80 bombs. Three Typhoons were lost; two pilots probably died in a midair collision. An official communique claimed that the Typhoons had put 162 tanks out of action with 81 destroyed and 54 seriously damaged. It was Wing Commander Green who told his messmates at dinner that evening, "You know, chaps, this has been the Day of the Typhoon and no bastard can take it away from us."

Actually, the poor "bastards" on the ground at Mortain were somewhat skeptical of the RAF's claims. Many GIs failed to see much evidence of the Typhoons' effectiveness.

"The only time we saw a Typhoon was when they hit us," said Lt. Tom Springfield, commanding the roadblock at L'Abbaye Blanche. The GIs had their recognition panels out and fired yellow smoke as the British fighters approached from the north. Still, several rockets exploded near Springfield's No. 3 and No. 4 guns, killing one man (the roadblock's first casualty) and wounding several more.

Colonel Birks complained to division headquarters that Typhoons had hit his Cannon Company. When VII Corps' air attache asked at 1802 hours if 30th Division was receiving air support, Capt. James Powers of the headquarters staff answered, "Our planes have bombed and strafed our troops on the hill east of Mortain, in Mortain and Barenton. Major [James] Bynum was killed and [there were] several other casualties."

Bynum, a National Guard veteran in command of the 120th's Service Company, was seated in the basement of a small building near the regimental headquarters when a cannon shell from a Typhoon entered through a small vent and struck the back of his head, just beneath his helmet. Captain Layton Tyner, who succeeded Bynum as commander of the Service Company, was strafed by another Typhoon a few minutes later and badly wounded.

There were many other errors. A Typhoon attacked four Shermans belonging to the 743d on a hill outside Mortain, destroying one American tank and killing its crew. Not all of the Typhoon mistakes were deadly. Sergeant Floyd Montgomery, manning the southern end of the roadblock at L'Abbaye Blanche, watched in amazement as the British pilots launched attack after attack on abandoned vehicles that the 823d TD gunners had knocked out earlier in the day.

Lieutenant Murray Pulver on Hill 285 also discovered that the airmen had trouble distinguishing live tanks from dead ones. "A British Typhoon buzzed us, circled around and cut loose a rocket aimed at the knocked-out tanks just in front of me. My God, the heat from that thing almost singed my hair! We all grabbed our gear and ran back to the next hedgerow, where there was a big hole. We dove in as two more Typhoons dropped their loads, circled around and came at us straight. The weapons carrier driver was killed as bullets broke through our cover. It's a puzzle why we weren't all killed."

It is easy to understand the contempt the GIs felt for the airmen. Two days in a row before the Cobra breakout, the 30th Division suffered heavy casualties at the hands of the Army Air Forces. Smaller attacks were so frequent as to be commonplace. Major Warren Giles, the 117th's intelligence officer, noted: "It got to the point where we were afraid to call on our air force for support." The foot soldiers lived a life of dirt and despair, whereas airmen lived comfortably, well behind the lines. The fliers were lionized by the press and the public. Captain Byrn of the 120th Infantry remembers with a passion undiminished over the years, "We hated the guts of the Air Force."

Between the extremes of the airmen's extravagant claims and the GIs' skepticism lies the reality of the situation. The Typhoons did inflict significant damage on the backed-up German armored columns that day.

"The activities of the fighter-bombers are almost intolerable," Funck reported. "The air attacks are of an intensity hitherto unknown."

General Lüttwitz, the superb commander of the 2d Panzer Division, phoned headquarters to ask where the promised Luftwaffe fighter cover was. "We can do nothing against their fighter-bombers," he complained. "They descend in their hundreds firing rockets on concentrations of tanks and vehicles."

A few GIs recognized the contribution of the air force. "If it hadn't been for the British air force that first day, well, Mortain would have been a different story," said Sgt. James Waldrop of the 117th Infantry. "I can still see those planes, flying so low they were coming up with branches in their air scoops."

Even Giles, no fan of the air force, described the events of August 7 this way: "We had gotten [the Germans] stopped, but there's no way in hell we could have held them without the British air force. We won the battle . . . with a whole lot of help from those Typhoons."

The exact distribution of credit for tank kills will never be known. A British Operations Research Group attached to the 21st Army Group reached the Mortain area shortly after the battle and examined seventy-eight armored fighting vehicles, four self-propelled guns, and fifty unarmored vehicles left behind by the Germans. More than half of these targets were destroyed by antitank weapons and artillery, although several of the kills were judged to be vehicles abandoned by their crews for fear of air attack, then later destroyed by the infantry. Even this study is misleading, since many of the tanks hit on the first day of the battle would have been recovered for repair or for use as spare parts. One observer on Hill 314 reported watching knocked-out tanks being towed to the rear. Tanks hit by aircraft in the German rear would have been the easiest to recover.

The official history of the Royal Air Force in World War II admits that the claim of eighty-one tanks destroyed on August 7 was "perhaps a little too optimistic." The same could apply to subsequent historians who have credited the Typhoons with turning the tide or even single-handedly winning the battle at Mortain. Allied air power played an important role on August 7. But so did the TD gunners, the artillery, and the infantry.

It is worth noting that when the sun went down on the Day of the Typhoon, and Wing Commander Green was toasting his pilots with an extra liquor ration after a hot meal at Le Fresne Camilly, the weary soldiers of the 30th Infantry Division were still stuck in their foxholes, bracing for a night of further combat.

CHAPTER 14: THE MOMENTUM SHIFTS

Some of the GIs on Hill 314 were denied even the meager refuge of a deep foxhole. Private First Class Leo Temkin of E Company found the ground too rocky to dig where his squad was positioned. "We tried to pick out positions where the rocks would give you some protection. I picked out a crack in a wall of soft rock. I can still hear the funny sound the German bullets would make when they hit." The composition of the hill's rock helped save the spotters from the 230th FA Battalion. Several 88mm shells hit an outcropping above their observation post, but the shells didn't explode on impact, instead bouncing over the hill and exploding in the valley below.

The German troops besieging Hill 314 left E Company's position alone during the afternoon hours of August 7, except for the incessant artillery and sniper fire. The day turned warm as the morning fog burned off and the sun rose in the clear blue August sky.

At approximately 1400 hours, the panzergrenadiers of the Goetz von Berlichingen Division mounted an attack from the west, toward Lt. Ronal Woody's G Company. The tired riflemen, many of whom had been awake for more than thirty-six straight hours, repulsed the assault with help from the company's two 60mm mortars. "I had two guys who could lean those mortars on their knees and drop their shells anywhere they wanted," Woody said. "Everytime we'd see the Germans forming up for an attack, we'd drop a few shells on top of them." G Company's victory was not without cost. The unit suffered several casualties. With all routes off the hill blocked by the Germans, there was no way to evacuate the wounded. Woody had the injured men placed in slit trenches. Medical supplies were already in short supply.

Lieutenant Tom Springfield had no such problems at L'Abbaye Blanche. Not only were his lines of communication still open, but the Germans had failed to inflict a single casualty on his position. The men wounded in the RAF attack were evacuated by one of the platoon's trucks. Meanwhile, Springfield's gunners continued to take a toll upon German vehicles moving up the hill from the dairy, destroying three more tanks (two Panthers and a Mark IV) and five other vehicles. Midway through the afternoon, the Germans asked for a truce in order to pick up their dead and wounded from the battlefield. Springfield's men watched as the enemy approached, waving large Red Cross flags. During this respite, the German officers trapped in the dairy barn made their escape, after having been stuck in hiding for eight long hours.

During the lull, Springfield met with Col. Hammond Birks, the commander of the 120th Infantry, whose command post was located in a farmhouse on a small hill just southwest of the roadblock. "I remember, he was covered with blood," Springfield said. "Birks wanted me to get a squad together to haul some ammo up the hill [314] for the infantry. He wanted us to go up that night." Birks later canceled the order, after another relief force ran into such stiff resistance.

The regimental commander was in radio contact with the three companies on the hill. The arrival of the 2d Battalion of the 117th Infantry (minus Company G) early in the afternoon finally provided the 120th's commander an opportunity to reestablish contact between his scattered units. He ordered Lt. Col. James Lockett to detach one of his companies to recapture Romagny. The remainder of the battalion, accompanied by four Shermans from the 743d's Company A, was to drive into Mortain from the northeast and reopen communications with the battalion on Hill 314.

Lockett led what amounted to a reinforced company through the railroad underpass and into the town. His troops encountered no resistance as they passed L'Abbaye Blanche, but as soon as his scouts reached the outskirts of Mortain itself, the Germans unleashed ferocious machine-gun and mortar fire. Lieutenant William Richards, commanding the lead platoon, decided it was impossible to advance farther. Lockett reluctantly agreed, electing to withdraw just far enough to cover the vital roadblock at L'Abbaye Blanche. The brief counterattack cost Lockett seventy-three casualties (twelve dead). Meanwhile, the four attached Shermans advanced into the center of town before Capt. Kenneth Cowan decided it was too dangerous to continue without infantry support. He pulled back and took up defensive positions on a small hill just northwest of Mortain, where one of his tanks was attacked and knocked out by the RAF.

Lockett's detached Company F had even worse luck in its attack toward Romagny. The small force, accompanied by four tanks and two self-propelled tank destroyers, approached Romagny from the west, using a trail that ran alongside a dry streambed. Approximately three hundred yards short of the village, the point of the column was ambushed. Six men were killed, two were captured, and several remained frozen in no-man's-land. Private William King worked his way forward and persuaded two of the frightened GIs to pull back. A third man was discovered four days later, hiding in a ditch.

The small task force was a victim of confusion and poor communications. Captain George Sibbald, commanding Company F, was told only to set up a roadblock west of Romagny. He had no idea the Germans had taken the town. The accompanying tankers were well aware of the situation, but they never thought to pass that information on to Sibbald. Fortunately, the American task force was on high ground when contact was made and was able to establish a strong defensive line. As darkness fell, one of Sibbald's platoons launched an attack upon the left and rear of the enemy position, causing the Germans to break off contact and withdraw into town.

Although none of these blows made significant progress, the limited counterattacks were evidence that by late in the afternoon of August 7, the Americans had wrestled the initiative away from the Germans. In the north, Combat Command B (CCB) of the 3d Armored Division had finally gone into action, driving north from Reffuveille toward Le Mesnil-Tove. The tankers slid into position alongside the 3d Battalion of the 119th Infantry. The arrival of the 12th RCT (the unit that General Hobbs wasn't sure he needed) allowed Lt. Col. Walter Johnson, commanding the 117th Infantry, to plug the gap on his right flank, where German infantry had succeeded in infiltrating behind his lines. The 1st Battalion of the 119th Infantry, which had spent most of the day guarding the division headquarters at La Bazoge, reached the 197th Field Artillery Battalion and helped clean out the German infiltrators still plaguing the exposed gunners.

In addition, Hobbs learned that the 35th Division would launch an attack at daybreak. Two regiments were scheduled to push north toward Mortain from a position south of the St.-Hilaire–Mortain highway.

Major General Paul Baade's weary division had taken almost six hundred casualties in its two-week battle to capture Vire. After being pinched out of the line by the advance of the XIX Corps across its front, the 35th was supposed to transfer to Maj. Gen. Walton Walker's XX Corps in the Fougères-Vitré area. On August 6, the division's lead element, the 137th Infantry Regiment (Harry Truman's old National Guard unit) boarded trucks and began the long drive south. The convoy rolled down the coast highway, passing within sight of Avranches. The GIs got a spectacular view of the sunset over the Bay of Mont-St.-Michel. The convoy turned east after crossing the Pontaubault Bridge and reached St.-Hilaire at midnight.

The convoy had almost cleared the bombed-out city when it was bombed by a large force of German planes. The Luftwaffe first dropped a long line of flares along the road to Fougères, then pounded the brightly lit highway. Despite the vulnerability of the long convoy, few vehicles were damaged, and the division lost only four men killed and three wounded in the raid.

Although the convoy was supposed to continue on to Fougères in the Third Army sector, the lead trucks pulled to an abrupt halt ten kilometers south of St.-Hilaire, near Louvigne du Desert. The division, halted by General Patton's midnight stop order (thanks to the warning provided by Ultra), moved into an assembly area just northwest of Louvigne. The confused GIs climbed off their trucks and tried to get some needed sleep while the brass figured out what to do with them.

General Baade was anxious to help the embattled 120th Infantry Regiment near Mortain, but his first order of business was to plug the gap in the American line south of the 30th Infantry Division. He elected to employ his "Santa Fe" Division (so-called because the prewar home of the National Guard division was Camp Doniphan, Oklahoma, near the eastern terminus of the old Santa Fe Trail) to establish a strong defensive line to cover the territory between St.-Hilaire and Barenton.

Shortly after 1500 hours, the men of the 137th Regimental Combat Team reboarded their trucks and rode ten kilometers to the northeast. They dismounted at St.-Symphorien, a small village approximately fifteen kilometers due south of Mortain. At 1830 hours, the regiment was ordered to begin an advance at 2000 hours. Despite the short notice, the attack got off on schedule, supported by a company from the 737th Tank Battalion and a company of the 654th TD Battalion. The regiment met no resistance as it advanced five kilometers to the small village of Villechien, where at sundown (about 2230), General Baade's men dug in for the night. To the west, the 134th RCT tried to keep pace on the 137th's left flank, but darkness and several pockets of German resistance slowed the regiment's advance.

A few miles to the east, Maj. Gen. Ted Brooks was trying to organize the odd collection of units in Barenton. The small town, recaptured from the Germans only that morning, now held the 3d Battalion of the 120th Infantry Regiment, Task Force X, from the 3d Armored Division, and Brooks's 2d Armored Division (minus Combat Command A). The latter unit, which had successfully disengaged from the 2d Panzer Division spearheads in the Sée River valley before dawn, had arrived in Barenton at 1600 hours after a long but unimpeded fifty-mile swing to the west and south. Along the way, French civilians lined the route and shared cognac, wine, and cider with the American tankers. Some enterprising GIs were able to trade cigarettes and chocolate for butter and eggs.

The holiday mood ended when the lead Shermans rolled into Barenton. Major General Collins, the VII Corps commander, ordered Brooks to organize an immediate strike north toward Ger. The 2d Armored's 41st Armored Infantry Regiment led the attack, supported by Task Force X. However, the ground north of Barenton was extremely hilly and thus unfavorable for armored attacks. Brooks's first thrust made little progress before being halted by darkness.

The 30th Division still had some major problems as darkness fell over Mortain at the end of the first day of battle. The 2d Battalion of the 120th was cut off on Hill 314, and the battalion headquarters staff was in hiding somewhere in Mortain. A platoon of C Company was also isolated in the northern end of town. The enemy maintained a foothold on Hill 285 and still had forces in the 120th's rear at Romagny. A wide gap separated the 120th Regiment at Mortain and the 117th

Regiment in front of Juvigny. The Germans still maintained deep penetrations on the division's flanks, southwest of Mortain and westward along the Sée River valley.

Still, General Hobbs could be forgiven for believing the worst was over. His division had withstood a surprise assault by three German panzer divisions without cracking. There was no longer any danger that the enemy could reach Avranches. Reinforcements were gathering, and the 30th's front was almost stable. Surely, the Germans must have realized that their attack had failed.

By the afternoon of August 7, Field Marshal von Kluge was ready to admit that Operation Lüttich was a failure. Hitler, as usual, had other ideas.

"I command the attack be prosecuted daringly and recklessly to the sea—regardless of risk," he ordered von Kluge. "Greatest daring, determination, imagination must give wings to all echelons of command. Each and every man must believe in victory. Cleaning up in rear areas and in Brittany can wait until later." To fulfill this grandiose scenario, Hitler ordered the II SS Panzer Corps (of three divisions) to be withdrawn from the line facing the British and thrown into the Mortain sector, "to bring about the collapse of the Normandy front by a thrust into the deep flank and rear of the enemy facing the Seventh Army."

Hitler also took time to indulge in recriminations. He accused his commander-in-chief West of clumsily executing the attack. Von Kluge was, he claimed, guilty of launching Operation Lüttich prematurely. He should have waited until the promised panzer reinforcements arrived, creating an irresistible striking force. In addition, Hitler said that von Kluge erred in committing the 1st SS Panzer Division at St.-Barthelmy, rather than south of Mortain, where the 2d SS Panzer Division had achieved a deep penetration against negligible opposition. Many historians have agreed with the latter criticism, pointing to the accepted tactical doctrine of reinforcing success, not failure.

However, given the tight timetable for Operation Lüttich and the limited road net around Mortain, von Kluge had little choice. In order to be in position to exploit a breakthrough, the 1st SS Panzer Division had to be set in motion well before the results of the initial assault were known. True, upon reaching the crossroads at La Dainie, the division could have turned south on Route 177, but in order to reach the open highway to St.-Hilaire, the armored column would have had to get past the formidable roadblock at L'Abbaye Blanche and the 1st Battalion of the 120th on Hill 285, a task that would have been at least as difficult as pushing the 1st Battalion of the 117th out of St.-Barthelmy.

General Hausser, commanding the Seventh Army, blamed the failure of the operation on three factors: stronger than expected American resistance, Allied air superiority, and the failure of the 116th Panzer Division to carry out its supporting attack north of the Sée River.

General von Schwerin, who refused a direct order to attack, claimed his division was unable to disengage because of the late arrival of the 84th Infantry Division, which was to relieve his unit. Actually, it is likely that von Schwerin, one of the July 20 conspirators, had simply given up hope of victory. Whatever his motives, the 116th remained on the defensive until 1600 hours, when von Schwerin was finally relieved of his command. Colonel Walter Reinhard, given command of the demoralized division, launched an attack at 1630 hours, but the feeble effort was stopped in its tracks by the U.S. 9th Infantry Division.

Hitler's demand that von Kluge renew the offensive left no room for argument. General Eberbach, who called C-in-C West's headquarters to beg for reinforcements for his Fifth Panzer Army, was told that his formation would lose two panzer divisions instead. Von Kluge all but apologized to his subordinate, explaining, "I foresee that the failure of this attack can lead to collapse of the entire Normandy front. But the order is so unequivocal it must be obeyed."

It is possible to defend the reasoning behind the original decision to launch a major counteroffensive at Mortain. It was a gamble, but not an unreasonable one. Even the German professionals came to see potential in the original plan. However, the failure to address Hitler's unrealistic expectations for Operation Lüttich was now bearing bitter fruit. Hitler's order to pursue the attack after August 7 had no redeeming features. It was sheer lunacy.

It was to present General Bradley the chance of a lifetime.

Bradley was not yet aware of the opportunity offered by Hitler's military obstinacy. The commander of the American 12th Army Group spent the morning of August 7 at General Patton's headquarters in Brittany, briefing the Third Army commander on his plan for a wide sweep past Paris. The two generals also discussed the Mortain counterattack. Neither was particularly concerned by the threat of a German break-through to Avranches. Bradley decided to hold on to Major General Walton Walker's XX Corps in case it was needed, but agreed to turn loose Maj. Gen. Wade Haislip's XV Corps to continue its advance toward Le Mans.

Bradley returned to his own headquarters outside Coutances for another important meeting later that afternoon. Prime Minister Winston Churchill had flown the Channel to lobby for the cancellation of Operation Dragoon, the scheduled landings in southern France. Forewarned by General Eisenhower, Bradley listened courteously to the prime minister's pitch, but refused to commit himself. Churchill departed late that afternoon for Eisenhower's headquarters, leaving the American commander to review the reports from the front. As Bradley pored over the maps in his headquarters trailer and read the reports on the Mortain fighting, he began to glimpse a great opportunity.

"It occurred to me that night, that Hitler's Mortain offensive had set the stage for an Allied coup de main," Bradley later wrote. By throwing so much of his armor so far west, the enemy was leaving himself open to a short envelopment. As Bradley considered the possibilities, he told his aide, Chet Hansen, "[This is the] greatest tactical blunder I've ever heard of. Probably won't happen again in a thousand years."

It was too early for Bradley to act on his idea. The situation at Mortain was still unsettled, and it wasn't certain how long the Germans would persist in the attack.

Also, one more major piece would have to fall into place for his plan to have a chance. Bradley knew that at midnight more than a thousand British heavy bombers would hammer the German 89th Division south of Caen to open General Montgomery's new offensive. Code-named "Totalize," the aerial bombardment was very closely modeled after Cobra. It was designed to blast a hole in the German lines for the Canadian II Corps, commanded by Lt. Gen. G. G. Simonds. His two armored divisions, backed up by two armored brigades and three infantry divisions, planned to drive twenty-one miles southeast to the town of Falaise, deep in the rear of the Germans fighting in Normandy. "We silently prayed the offensive would go well," Bradley wrote. "If it did, it was bound to take considerable pressure off Joe Collins at Mortain."

It would also set the stage for the scheme growing in Bradley's mind.

CHAPTER 15: RADIO BATTERIES

I t was anything but a quiet night on Hill 285. Sporadic firing persisted during the brief hours of darkness, but the German and American positions were so intermixed that it was impossible for either side to mount a real attack. Isolated riflemen spent the night crouching in their foxholes, hoping the dawn would relieve the confusion. Each side launched patrols to probe the dark countryside.

Just before first light, a German patrol sweeping southeast of Hill 285 stumbled across the 2d Battalion aid station. The aid station originally had been set up in a church in town, but the previous night's attack had forced a hasty evacuation. The medical unit pulled back to a small French house near an intersection just a few hundred yards away from the regimental headquarters. Most of the weary doctors and medics were asleep when the Germans appeared.

"*Raus! Raus! Raus!*" medic Robert Bradley heard as he woke. "The next thing I knew I was being jolted suddenly awake by the stomping of hobnail boots on my ankles."

Gunnar Teilmann, the regimental chaplain, was also captured, along with his aide, T. Sgt. Jack Thacker. "I was asleep in a pretty nice foxhole," Thacker said. "I remember being prodded. As I woke up, I heard two unfamiliar words—'*Raus mitten.*' I assumed it meant 'Get up and come along.' When I peered out of my foxhole, I saw several German soldiers, all heavily armed. They had captured about ten of us: two or three doctors, some aid men, the chaplain, and myself."

The German patrol got the small group of prisoners away quickly, grabbing as many medical supplies as possible. "They were particularly eager to get morphine and water purification tablets," Bradley recalled. Captain Frank Towers, the liaison officer between division headquarters and the 120th, was making a predawn run between La Bazoge and Colonel Birks's command post when he discovered the abandoned aid station. "They must have just left in a big hurry," he said. "I didn't know what had happened. Nobody was there, but there were a couple of Bunsen burners still burning."

The Germans got in the first blow on Hill 285 just a few minutes later, attacking at first light, striking between A Company and the tank-destroyer platoon on the northern face of the hill. Using two flamethrowers to spearhead the assault, the Germans forced A Company back over the crest of the hill, exposing the TD gunners. However, Lt. Francis Connors, commanding the battery, mounted a counterattack using his security squad and a handful of stragglers he had collected to halt the German advance, capturing one of the flamethrowers in the process. The action ended with the Germans in possession of an orchard near the top of the hill and most of the northern slope. The American line curved below the crest, occupying Hill 285's eastern, western, and southern slopes. The bald crest of the hill was no-man's-land, offering no cover from fire from below.

Lieutenant Murray Pulver of B Company decided soon after dawn to check in with the 1st Battalion CP. His company had been out of touch with higher command since his radio was blasted by a mortar shell early in the previous day's fighting. His men had no food and their ammo was running low. "I took a 1st Platoon runner with me," Pulver wrote. "On the way, we were caught in a mortar barrage. I was hit in the face with a piece of shrapnel or stone. It shattered my lower front teeth and chipped my upper teeth. Outside of a fat lip, however, I was okay. My runner was also hit. He ran around in circles yelling. I had to tackle him to quiet him and dress a nasty wound behind his ear. All the while, he kept apologizing for his behavior."

Pulver finally reached his destination, where he reported to Lt. Col. William Bradford, the commander of the 1st Battalion. "When I walked into the CP, a strange expression came over Colonel Bradford's face," Pulver recalled. " 'How did you get away?' he asked. 'Away from what?

I've been right up there where I was supposed to be for the last two days.' He said it had been reported that all of Company B had been captured. I told him, 'Colonel, all I need is a new radio, some ammunition and some food.' I was soon on my way back to Company B with the necessary supplies."

The Germans were content to maintain their foothold on Hill 285, but they obviously had to do something about the troublesome roadblock at L'Abbaye Blanche. Under cover of the light predawn fog, the Deutschland Regiment of the 2d SS Panzer Division prepared a major attack to reduce the position.

The defenders at L'Abbaye Blanche had endured a long, difficult night. The roadblock received sustained German artillery fire during the hours of darkness. Most of the flat-trajectory 88 shells, fired from positions below the humpbacked ridge where the Americans were dug in, passed over the roadblock and exploded in the woods to the west. However, several mortar and nebelwerfer salvos did fall on the ridge, wounding four men, the first casualties the Germans were able to inflict on the roadblock's defenders.

At first light, the security squads covering Lieutenant Springfield's No. 3 and No. 4 guns detected a German patrol in the orchard just northwest of the two antitank weapons. The GIs opened up with their heavy machine guns and bazookas, killing five panzergrenadiers and forcing the rest of the patrol to withdraw deeper into the woods. At the same moment, another German patrol attacked the outpost at Villeneuve, a hundred yards to the east, and were driven off.

The main assault developed a few minutes later. The Germans in the orchard reappeared, this time supported by armor: three Mark IV tanks and four half-tracks. Lieutenant Springfield's gunners soon eliminated all seven vehicles. Six were positively destroyed. One of the tanks may have been able to withdraw successfully. Even with the armor eliminated, the Germans continued the infantry assault, supported by several light machine guns and a flamethrower. The firefight continued for almost two hours, finally ending when Springfield led his five-man strike squad in a counterattack, which succeeded in killing the flamethrower operator and capturing fifteen panzergrenadiers.

"It was nip and tuck there for a period," said Springfield, who just missed immolation when he was targeted by the flamethrower. "They hit a tree next to me and that was it. And that guy [with the flamethrower] got burned. When we hit him, I guess we hit the tank, too. I was kind of mad."

While Springfield's men were busy repelling the attack from the northwest, one of Lieutenant Stewart's squads was holding off an attack from the southeast. Private First Class Robert Vollmer, armed with a bazooka, and five riflemen were occupying foxholes covering one of the bridges over the Cance, just below the abbey. Their position came under heavy fire from a machine gun across the river and from artillery, which dug up huge craters within fifteen yards of the squad's line of foxholes. That didn't stop Vollmer from destroying an armored car that tried to approach the bridge. The crew bailed out and took refuge in a house about two hundred yards away. A squad of German riflemen was occupying the dwelling, and from time to time these soldiers would emerge to take potshots at Vollmer. They were engaged by the American riflemen while Vollmer continued to blast vehicles approaching the bridge. He hit a motorcycle about thirty yards behind the wrecked armored car. Not long afterward, another armored car approached. When the driver tried to pass the hulk of Vollmer's first victim, the private's bazooka roared again, setting the car on fire. Only one German escaped the wreckage, and he was so badly burned that he dropped dead within sight of the American defenders. Vollmer finally used his bazooka to knock out the troublesome machine gun firing from across the river. He later added a German gasoline carrier to his score.

Surprisingly, the Germans continued to try and run vehicles up the hill past Pont de la Vacherie. Springfield's gunners compared their position to a shooting gallery. His No. 1 and No. 2 guns couldn't miss the slow-moving vehicles at ranges of three hundred to four hundred yards, adding two more Panthers to their growing score.

Rations were already in short supply on Hill 314. Most of the men on the hill had been fed a hot meal Sunday night and were issued two K rations at that time. By Tuesday morning, many GIs were already starting to feel the pangs of an empty stomach. Lieutenant Ronal Woody's G Company was also running low on rifle ammunition. However, the two most critical shortages on the hill were medical supplies and radio batteries.

"We were watching men die because we had no disinfectant, no bandages, except what was in the tiny first-aid kits we carried," Capt. Delmont Byrn said. "We didn't have morphine, clean bandages . . . anything." Lieutenant Ralph Kerley added, "We made the wounded as comfortable as possible. They were collected in each company and placed in slit trenches. No medical aid was available."

The shortage of radio batteries was potentially even more serious. The continuation of accurate artillery support was vital to the security of the three companies on Hill 314. That accuracy was possible only as long as spotters like Lt. Robert Weiss remained in radio contact with their guns west of Mortain. Unfortunately, the small square battery of the "300" radio (about half the size of a car battery) had a very limited life span. The batteries on the hill were beginning to grow weaker and only a few spares were available.

Both Colonel Birks and Major General Hobbs were aware of the problem. Birks wanted an immediate supply drop. Hobbs explained to his subordinate that he would have to send back to England for C-47s to make a supply drop. "I don't care if you have to send back to the States for 'em," Birks answered. "My boys need those supplies!"

Before dawn, Hobbs contacted the VII Corps air liaison officer and asked for him to arrange a supply drop. "We have to get supplies to that unit that is cut off up at Mortain," he said, although he mistakenly listed ammo and water as the most urgent requirements. "They will mark the place with a big X on the ground with whatever color panels they have. I don't see how the planes can miss it as it is on high ground. We must get supplies to them and we can't reach them."

The response from VII Corps was an astonishing telephone call from General Collins's operations officer (code-named Jayhawk 3) to Hobbs's G-3 (Custom 3). The 30th Division's phone journal recorded this bizarre exchange:

Jayhawk 3: With regard to dropping those supplies, how far are they cut off?
Custom 3: About 800 yards. We've been trying to get them all day and we are getting another attack [ready] right now.
Jayhawk 3: G-4 [supply officer] told me it would take at least 36 hours to make arrangements for dropping supplies.
Custom 3: This is an emergency and it must be done.

Jayhawk 3: It seems to me you should be able to get through 800 yards to them.

Custom 3: It's only 800 yards, but there's a town in there.

Jayhawk 3: There is a memorandum giving details on the dropping of supplies and it will take at least 36 hours to complete arrangements. There are certain things we will have to know. Have your G-4 call me at my office, but have him look at this memorandum before he calls.

While the paper shufflers back at VII Corps headquarters tried to decide whether to arrange for an airdrop, the men on the hill took what action they could to secure their position. German activity was fairly light after a large attack just after midnight was beaten off. The infantry assault was supported by a single tank, which climbed the dirt road to the crest of the hill. Lieutenant Kerley's men had no antitank weapons, but the tank simply withdrew when its supporting infantry was driven off by accurate American artillery fire. "We were in positions where it was hard for armor to reach," noted Lt. Joe Reaser, commanding K Company. "Hard, but not impossible. If they had tried, they would have been successful. We didn't have much ammo for our bazookas."

The three companies on the hill finally established contact with each other that morning, thanks to Captain Byrn. "I was sort of on my own," he said. "All my [heavy weapons] units were farmed out. I had no real command, so I tried to help where I could." He volunteered to lead a patrol from E Company's area to locate the other two companies on the hill. His journey was extremely hazardous, since German mortars and artillery poured shells on the crest of the hill and German troops below fired at anything that moved. Byrn showed remarkable composure under fire as he discovered a path that led to the position held by G and K companies. "As I had not learned to be scared yet, I made a fairly good example," he said. "Later I learned to fear rifle fire—you couldn't duck it."

Some of the enterprising enlisted men did what they could to solve their shortages. They dug potatoes and cabbages from the fields on an abandoned farm within the American lines and plucked small green apples from the orchard growing on the south end of the hill. Some GIs found a well just outside their lines and risked their lives to fill their canteens. "You could live without food, but not without water," noted Sgt. Charles Herndon of E Company.

And the men on Hill 314 couldn't live without radio batteries. For the time being, the only action possible was to restrict calls and hope the batteries would last until relief arrived.

Lieutenant Colonel Eads Hardaway was also worried about his radio batteries. Still hiding with his command group in a building in Mortain, the 2d Battalion commander radioed Birks at 0915 hours, informing the regimental commander that he would be able to keep his radio open only from ten minutes before the hour until ten minutes after.

That was the last message from Hardaway. Regiment assumed that he was captured, but Hardaway simply had nothing to report and didn't want to waste his batteries. Instead, the battalion command group remained in hiding all day Tuesday, August 8.

There were other pockets of resistance in Mortain and one of them had better luck than Hardaway's group. Early Tuesday morning, a supply sergeant from the 120th reached the position just north of town where E Company of the 117th Regiment had established itself the evening before. The sergeant told Lieutenant Colonel Lockett that forty-five survivors of C Company, many of them wounded, were marooned in town, surrounded and without food. Lockett could see considerable German activity from his CP. The approach to the isolated company would not be easy. But Sgt. Walter Stasko reconnoitered a route and volunteered to lead a patrol to rescue the stranded men. Lockett's group had already picked up several stragglers from C and D companies of the 120th, and eight of these men volunteered to join Stasko's patrol. An additional twelve men were added to the tiny force as litter bearers.

Stasko led the twenty men down a steep hill, under a bridge, then up a trail under constant artillery fire. A mortar squad from H Company covered the patrol with some accurate fire from their 81mm mortars. At one point, two shells were fired at a pair of German soldiers who were spotted urinating on the side of the opposite hill, killing both. Stasko reported he had little trouble, except for the rough terrain "and a burp gun which chased us up a steep hill." The patrol reached the isolated GIs without loss, but the route was so rough that it was impossible to evacuate the wounded on litters. Instead, the fifteen C Company casualties were carried on the backs of the litter bearers. The entire group returned safely to the American lines.

There was very little movement along the front on the second day of the battle. Lieutenant Colonel Walter Johnson, his battered 117th Infantry reinforced by a battalion from the 12th Infantry Regiment (on loan from the 4th Division) and by a company of self-propelled tank destroyers, was attacked at dawn by German infantry—with no armored support on this occasion.

The assault hit Lt. Col. Ernest Frankland's weary B Company, still clinging to its sunken road. The battle soon degenerated into close-quarters combat in the foggy half-light. There was such confusion that at one point a German soldier jumped into a foxhole with a wounded medic from the 2d Platoon.

"Got a gun?" the German asked in English.

"No," the surprised medic answered.

The German apologized and promptly climbed out of the foxhole. He was immediately mowed down by T. Sgt. Grady Workman, who killed at least six enemy soldiers with his tommy gun.

The hand-to-hand combat lasted about thirty minutes before the Germans withdrew. B Company's casualties were surprisingly light, except in the 3d Platoon, where some accurate German mortar fire killed or wounded almost two dozen men.

Johnson launched his own attack two hours later in an attempt to recapture St.-Barthelmy. The advance gained about two hundred yards but bogged down short of the objective and soon turned into a static exchange of artillery fire. Johnson wasn't too happy with the performance of his reinforcements from the 12th Infantry, complaining to Hobbs, "This battalion we got [2d Battalion, 12th Infantry] is not doing so hot. I think they all have battle fatigue."

That assessment was seconded by Lt. William L. Anderson, the battalion's intelligence officer (S-2), who noted the loss of thirty men, including a platoon leader, from "combat exhaustion" during the battle. Anderson blamed it "primarily on the terrific artillery fire they received . . . This at one time became so intense as to compare with some of our American artillery barrages and some of our men became quite jittery."

The battalion was trying to push east from La Chevalaye across the fields to close the gap south of the 117th Infantry. It made steady progress against little more than sniper fire but ran into a German strongpoint where the trail they were following crossed a streambed. The GIs from the 12th Regiment counted twenty-three tanks and a number of infantrymen digging in. The battalion commander bypassed the strongpoint and continued the advance to a small orchard near the tiny hamlet of La Delmiere.

"Just about this time, we started receiving fire," Lieutenant Anderson reported. "A German tank opened up right down the middle of the road with machine-gun fire. A second tank began firing northward in the direction of the first tank. It seems the Germans had sited these two tanks to fire almost directly at each other, but so as not to hit each other. They were both covering the road so as to knock out any movement from the orchard."

The battalion hung on to the orchard until darkness, when the battalion commander decided to withdraw. At almost the exact moment he gave that order, one of the dug-in tanks knocked down the house next to the battalion's CP.

"Colonel Johnson [not to be confused with Walter Johnson of the 117th] was very calm and he held the group together," Anderson said. "He remained on the telephone and kept complete control of the movement. The withdrawal was carried out in an orderly fashion, all the equipment being brought back across the road . . . Colonel Johnson witnessed the withdrawal of all the units during the night and early morning hours, then turned around and saw only his CP group left. He said, 'We're the only troops in the area,' and laughed, 'so let's go!'"

Johnson pulled his battalion south of the orchard, where he linked up with the 12th Infantry's 3d Battalion just after dawn, Wednesday, August 9. The attack by the 12th Infantry Regiment had bogged down far short of its objective, the road junction at La Dainie.

There was only minor movement anywhere on the battlefield that Tuesday. The 1st Battalion of the 119th Regiment was attached to the 120th Infantry to support the attempt to recapture Romagny, but due to a breakdown in communications, it operated for a full day without orders from Colonel Birks. The 119th's 3d Battalion, committed on the other side of the battlefield, had better luck. Advancing north with

CCB of the 3d Armored Division, the troops drove through strong opposition to reach Le Mesnil-Tove, pinching seven kilometers off the 2d Panzer's penetration down the Sée Valley. For the first time since the 30th Division's arrival, its troops were in direct contact with the 9th Division on its left.

To the south, the 30th Division's right flank remained up in the air. The 35th Division resumed its attack northward from Villechien at 0720, but soon ran into armor just north of Notre Dame de Touchet. The 134th Regiment, on the left (just south of the St.-Hilaire–Mortain road), met such heavy resistance that Major General Baade loaned the regiment a battalion from the 137th Regiment. The rest of that regiment succeeded in linking up with the 3d Battalion of the 120th Infantry in Barenton, securing the right flank of the 35th Division. But the left flank was still dangling in thin air, slowing the advance toward Mortain. By nightfall, Baade's troops still had a long way to go.

So did Maj. Gen. Ted Brooks's 2d Armored Division north of Barenton. He followed up the previous night's hastily prepared attack toward Ger with a much stronger assault at 0800 hours Tuesday morning. Two battalions of the 41st Infantry Regiment attacked abreast and advanced more than three miles through a maze of minefields and antitank guns. The two battalions halted at nightfall and dug in along a ridge about halfway along the road to Ger. Capture of that important town would cut off the 2d SS Panzer Division, still fighting the 120th Infantry in Mortain.

It was obvious to Colonel Birks that his troops on Hill 314 would have to spend another night without relief. Prospects for a supply drop remained dim, even though Brig. Gen. James Lewis, the 30th's artillery commander, volunteered his small spotting planes to make an attempt the next day. The offer was a measure of the high command's growing desperation: The tiny, single-engine planes simply couldn't carry enough supplies to fill the isolated battalion's needs.

Birks resolved to take action on his own. He visited his 1st Battalion headquarters, where he discussed the matter with Lieutenant Colonel Bradford. The two officers summoned Lieutenant Pulver back from Hill 285. Birks explained the situation to the young officer. He told him that the battalion on the hill couldn't survive much longer without supplies.

"Lieutenant," Birks said, "tomorrow morning I want you to pull your company out of line, fight your way through the enemy line here [he pointed to a place on the map], and deliver radio batteries and medicine."

As the two colonels began arguing how it was to be done, Pulver nodded off, almost falling from his stool. Bradford shook his head. "Look," he said to Birks, "the man is exhausted and so are his men. This mission is just impossible. I don't believe anybody in his company has had any sleep in the last forty-eight hours."

Birks was sympathetic, but he wouldn't budge. "We have to make a try," he said. "We can't lose half the regiment."

Pulver had to follow orders. He returned to his company and began to pull out of line, one squad at a time, as A Company extended its lines to cover the front. The entire maneuver was accomplished under mortar, artillery, and machine-gun fire. By dawn, Pulver's weary company was ready to move in a desperate attempt to save the men on Hill 314.

Something had to be done. Just before midnight, a message from Captain Erichson was relayed to 30th Division headquarters from an artillery post in radio contact with Hill 314: "They need batteries for the 300 and 600 radio series. They need food and medical supplies. They are not worried about the situation as long as the artillery fire continues."

The artillery fire would last only as long as the observers on the hill could radio in their fire missions. As Tuesday, August 8, became Wednesday, August 9, the fate of the 2d Battalion on Hill 314 depended upon the life span of a dozen dying radio batteries.

CHAPTER 16: THE SHORT ENVELOPMENT

Major General Wade Hampton Haislip was blessed with a famous name. There was a Wade Hampton who fought for Nathanael Greene in the American Revolution. A wealthy South Carolina planter, he became a general in 1812 and was one of the heroes at the Battle of Plattsburg. His grandson, also named Wade Hampton, became one of the Confederacy's finest cavalry commanders. He fought alongside Col. George S. Patton in the 1864 Shenandoah Valley campaign and succeeded "Jeb" Stuart after the famed commander of Lee's cavalry was killed at Yellow Tavern. After the war, Hampton became a force in South Carolina politics, serving both as governor and United States senator from the Palmetto State.

The stocky, round-faced, balding Haislip was neither a South Carolinian nor a cavalryman. Nor was he one of the favorites of Gen. George S. Patton, Jr., the grandson of the Civil War warrior. Haislip was a native Virginian. He graduated from West Point in 1912 (three years before the stars fell) and saw combat in World War I. He was one of Dwight Eisenhower's best friends, and he introduced Ike to the woman who would become his wife. But Haislip's background was infantry, and that was a major drawback for Patton, who complained that his new corps commander "has been sitting around the War Department in swivel chairs so long, he's muscle-bound in the ass."

If Patton had doubts about the XV Corps' commander, Gen. Omar Bradley questioned the quality of the divisions assigned to the new formation. "I privately worried about the troops under Haislip's command, wishing they were more battle-wise," he later wrote. "My decisions would, in part, be influenced by misgivings I had about these five divisions."

There wasn't a proven combat unit in the XV Corps. Major General Lunsford Oliver's 5th Armored Division was Bradley's least-experienced tank force. Major General Horace McBride's 80th Infantry Division was "newly-arrived and utterly green." The corps' other armored unit presented a different kind of problem. To the naked eye, the 2ème Division Blindée appeared to be an ordinary American unit. The Free French formation was in fact equipped and organized as an American armored division. But at its heart was the Régiment de Tirailleurs Sénégalais du Tchad, commanded by Philippe François Marie de Hautecloque. The world was to know him as Jacques Phillipe Leclerc, a name he adopted to protect his family in Occupied France. The Gaullist officer had taken command of the regiment in Chad in December 1940. Two years later, he led his troops across the Sahara Desert to join the British Eighth Army in Tripoli. Leclerc's division—his original regiment reinforced by Free French soldiers from outposts all over the world—landed on Utah Beach on July 30 and created a sensation whenever civilians spotted the tricolor or the Cross of Lorraine painted on the division's Sherman tanks. Bradley was less enthused. Leclerc's troops had some combat experience, but the French Général de Division was "notoriously undisciplined and did not speak English. His sole ambition seemed to be the liberation of Paris." The language problem did not bother Haislip. Between wars he had graduated from the École Supérieure de Guerre.

The XV Corps was originally supposed to include the 83d Infantry Division, but circumstances forced Haislip to take the 79th Infantry instead. Major General Ira Wyche's division got off to a bad start. Not only did it perform poorly during the opening stages of the St.-Lô campaign, but when Eisenhower and Bradley visited Wyche's CP, "we found both Wyche and his assistant division commander there. One of them should have been at the front." Bradley's aide, Chet Hansen, recorded the incident, noting, "Brad did not like that and it did not set too well with Ike." Wyche came very close to losing his job that night. He stayed in command, but throughout July his division was denied an important role in the campaign.

Yet compared to the 90th Infantry Division the 79th might have been Old Hickory or the 1st Infantry Division, the famous Big Red One. Quite simply, the 90th was regarded as the single worst division in the European theater. When first thrown into action, as part of the force attempting to capture Cherbourg, the 90th performed so poorly that Bradley was forced to relieve Maj. Gen. Jay MacKelvie and two of his regimental commanders. Major General Gene Landrum, the deputy commander of the VII Corps, took command, but two weeks later, the 90th botched its attack in the first stages of the St.-Lô offensive, and Bradley had to sack Landrum, too. His first choice for a replacement was Maj. Gen. Theodore Roosevelt, Jr., the assistant commander of the 4th Division and the son of President Teddy Roosevelt. But Roosevelt died of a heart attack before he could take the job.

Bradley didn't know what to do with the ill-starred 90th. There was talk of breaking up the division and parceling the men out as replacements. Instead, Bradley did something even more radical: He gave command of the 90th to Brig. Gen. Raymond S. McLain. The appointment was unique because McLain was not a professional soldier. He was an Oklahoma banker who entered the army in 1940 with the National Guard. McLain came up through the ranks, winning recognition for his performance as artillery commander of Maj. Gen. Troy Middleton's 45th Division in North Africa, in Sicily, and at Anzio. McLain was transferred to the 30th Division in May 1944, joining Old Hickory in England. He ably commanded the 30th's artillery through the hedgerows and the St.-Lô campaign.

Despite McLain's undeniable excellence, he was never popular with Leland Hobbs. "Hobbs threw a damn fit when they gave him a National Guard officer as his artillery commander," said one of Old Hickory's veteran guardsmen. "They never got along. He did everything he could to get rid of him."

McLain was ordered to the 90th on July 24, the day before the Cobra breakout. He was with the division barely a week before it was assigned to the XV Corps and ordered to follow Troy Middleton's VIII Corps down the coast highway to St.-Hilaire. General Patton met McLain's new command on the march and came away with a terrible first impression: "The division is bad, the discipline poor, the men filthy, the officers apathetic, many of them removing their insignia and covering the markings on [their] helmets."

Nevertheless, on August 2, less than twenty-four hours after the unfortunate encounter with Patton, a task force commanded by Lt. Col. George Randolph reached St.-Hilaire and captured intact the bridge over the Selune River. A larger force, commanded by Lt. Col. Christian Clarke, followed up quickly and eliminated all resistance in the town. It wasn't a miraculous feat of arms by any means, but the capture of St.-Hilaire was carried out swiftly, efficiently, and with a minimum of casualties. It was the first sign that the "inept" 90th Division might be worth saving after all.

Neither Bradley nor Patton ever planned to give the XV Corps the key role in the Third Army. Originally, Haislip's formation was assembled around Fougères (seven miles due south of St.-Hilaire) to protect the exposed flank of Middleton's VIII Corps, which was rampaging through Brittany. There was some initial confusion as the 79th and 90th divisions made contact on August 3 near Fougères. Haislip's headquarters had no secure wire communication with either of the two divisions. However, both formations just happened to be oriented toward the southeast, just as the Allied high command reached a momentous decision.

The preinvasion Overland plan had called for Patton's full Third Army to clear Brittany first, securing ports to support the Allied drive across France. But Ultra intercepts revealed that von Kluge had virtually stripped Brittany of troops to fight in Normandy. The few defenders left in the region retreated into the vital port cities, where they prepared for long siege operations. "Accordingly," Bradley wrote, "I made the decision to greatly reduce our commitment of forces to the Brittany campaign. We would do it with one corps . . . Patton's other corps could thus be available to throw against the Germans in the east."

On August 3, the same day the 30th Division was resting at Tessy and the 79th Division was occupying Fougères against light opposition, Bradley issued an official 12th Army Group letter of instruction stating that Patton was to clear Brittany with "a minimum of forces" while the rest of the American army was to drive eastward and expand the lodgement area. The plan was approved by Eisenhower and by British Gen. Bernard Law Montgomery, who resisted "considerable pressure" from his staff to send more troops into Brittany to secure the ports.

If Bradley could have shuffled his forces like a deck of cards, he would have dealt General Collins's VII Corps—"the best troops I had in my command"—the prime assignment to lead the thrust into the heart of France. Patton would have preferred to see Maj. Gen. John Wood's 4th Armored Division as the spearhead. Instead, the momentous movement would be led by two untrustworthy infantry divisions commanded by the infantryman who was "muscle-bound in the ass." McLain assigned his assistant division commander, Brig. Gen. William Weaver, to command the 90th's spearhead. Just before dawn on Saturday, August 5, the men of the 357th Infantry Regiment (motorized) climbed into trucks borrowed from the 5th Armored Division and, accompanied by the division's recon troop, a company of Shermans from the 712th Tank Battalion, and the 343d FA Battalion, prepared to advance on Mayenne, a town thirty-one miles to the southeast, which commanded a difficult crossing of the wide Mayenne River.

"Nobody knows anything about the enemy, because nothing can be found out about them," stated the XV Corps intelligence officer.

There was, in fact, a temporary vacuum in front of the XV Corps. It wouldn't last long. The German Seventh Army was even then trying to fill the gap, rushing elements of the 708th Infantry Division and the 9th Panzer Division from Le Mans toward the Mayenne River.

The reinforcements didn't arrive in time. Moving with a boldness worthy of Wade Hampton, the Confederate cavalryman, Haislip's forces raced forward on a narrow front, their flanks protected only by Pete Quesada's Jabos.

"Don't stop for any goddamn thing," Patton commanded. Weaver followed his order to the letter. Driving behind a light screen provided by the 106th Cavalry Group, Weaver's task force overran several roadblocks, bypassed pockets of resistance, and reached the west bank of the river before noon, having covered an astonishing thirty miles in less than seven hours.

Weaver could see Germans mining the last remaining bridge over the Mayenne. He quickly dispatched two of his three infantry battalions on a wide flanking movement to the south. They found two old wooden skiffs and, knocking down a nearby fence to use the staves as paddles, began to cross the river to get in position to attack the Germans from behind. But Lt. Col. John Hamilton's battalion had slipped into town from the northeast, so the impatient Weaver ordered a frontal assault on the bridge. Racing over one hundred yards of open ground in the face of heavy rifle and machine-gun fire, Hamilton's men reached the bridge and began tearing away the demolition charges. The wild

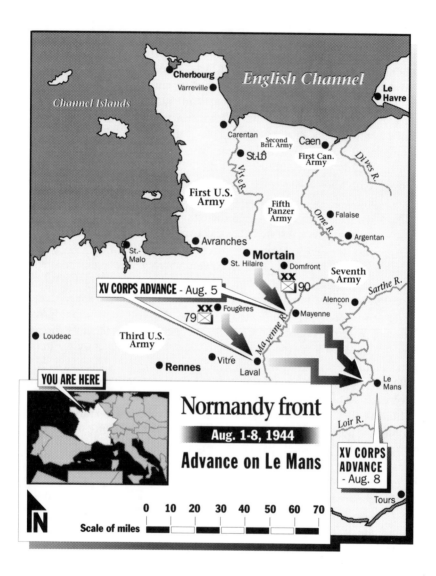

YOU ARE HERE

XV CORPS ADVANCE - Aug. 5

Normandy front

Aug. 1-8, 1944

Advance on Le Mans

XV CORPS ADVANCE - Aug. 8

0 10 20 30 40 50 60 70
Scale of miles

attack not only secured the bridge but collected more than 150 German prisoners—all long before the flanking battalions penetrated the eastern edge of the town.

The balance of the 90th Division reached the Mayenne River south of the town, where engineers began to construct bridges over the wide but shallow river.

The 79th Division on the right flank moved almost as swiftly, driving toward Laval. Colonel Sterling Wood's motorized 313th Infantry Regiment raced southeast along the Fougères-Laval highway. A strong roadblock delayed the advance for almost two hours until Quesada's Thunderbolts could smash the obstacle. Wood's spearhead finally reached the river just before midnight, only to find that the Germans had destroyed every bridge in the vicinity and then withdrawn to the east. The next morning, the division crossed the river (most riflemen by boat; one battalion led across a dam by a French policeman) and occupied Laval while engineers began work on a floating Bailey bridge. It was completed by noon, August 7, just as the British Typhoons were arriving to rain destruction on the Germans at Mortain.

By that time, Haislip's spearheads were already on the move again, converging on Le Mans, the headquarters of the Seventh Army. This time, the 5th Armored Division was driving forward on the 79th Division's right flank.

"Push all personnel to the limit of human endurance," Haislip ordered. "Your actions during the next few days might be decisive for the entire campaign in western Europe."

It wasn't supposed to happen that way, but in the first days of August, Wade Hampton Haislip and his second-rate divisions had become the sharp point of the spearhead for the entire Allied army in France.

General Bradley awoke on the morning of August 8 to good news. The first reports on Totalize were encouraging. General Simonds's two lead divisions, the 4th Canadian Armored and the 1st Polish Armored, striking south of Caen, had advanced three miles behind a shattering air bombardment before running into stiff resistance from the 12th SS Panzer Division.

There was more good news. Ultra intercepts revealed that the Mortain offensive had been ordered by Hitler himself, and the Germans had no intention of calling off the attack and withdrawing.

"These were some of Ultra's most prolific days of the entire war," wrote Ralph Bennett, who was working in Hut 3, where Wehrmacht communications were decoded. "Unprecedented amounts of Enigma traffic were being intercepted, and most of it was decoded with such rapidity that signal after signal could be prepared so close to the German time of origin that each seemed more urgent than the last . . ." In Hut 3, the Ultra magicians decoded a message from General Hausser to General Funck sent late in the evening of August 7, ordering the continuation of the attack.

That was the message Bradley was waiting for.

The opportunity for a decisive victory that Bradley had glimpsed the night before suddenly seemed to be a real possibility. If Collins's VII Corps could hold on at Mortain without further reinforcement, then a sudden swing north by Patton's Third Army could effect a linkup with General Montgomery's British and Canadian troops west of the Seine, trapping the two German armies fighting in Normandy.

It was a remarkably cold-blooded scheme. Instead of providing relief for the embattled troops at Mortain, Bradley proposed to use their precarious situation as bait to keep the German forces in his trap. Bradley's daring plan depended upon the resolve and courage of troops who had already given more than any commander could expect.

Bradley outlined his idea to his staff officers, then left them to work out the details while he set off for Patton's command post to explain his scheme to the Third Army commander. "He was curiously cool to the idea," Bradley recorded. Instead, Patton preferred Bradley's earlier scheme for a deeper and wider envelopment along the Seine, "perhaps because it was more dramatic," Bradley speculated, "perhaps because the success of my proposed shorter envelopment was heavily dependent on the Canadian army closing the gap from the north. Typically, the fact that logistical considerations argued for the shorter envelopment carried no weight with Patton."

The key to Bradley's new plan was Haislip's XV Corps, which was still driving east against stiffening resistance toward Le Mans. Upon capturing that important city, Haislip's spearheads were to turn north and drive like hell for Alençon (thirty miles north of Le Mans), which commanded one of the three vital east-west highways linking Normandy with the heart of France. The other two key German supply routes ran through Argentan (twenty miles north of Alençon) and Falaise, the Canadian objective of Totalize. Both Argentan and Falaise were in the British zone of operations.

Bradley proposed that while the XV Corps was driving north, the rest of the 12th Army Group would wheel behind it like a giant scythe, pivoting on Mortain, and trap the Germans against the British troops driving south. To strengthen the hard tip of his scythe, Bradley would finally release the 80th Infantry Division and the 2d French Armored Division, which had been waiting near St.-Hilaire since Sunday night just in case they were needed to help contain the breakthrough at Mortain. General Leclerc's Free French unit would join Oliver's 5th Armored Division in the van of the advance, while the untested 80th would protect the XV Corps' left flank and rear.

Bradley still needed final approval for his radical change in plan. To get it, he arranged a meeting with General Eisenhower, who was touring the First Army's front. The two generals met on the road to Coutances. Ike was riding in a giant Packard Clipper with his long-time driver, Kay Summersby, at the wheel. Bradley explained his scheme over lunch—which was K rations consumed on the side of the road.

"We must destroy the enemy rather than win territory," an approving Eisenhower said. "Now and not tomorrow."

Bradley was frank about the risks his plan entailed. By releasing the 2d French Armored and 80th Infantry divisions, there wouldn't be any reinforcements in position should the Germans break through the 30th Division and reach Avranches.

Eisenhower said he was willing to take that risk. Besides, if the forces south of Mortain were "temporarily" cut off, Eisenhower promised to airlift two thousand tons of supplies a day to the Third Army. That wasn't a lot. The average American division consumed seven hundred tons of supplies a day, and there were the equivalent of twelve American divisions south of Mortain. But it was enough to convince Bradley to go ahead with his gamble.

Eisenhower approved his subordinate's plan on the spot. The two returned to Bradley's trailer to phone General Montgomery with the news. "Montgomery . . . expressed a degree of concern about the Mortain position," Eisenhower said. "He agreed the prospective prize was great and left the entire responsibility for the matter in Bradley's hands."

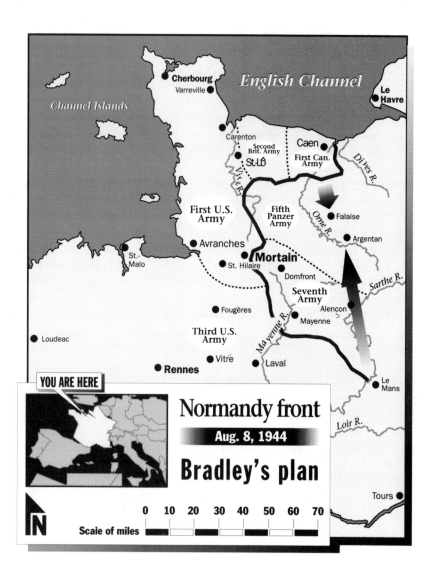

Channel Islands

English Channel

Cherbourg
Varreville

Le Havre

Carenton
Second
Brit. Army
St.-Lô

Caen
First Can.
Army

Dives R.

Vire R.

First U.S.
Army

Fifth
Panzer
Army

Orne R.

Falaise

Avranches

Argentan

St.-Malo

Mortain

St. Hilaire

Domfront

Sarthe R.

Seventh
Army

Alençon

Fougères

Mayenne

Loudeac

Third U.S.
Army

Mayenne R.

Vitré

Laval

Rennes

Le Mans

YOU ARE HERE

Normandy front

Aug. 8, 1944

Bradley's plan

Loir R.

Tours

N

0   10   20   30   40   50   60   70

Scale of miles

The British commander approved the plan (later claiming it as his own) and suggested Argentan as a boundary line between the two armies. Monty was confident that the Canadians would smash through Falaise and reach Argentan well before Haislip's spearheads arrived. Bradley agreed with the suggestion, even though he had reservations about Montgomery's optimism. Eisenhower left Coutances to visit the British headquarters and make sure the cautious Montgomery would pursue Totalize aggressively.

Bradley remained to work on the details of his plan. The First Army commander, Lt. Gen. Courtney Hodges, reported that Hobbs was confident the 30th Division could hold at Mortain. Hodges was visiting General Collins's headquarters when the VII Corps commander put in an early-afternoon call to Hobbs.

"We are holding and getting in better shape all the time," Old Hickory's commander reported. "It was precarious for awhile, but as it stands now, it doesn't look like they're going to get through. We're doing everything in God's power to hold."

That assurance was exactly what Bradley wanted to hear. Looking at the map, he still couldn't believe his opportunity.

"The German is either crazy or he doesn't know what's going on," he told Chet Hansen. "I think he's too smart to do what he's doing. He can't know what is going on in our sector. Surely the professional generals must know the jig is up."

Indeed, the generals on the other side of the hill knew just how dangerous the continuation of the Mortain attack was. At almost the same moment that Bradley was meeting with Eisenhower to win approval for his plan, Field Marshal von Kluge was talking to General Eberbach about the new Canadian threat.

"We didn't expect it to come so soon," von Kluge said, "but I can imagine it was no surprise to you."

"No," Eberbach answered. "I have always awaited it and looked toward the morrow with a heavy heart."

Hitler's new offensive at Mortain was scheduled for the afternoon of August 9. Eberbach was to command the assault, which would include two panzer corps: the XLVII, which included the same four battered divisions that had been halted on August 7, and the LVIII, which included the powerful 9th and 10th SS panzer divisions, a Panther tank battalion from the 9th Panzers, and two rocket brigades. The offensive would be reinforced by the 12th SS Panzer Division and the 85th Infantry Division.

Operation Totalize disrupted those plans. The 10th SS Panzer Division had already pulled out of the line south of Caen, but the 9th and 12th SS panzer divisions were rushed to close the gap in front of Falaise. The tank battalion from the 9th Panzer Division and a rocket brigade were also diverted from Mortain to the Falaise defenses.

Late in the afternoon of August 8, von Kluge was forced to postpone the second attack at Mortain. Hitler issued an order the next day supporting that delay, but he refused to cancel the attack. He still blamed von Kluge for bungling the first assault, claiming that it was launched "too early, too weak, and in unfavorable weather." (He apparently blamed his C-in-C West for the lifting of the morning fog on August 7.) In order to ensure proper execution of the second attack, Hitler reserved the right to designate H hour. Eberbach turned over command of the Fifth Panzer Army to Gen. Josef ("Sepp") Dietrich and set up a new headquarters, Panzer Group Eberbach. Its sole purpose was to prepare for the second attack at Mortain. Hitler tentatively ordered that the attack be launched on Friday, August 11.

As Eberbach suspected, events were rushing to overtake Hitler's orders.

The Germans evacuating Le Mans had blown all the bridges but one. The Gambetta Bridge over the Sarthe River was retained to allow the retreating troops a final escape route to the east. A squad of engineers had prepared the bridge for destruction, planting forty-two powerful mines beneath the structure.

Nine Frenchmen, a "commando" of the Maquis, were keeping watch on the bridge from within a shed on a nearby quay. They knew the Americans were nearby. Yet it didn't seem possible that anything could be done to save the last remaining bridge over the Sarthe. The Americans would have to stop and rush bridging equipment to the front of the column. The advance would be delayed for hours.

"And then the incredible happened," said Canon Breteau, a member of the commando. "The Germans suddenly abandoned the bridge and rushed to blow up the radio station."

The waiting Frenchmen seized the opportunity, racing to the bridge, where the members of the commando began to cut every wire they could find. Rifle fire from German positions on the opposite bank wounded two of the resistance fighters, but the work went on. A former soldier began to defuse the mines, while two teenage boys ripped out the wires as soon as they were cut. A seventeen-year-old girl, Jacqueline Debray, was dispatched to alert the Americans that the bridge was in French hands. She found a column of tanks near the Croix d'Or and persuaded the NCO in charge to advance immediately on the bridge. Guided by a local veteran, the Sherman reached the bridge and silenced the fire from the opposite bank with two well-placed shots from its 75mm cannon.

The soldiers following the tank belonged to the 79th Infantry Division. Wyche's troops had won the race to Le Mans.

It was a near thing. McLain's 90th Division actually started first, pushing off on the morning of August 6. Weaver's task force, again in the van of the division's attack, had no sooner left Mayenne than it ran head-on into strong opposition from German armor and infantry.

Another column, commanded by Col. George Barth, made better progress on the right until it reached the hamlet of St.-Suzanne at 1700 hours. There, Barth discovered that the Germans had cut his line of communications and were massing a regiment-sized force to assault his isolated column. Darkness was falling when one of Barth's patrols detected the unmistakable clank of approaching armor. "Now I know how General Custer must have felt when he made his last stand at the Battle of Little Big Horn," Barth thought. Luckily, the approaching tanks turned out to be ten Shermans from the 712th Tank Battalion, carrying the men of Lieutenant Colonel Hamilton's infantry battalion piggyback.

Barth's reinforced regiment beat off the German counterattack, then teamed with Weaver's task force to push through the wooded terrain south of the St.-Suzanne–Bernay road. By late afternoon of August 8, both units were on the outskirts of Le Mans. In the two-day drive from Mayenne, the 90th Division had taken twelve hundred prisoners and destroyed the reconnaissance battalion of the 9th Panzer Division and a regiment of the 708th Infantry Division.

The 79th Division started its drive to Le Mans on the morning of August 7. Colonel Wood's task force, again leading the way, covered almost half the distance to its objective against light opposition before letting Lt. Col. John McAleer's 315th Infantry take the point for the final sprint to the prize. Wood's men barely beat the fast-closing spearheads from Oliver's 5th Armored Division, which had actually forded the Sarthe River south of Le Mans and were in the southern and eastern outskirts of the city when McAleer's men seized the Gambetta Bridge.

It was at 1700 hours, August 8, when Haislip's lead tanks rolled across the Gambetta Bridge and into the center of Le Mans. There were no organized defenses between his spearhead and his ultimate objective, Argentan. If the 30th Division could detain the Germans at Mortain for just a little longer, the great opportunity that Bradley had first seen the night before would become a reality.

CHAPTER 17: COME AND GET US

One of the oddities of combat is the vast difference in conditions experienced by soldiers stationed very close together. On Hill 314, many of the GIs had endured hand-to-hand combat and seen German tanks roll toward their foxholes. Others were exposed only to the constant danger of artillery and sniper fire. For Sgt. Luther Myers, manning a .30-caliber machine gun on the slope below E Company's front, the first two days and nights on the hill were relatively quiet.

"We didn't see much of the Germans," Myers said. "All we got were artillery, mortars, that kind of thing." That changed during the night of August 8–9. "Two of my boys were sitting on the edge of their foxholes when two Germans came around a hedgerow. They were close enough we could have thrown our guns at them, but they ran off before anybody fired."

It was very dark when a German patrol launched a sudden attack on Myers's squad. "The first thing we knew, they were throwing hand grenades at us. One of the grenades rolled under my gun before it went off." Myers's machine gun wouldn't fire after the explosion, so he proceeded to fieldstrip the weapon in the dark. He counted tracers from five burp guns as the Germans advanced. One of his riflemen was wounded in the elbow and began to crawl back to the sergeant's position. Within seconds, Myers had repaired the machine gun and broke up the attack by firing it over the heads of the advancing Germans. "I could have got 'em all, but it wasn't worth it, not with my man crawling across my field of fire."

Not long after the brief action, a German officer appeared and began to pick up weapons his soldiers had discarded in their haste to escape. "I shot him with an M1," Myers said. "I didn't even have to use the machine gun. I wasn't trying to stir up trouble. We weren't trying to win the battle so much as survive."

The survival of the men on Hill 314 was very much in question on the morning of August 9. Less than a mile away, Lt. Murray Pulver of B Company led his relief expedition into no-man's-land at dawn. "We made our way cautiously down the hill, leapfrogging from one hedgerow to the next," he said. "We moved slowly into a valley, to the village of Le Neufbourg, just west of Mortain. On the way, we ran into two large German patrols but scattered both of them. In the process, we lost three men."

After a cautious four-hour advance, Pulver's company ran into elements of the 30th Division Recon Company on the outskirts of Mortain. "They were really happy to see us," he said. "They thought we were sent to reinforce them. When I told the captain of the recon unit that our mission was to break through to Hill 314 with supplies, he said, 'Are you kidding? Come with me.' " Pulver followed the recon captain to an observation point that provided a good view of the hill. "My God," Pulver said, "the road winding up the hill was choked with German vehicles of all kinds. Through my binoculars, I spotted at least three hundred Germans. The place where Colonel Birks had told me to break through was sheer cliff. Even a mountain goat couldn't get up. All other places that were accessible were crawling with Germans. We studied the area for an hour and could find no possible way to get up the hill."

Pulver radioed battalion headquarters and explained the situation. Half an hour later, Lt. Col. William Bradford called back and ordered Pulver to wait until dark, then return to Hill 285. The attempt to break through to Hill 314 on the ground had failed. Colonel Birks would have to find another way to reinforce his "lost battalion."

Pulver's company was not the only American unit trying to break through to Hill 314 on the morning of August 9. Lieutenant Colonel

Hardaway's 2d Battalion command group was finally flushed from its hiding place in Mortain.

"One of our men got upset," said Lieutenant Hagen, the battalion communications officer. "He was sure the Germans knew we were in the house. That's when we decided to leave. We snuck out the back door. We had no problem getting to the edge of town." The twenty-seven members of the command group carried their rifles, but still had no ammunition. For the previous forty-eight hours they had been without food and had only the water in their canteens. Hardaway led the column out of town and toward Hill 314. "We crossed a couple of fields and were just starting to climb up the hill," Hagen said. "Lt. [Willie] Irby and I were at the rear of the column. We were maybe thirty or forty feet behind the front, alongside a ten-foot cliff. Suddenly, we heard a burp gun and somebody ahead of us yelled, 'Hands up!' Someone nearby said 'Let's jump!' so a few of us jumped off the cliff and rolled down an embankment. I think [the Germans'] attention was on the surrender and they never knew we jumped."

Hagen, Irby, and four enlisted men made good their escape. They reached a wheat field below the hill and elected to hide out in it for the rest of the day. "There was about a three- or four-acre field of the stuff, about three feet high. We just lay in it, not moving." Sometime before nightfall, the six GIs in hiding heard German voices and the sound of activity. "They were digging all around us. We finally figured out it was an artillery area and they were digging in their guns between us and the hill."

No member of the command group was to reach Hill 314. The barrier around the hill was impenetrable.

The 2d Armored Division, fighting more like an infantry unit than the dashing tank force George Patton nicknamed "Hell on Wheels," was doggedly slogging its way toward Ger on the morning of August 9.

A patrol from H Company of the 41st Infantry Regiment was assigned to seize the tiny village of Le Guy Rochoux, just three miles south of Ger, while a line of Shermans supported the advance from firing positions a mile away. As Lt. Roy Green led his men toward a stock shed on a hill overlooking the Barenton-Ger road, he ran into a German patrol, apparently on the same mission. After a brief firefight,

Green's men drove the Germans off the crest. He set up a command post overlooking the area where the Germans were trying to mass for their counterattack. Using his radio to direct the fire of his supporting tanks, Green was able to halt several attacks before they could be launched.

The Germans belonged to the 19th SS Panzer Division, committed by Field Marshal von Kluge to defend Ger and keep the lines of communication open to the 2d SS Panzer Division in Mortain. The 19th SS Panzers dispatched two parallel armored columns against the 2d Armored Division.

The first, striking south along the Barenton-Ger road, was intercepted by the tank destroyers of the 702d TD Battalion. Their 3-inch guns blasted five Mark IV tanks without a loss, forcing the German column to withdraw.

The second column, slamming against the western flank of the 2d Armored Division, struck the high ground that had been seized the night before. A rapid and vigorous counterattack by the 3d Battalion of the 67th Armored Regiment and the 102d Armored Infantry Regiment forced the second German column to withdraw with heavy losses.

Still, while the counterattacks by the 19th SS Panzer Division were costly to the Germans, they did succeed in bringing the 2d Armored Division drive on Ger to a halt.

The 30th Division's staff was still trying to break through the wall of bureaucratic inertia and schedule a supply drop for the surrounded battalion.

A captain at VII Corps phoned at midday with a cheery report: "Here's something for you. On this question of supplying that battalion of yours by air, Master wants to know the following: Can unit give night communications signals? What kind? Can unit signal wind direction? What is the approved boundary of the area occupied by the battalion?" When asked why all that information was needed, the captain responded, "That is so they can drop the supplies on a pinpoint."

An hour later, a division staffer was forced to admit, "We cannot give you an answer on any of those questions. The only thing we can do is mark the area with an *X*." The officer ended the conversation with a plaintive plea: "See if you can't do something with some of those yardbirds up there and get something for us." Two hours later, VII Corps responded, "It's up to G-4 now."

While the higher echelons quibbled over details, Brig. Gen. James Lewis, commanding the division artillery, made his first attempt to get supplies to the men on the hill. Two small spotting planes were loaded with radio batteries and medical supplies. When the morning mist lifted, they took off and flew at low altitude toward Hill 314. Unfortunately, both aircraft were hit by antiaircraft fire as soon as they crossed the German lines. Neither plane could get close to the hill. One pilot was forced to bail out. He landed behind German lines and was captured. The other Cub returned to base, badly shot up.

It is not surprising that the artillery staff took risks to maintain the 2d Battalion positions on the hill. The Battle of Mortain had become an artillery duel, and observation from Hill 314 gave Lewis's gunners a decided edge in the exchange. During one sixty-minute period that Wednesday (August 9), the division was able to fire thirty observed counterbattery missions, believed to be a record in the European theater.

"After these missions, we heard very little more from German artillery," Lt. Col. F. C. Shepard noted.

Late in the afternoon, the division massed the fire of ten field artillery battalions—120 guns—on a concentration of German armor moving along the Mortain-Ger road, causing considerable destruction.

It was Lewis's opinion that "without observation from the hill east of Mortain, we would have been much in the dark. Not only did the artillery observers on the hill spot counterattacks forming up against the hill, they were able to locate a number of targets in the north."

The life-or-death question was: How much longer could the observers on the hill keep up their reports? An ominous message was received just after sundown. Captain Robert Stewart of the 230th FA Battalion passed on a message from Lt. Robert Weiss on Hill 314 to divisional headquarters: "We had a report from the observer on the hill that the Germans are building up strong reserves on all sides. We are laying a ring of fire. I couldn't get much dope because his radio [has been] running on one battery for three days."

The divisional artillery did have other sources of information. The light spotting planes, like the pair shot up trying to drop supplies on

Hill 314, did invaluable duty and were particularly effective late in the afternoon, when the low angle of the sun in the west exposed German positions. Also helpful were the Cannon Company observers up front with the rifle companies. Each regiment was assigned six short-barreled 105mm howitzers, which were controlled by the infantry, not the artillery. The cannon companies were created to address the infantry's feeling that the artillery battalions weren't always responsive to their needs. One artillery officer dismissed the short-barreled cannon as "popguns," but the system actually worked to the artillery's benefit, since the Cannon Company observers, constantly up front with the riflemen, were tied into the artillery's phone net and often provided targets for the big guns.

Sergeant Hubert Pennington of the 119th's Cannon Company was up front with a patrol from K Company when his report triggered a major concentration of fire at Mortain. "We were crawling up the side of a hill when somebody spotted a German soldier across the way," Pennington recalled. "I tried to lose myself in the hill. Then I raised my head carefully. I saw a little house; it looked like it was made of cement blocks. We could see activity behind the house. Then I heard the sound of a tank engine starting up. I couldn't see it, just hear it. I called the radio operator over and called in a fire mission. I gave them the coordinates and asked for phosphorus. Well, they gave me smoke, not phosphorus. That was so I could spot the fall of shot. They made an adjustment, then they came in with phosphorus. What I didn't know was, the division had been monitoring my report and all of a sudden they let everything loose. That's the first time they ever concentrated on me. It's one thing to sweat out one or two guns, but this . . . it was a harrowing experience. They were sending in 105s, 155s, everything. The shells were landing all around the house. We could hear [the Germans] screaming. It was deadly. It only lasted a few minutes. When it was over, we were able to walk in there. Most of the Germans were dead or badly wounded. A few were walking around in a daze. The tank was wrecked. It was only a Mark IV. I was hoping we'd gotten a Tiger."

The Germans were hoarding most of their surviving armor, trying to reconstitute striking forces for the attack scheduled for August 11. The situation produced a boring day for Lieutenant Springfield's force on the L'Abbaye Blanche roadblock. His gunners recorded only three kills on August 9, none of them tanks. German artillery damaged the gunsights of Springfield's No. 1 and No. 2 guns, but the enterprising gunners took the sights of their other two guns and replaced them. The No. 3 and No. 4 guns were bore-sighted on the road where it emerged from behind the orchard.

Springfield's eastern flank was well protected by Colonel Lockett's task force from the 117th Infantry, which spent the day exchanging mortar and artillery fire with the Germans holding Mortain. Captain Bernard Pogerel, the battalion surgeon, moved his aid station forward to within two hundred yards of the front lines just before the Germans cut off all routes of evacuation to the rear. For several hours, Dr. Pogerel provided the only source of medical aid for Lockett's battalion, Springfield's roadblock, and a portion of the 120th Regiment on Hill 285. His aid station came under observed fire, but Dr. Pogerel continued to perform surgery, at one point amputating a gangrene-infected leg as screaming meemies landed nearby.

North of L'Abbaye Blanche, the 117th Infantry retained the initiative in its struggle with the Germans holding St.-Barthelmy. Lieutenant Colonel Walter Johnson's weary troops launched an attack at 1400 hours with the 1st Battalion of the 117th Regiment on the left, the 3d Battalion of the 12th Infantry Regiment in the middle, and the 2d Battalion of the 12th on the right. Starting from Johnson's command post at La Rossaye, the attack quickly gained two hedgerows, despite fierce artillery and mortar fire, before the two battalions from the 12th Infantry lost contact with each other. The advance ground to a halt.

On Johnson's left, the 3d Battalion of the 119th Infantry was trying to wrest the high ground just east of Le Mesnil-Tove from the 2d Panzer Division. A tank force from CCB of the 3d Armored Division was supposed to support the battalion's advance. Lieutenant Colonel William "Jug" Cornog had called a commanders' meeting in a small building near a large farmhouse destroyed by shellfire. Cornog, concerned that the tank-infantry team was moving too slowly, had just begun to exhort his subordinates to step up the pace. But as he talked, a large-caliber shell struck the small building, penetrating the flimsy roof before exploding. Every man inside was killed, except for Lt. Walter May, who was lying on the floor next to a wall as Cornog spoke.

For the next thirty minutes, German artillery poured a terrific volume of fire on the tankers around Juvigny. Colonel Dorrance Royston, commander of the 3d Armored Division's Task Force 1, had to huddle under a tank with members of his staff while large-caliber shells (up to 150mm) pounded his command post. One shell blew up a half-track belonging to Royston's exec, Lt. Col. Rosewell King; another explosion rocked Royston's own half-track, loaded with vital communications equipment. Shell fragments ripped apart the thin-skinned vehicle.

The brutal barrage left the tankers leaderless and shaken. Losses were so heavy that S. Sgt. George McLemore found himself in command of his company. CCB was able to provide little support for the 119th's advance. The riflemen attacked anyway and gained about a thousand yards before being stopped by darkness and heavy machine-gun fire.

The 1st Battalion of the 119th, operating on the other side of the battlefield, finally got into action on Wednesday, August 9. Major Robert Herlong pushed his patrols into Romagny, where Lt. Robert Henglein accomplished the amazing feat of killing a Tiger tank with two rounds of bazooka fire (it was the only confirmed Tiger kill of the battle). The Germans retreated out of the shattered town just before dark, falling back to a strong defensive line a few hundred yards to the east. Herlong's battalion still had a long way to go to relieve Hill 314.

So did the 35th Division, pushing north by northeast from its position south of the highway from St.-Hilaire. Even without large commitments of armor, the 2d SS Panzer Division was strong enough to slow the advance to a crawl. General Baade was forced to commit his reserve infantry regiment to the front lines in order to keep the division moving forward. His troops could see Hill 314 rising in front of them, a galling reminder of how far they still had to go.

The slow progress of the 35th Division toward Mortain wasn't as much of a concern to General Bradley as was the slow progress of the Canadians toward Falaise. Bradley's plan required Montgomery's troops not only to reach Falaise, but to continue on and close the fifteen-mile gap between that city and Argentan. However, Montgomery's spearheads were still far short of Falaise, slowed by the inexperience of the Polish and Canadian armored divisions in the van.

A counterattack by the 12th SS Panzer Division—the Hitler Youth—struck the Poles and Canadians just after noon. General Kurt Meyer, the thirty-three-year-old commander of the Hitlerjugend, was able to assemble just forty-two panzers, which he divided into two Kampfgruppes (each approximately the equivalent of an American regimental combat team), one to attack on each side of the Caen-Falaise road. At Cintheaux, one of his groups knocked out twenty-six Polish tanks while losing just six Tigers. A single 88mm gun claimed nine of the Polish Shermans. The crew of its last victim scored a direct hit before dying and finally put the lethal weapon out of action.

Meyer's riposte was only temporary. The Canadians recaptured Cintheaux and resumed their advance. The Germans weren't the only reason for the painfully slow progress of the offensive. General Montgomery had committed his least experienced troops to the attack. Their inexperience showed. One promising breakthrough near the village of Potigny was brought to a halt when tanks of the British Columbia Regiment lost their bearings, reported the wrong position, then were mistakenly attacked by rocket-firing Typhoons and shelled by the guns of the neighboring 1st Polish Armored Division. A battalion of Panthers arrived to finish the job, virtually annihilating the unfortunate regiment. The regiment lost forty-seven tanks and 240 men.

In all, the Polish division was able to advance only a few thousand yards on the second day of the attack; the Canadians were hung up clearing the tiny hamlet of Bretteville-le-Rabet until dark. It was obvious that Totalize was grinding to a halt, well short of the high ground overlooking Falaise.

Bradley didn't let his concern for these developments show when Secretary of the Treasury Henry Morgenthau visited his headquarters in Coutances just after breakfast on August 9. Bradley gave in to his enthusiasm as he outlined the situation for his important visitor. "This is an opportunity that comes to a commander not more than once in a century," he said. "We're about to destroy an entire hostile army. If the other fellow will only press his attack here at Mortain for another forty-eight hours, he'll give us time to close at Argentan and there completely destroy him. He'll have nothing left with which to oppose us. We'll go from here to the German border."

Bradley allowed his aide, Chet Hansen, to escort Morgenthau on a tour of the front. The visiting VIP left that evening with the impression that everything was going well. "[Bradley] made an excellent impression," the secretary wrote in his diary. "Very quiet, complete self-control, complete balance."

*   *   *

Morgenthau never got a chance to meet Lt. Ralph Kerley, but if he had, it is likely he would have used very different words to describe the tall, sandy-haired Texan, the commander of the 120th Regiment's E Company.

"Kerley was kind of a loose cannon," said Capt. Delmont Byrn, the H Company commander. "A great combat leader, utterly fearless. He was rough, tough, unkempt, unshaven, profane, a heavy drinker and disdainful of red tape and protocol."

Kerley, a native of Houston, had tried to enlist the day after Pearl Harbor, but the army turned him down for medical reasons. Four months later, he passed the physical and was accepted. He was a platoon leader when he first distinguished himself during the St.-Lô fighting. Sent to reinforce the 3d Battalion, which was reeling under a German counterattack, Kerley elected instead to launch his own counterattack. Caught by surprise and unaware of the tiny force assaulting them, the Germans broke off the attack and withdrew.

"You couldn't find a better officer," said Sergeant Myers. "He wasn't one of these guys who directed an attack from a French cellar. He was always in the front lines. There wasn't a better officer in France."

Kerley might have been personally fearless, but by Wednesday morning, August 9, he was fearful for his unit's chances. "Attempts by regiment and the remainder of the division to relieve the battalion had failed," he wrote. "The ammunition supply had dwindled to almost nothing. Several of the severely wounded died during the night. The bodies of the dead, both our own and the enemy, were deteriorating fast in the warm August sun and the stench on the hill was nauseating. The future looked anything but bright and morale was on the decline."

The failure of the first attempt to airdrop supplies that morning didn't help morale. Neither did the promise of a C-47 drop for the next day. "Due to past unpleasant experiences with close supporting air, there was some doubt of success in the minds of the men," Kerley wrote.

Private John Weekly of H Company was attached to Kerley's company. He was sure the end was near. "I buried my dog tags and my wife's class ring," he said. "If they took me, I didn't want them to know who I was. I really don't know why. Maybe I was afraid they'd pick on my relatives. All I know was, there wasn't any time they couldn't have walked over us."

The lack of water was what bothered Sgt. Charles Herndon and his men the most. "One of my men heard there was a well down below us," Herndon said. "He said he was going to go down and try and find some water. I told him, 'I'm not going to tell you to go and I'm not going to tell you not to go.' He left, but he came back a few minutes later and said, 'Sarge, there's a German officer down there who wants to talk to our leader.' I sent a man up to tell Lieutenant Kerley."

Lieutenant Elmer Rohmiller, Herndon's platoon commander, arrived along with S. Sgt. William Wingate of G Company. It was just after 1800 hours when they reached the German officer.

"He was carrying a large white flag," Kerley reported. "He [told Rohmiller] he was an officer in the SS and he was prepared to offer generous terms for an honorable surrender. He said he personally admired the stand made by the battalion, but he was very careful to point out, however, that the situation was hopeless."

The German officer explained that his troops had captured the battalion command group, naming a Lieutenant Pike (the battalion S-2) and a one-star officer (evidently mistaking Hardaway's silver oak leaves for a brigadier general's star).

"He further pointed out it would be no disgrace to surrender under the circumstances and promised the men would be well cared for and the wounded would be given every consideration. His last promise was that if his offer was not accepted by 2000 hours, the battalion would be blown to bits."

Rohmiller's inclination was to reject the offer out of hand, but he blindfolded the German officer and escorted him back to E Company's command post. Kerley was directing his company from the top of a large flat rock. Captain Erichson, in command of all the American troops on the hill, was with him. Just below the two dirty, unshaven officers, E Company's wounded were lying in crevices and slit trenches, waiting untreated for either death or rescue.

"I am an officer in the SS," the German said in faultless English. "You are the 2d Battalion of the 120th Regiment, 30th Infantry Division," he added. Kerley assumed that the statement was intended to demonstrate the efficiency of German intelligence.

"I have come to request your surrender," the officer continued, "and to offer you and your men safe escort off this hill. You realize, of course, that your position here is hopeless."

The exchange was overheard by the wounded GIs lying nearby. At the last comment, they started jeering at the SS officer. Several shouted, "Don't surrender!"

"As you hear," Erichson said, "my men are prepared to argue that one."

"They are fools, you are not," the German answered. "As their commander, it is your duty . . ."

"I'm aware of my duty," Erichson interrupted. "Do you have anything more to say?"

"Only this," the German said. "If you do not surrender by 2000 hours today, your battalion will be annihilated."

Kerley broke in. Three days later, in an interview with Associated Press correspondent William Smith White, the young officer would claim that his response had been: "I will surrender when every one of our bullets has been fired and every one of our bayonets is sticking in a German belly." What he really said "wasn't quite so dramatic," Kerley later wrote. "It was short, to the point, and very unprintable."

Erichson reported the German ultimatum—and Kerley's colorful response—to Colonel Birks.

"That's telling the son of a bitch," Birks responded. "You guys have been playing hero up there long enough. The 119th is trying to reach you."

"They'd better move fast," Erichson replied, clicking off abruptly to save the radio battery.

While Erichson was talking to Birks, Sergeant Wingate reported the surrender demand to Lt. Ronal Woody of G Company. His response was also short and to the point: "I told them to go to hell," he said. "If you want us, come and get us."

That's what the Germans tried to do. The battle group from the 17th Panzergrenadier Division launched a major attack on Kerley's position at approximately 2015 hours, with the sun low in the western sky. A company of Panthers belonging to the 2d SS Panzer Division was in support. The forty-five-ton tanks rolled toward E Company's frail defensive line. Kerley's men had little ammunition left with which to defend themselves.

"I couldn't fire too much; I didn't have a good barrel," said Weekly, who was manning a .30-caliber machine gun. "I fired just enough to make them think we had plenty of ammo." Actually, Weekly's gun had enough ammo for less than five minutes of sustained fire.

"Things looked very bad that night," wrote Lt. Robert Weiss, the observer from the 230th FA Battalion. "We were saved by a ring of fire set up by seven battalions of artillery. One tank came within fifty yards of our OP [observation post], fired a few rounds, called for us to surrender or die, and left."

At the height of the attack, with E Company's front line in danger of being overrun, Kerley called in artillery fire on his own position. The GIs, huddling in their foxholes or in rocky crevices, had more protection than the exposed attackers. Hammered for five terrible minutes by the devastating fire of eighty-four American cannon, the panzer-grenadiers broke and retreated down the hill, leaving the crest littered with casualties—both German and American.

The surrender ultimatum and the repulse of the furious German attack that followed had a curious effect upon the men holding Hill 314. Their despondency disappeared. Despair had been replaced by anger—and resolve.

Kerley noticed the transformation, but he couldn't explain it. His men were still without food and medical supplies, were shorter on ammunition than ever before, and were totally dependent on a handful of dying radio batteries.

But a new feeling gripped the men on Hill 314. "It was like nobody expected to live anymore," Byrn said, trying to explain the curious transformation. "Once that decision was made, you could go on, just doing what you were doing, living day to day, hour to hour."

Private First Class Leo Temkin, with G Company, put it differently: "You can only be scared so long, then there's no such thing as being scared. You become like a zombie. You do what you have to do."

CHAPTER 18: STALEMATE

Lieutenant Hagen and his companions knew they had to escape the wheat field under cover of darkness. Sometime after midnight, they heard odd noises from the Germans surrounding the field. "They had gotten into some cognac and were pretty drunk," Hagen said. "We pretended we were drunk, too. We stood up and took our time crossing the field. We didn't hurry. Either they were too drunk to see us or they thought we were drunk Germans, too."

Hagen led the other five refugees toward a barn he had spotted Sunday night while stringing the battalion's phone net. It was on the edge of town. They reached it safely and climbed into the loft. Only when morning came did they realize how precarious their new hideout was. The Germans were using the building next door as a field hospital. "We were really stuck there," Hagen said. "There were Germans all around the barn. Right below us, there was a little watering hole for animals. We watched Germans bathing in it."

That same morning, Sgt. John Whitsett's solitary odyssey behind enemy lines ended. He had spent the last three days moving by night and hiding by day, trying to reach safety. He was without food and sleep during his ordeal and had very little water. At times, he was bothered by hallucinations. "I realized things were getting abnormal," he said. "I could make myself see anything. If I looked at a bush long enough, it would turn into a tank."

Only one thing kept Whitsett from giving up—the memory of his terror when the 120th was bombed before the Cobra breakout. "That experience was so terrible, I was determined not to go through it again. I was sure if I was captured, I'd get bombed by our air force back in Germany."

Whitsett found a road just after dawn on the morning of August 10 and began to follow it in what he hoped was the right direction. He hadn't gone too far when he found one of his company's 57mm antitank guns. "Nobody was around it. I kept walking and pretty soon I heard somebody shout, 'Halt!' I put my hands over my head." Whitsett's captor was a GI. It took the relieved sergeant several minutes to understand why the wary soldier kept his rifle pointed at him and refused to answer his questions. "He must have thought I was a German. I was blond and I had taken off my insignia when I thought I might be captured."

Whitsett finally convinced his captor to provide directions to battalion headquarters. He had missed more than three days of combat, but there was still plenty of fighting left in the Battle of Mortain.

Except for the saga of the trapped battalion on Hill 314, the fighting was not very dramatic after the first hours of the German attack, but the combat was no less intense. The murderous struggle in the Sée River valley, on the ridge road between St.-Barthelmy and Juvigny, around the village of Romagny, and on Hill 285 continued with unabated fury. It was as if the war had reverted to the stalemate before St.-Lô. Progress was measured in yards again, not miles. The gain of a hedgerow and the field it enclosed was a major victory. The front lines were so close, it was often impossible for the Americans to use their advantages in artillery and air power. It was a rifleman's war again: dirty, slow, dangerous, and unglamorous.

Neither side had the strength to move the other. The Germans were motivated by the knowledge that a new offensive was planned for Friday, August 11. General Eberbach was reluctant to commit his precious remaining tanks in the killing fields where so many panzers had died in the first attack. But some armored support was required if his panzergrenadiers were to retain the ground gained on August 7 as a starting line for the new assault. The Americans were limited by General Bradley's decision to gamble on all-out victory. The only reinforcements committed between the Sée River and the Mortain–St.-Hilaire highway were one regiment of the 4th Division and one combat command of the 3d Armored Division. Just south of the highway, the 35th Infantry Division was still advancing slowly to the relief of the battalion on Hill 314. In all, the U.S. Army had the equivalent of three divisions in the battle zone, facing three panzer divisions (the 116th was engaged north of the Sée). No wonder the battle became a stalemate.

A stalemate was exactly what Bradley wanted, even though his strategy meant misery for the GIs fighting in and around Mortain. "It isn't very easy," a 30th Division staffer wrote on August 10, "to tell the man in the front lines that the battle is going well when he's still up against the old combination of machine guns, burp guns, mortars, 88s, artillery, tanks—and terrain . . . But the battle is going well and it's worth saying."

It would have been hard to convince Lt. Ed Arn that the battle was going well. His platoon, part of the 119th Infantry, was working with Team 3 of Combat Command B of the 3d Armored Division, trying to reach the important intersection at La Dainie. One of the battalion's companies was down to just one officer and twenty-seven men, so on Thursday morning, August 10, 1st Sgt. Thomas Kirkman returned to Le Neufbourg to pick up replacements. "There were thirty-six of them," he said. "I brought them up to L'Abbaye Blanche in two two-and-a-half-ton trucks, but we had to snake across the railroad bridge on our bellies because of the hot artillery fire the Jerries were throwing. By the time we got back to the CP, we were getting hit with everything. We got a tree burst and the guy next to me got a fragment that went in the back of his head and came out his face. I was standing right next to him and didn't get touched."

Arn's platoon was one of two assigned to support an attack by a platoon of tanks commanded by Lt. Edmund Wray. The small force was to cross a grain field, then capture the vital intersection. "Wray, who was going to be out front, didn't believe it had a chance," Arn said. "He called it a suicide mission. As I was waiting, I got word to report to the Battalion CP and pick up some replacements. So I went to the CP and saw the Top [Sergeant Kirkman]. He told me he had seven replacements for me. 'Where?' I asked. He pointed, 'There—under that tank.' My replacements were all flat under a tank."

Arn took the frightened newcomers forward and put them into line before the attack jumped off. The other platoon was pinned down almost immediately, but Arn's men kept up with the tanks as they moved slowly across the grain field. Suddenly, "Wray's tank, spearheading the attack, exploded with a direct hit. The crew crawled out. Lieutenant Wray was terribly burned. He got out and fell to his hands and knees beside the tank. Then he pulled himself to his feet and started back to the hedgerow he had just busted through. It seemed as if he remembered something, because he went back to the tank and tried to pull somebody else out. He helped get the other man out and they both started to run, but the Jerries cut them down with a burst of machine-gun fire."

Arn's men retreated to the hedgerow. "That attack didn't have a chance," he said. "And, you know, a funny thing happened. The Jerries wandered out into the open to look at that burned tank. They came out in little bunches and stood around it. Curiosity, I guess. But from behind the hedgerow, we let 'em have it. Mowed them down."

The 119th took the intersection two days later, making an infantry attack without tank support. An army investigator interviewing GIs after the battle found that some of the riflemen preferred not to have armored support. "They draw too much fire," an unidentified infantryman was quoted as saying. Arn agreed that it was sometimes easier without tanks. "The tanks don't like to mix it up. They want the infantry to get in front while they stay back and pop away at located targets. Still, I don't blame the tankers for fighting the way they do. They risk the hell of being burned to death in a hot little iron prison. And those tanks are so blind. They lead a rough life."

The tankers of the 2d Armored Division were living a rough life on the road from Barenton to Ger. Their positions in the hills overlooking the vital road were under attack most of the night. On the morning of August 10, Private "Tiny" Hurtado reported to an aid station and complained that he could barely move his arms. When an examination failed to show any damage, a medic questioned the GI and learned that he had thrown six bags of grenades at the attacking Germans the night before. The doctor gave Hurtado a bottle of liniment and told him to apply it liberally for a condition he called a charley horse. That day, Hurtado's position was attacked again and the arm-weary private tossed almost half a sack of the heavy grenades at the enemy. Five German potato mashers came back—four bracketing his foxhole, one bouncing off his helmet. Hurtado survived the experience uninjured, except for aggravating his sore arm.

Pressure on the 2d Armored Division became so heavy that the division's engineers blew up the bridges on the Barenton-Domfront highway to forestall a possible German attack from that direction. The 3d Battalion of the 41st Infantry was so hard-pressed that its commander, Lt. Col. Marshall Crawley, was afraid his men were facing extermination. Their salvation came in the form of a savage grenade and bayonet attack, led by Capt. Thomas Carothers.

Conditions were far better on the roadblock at L'Abbaye Blanche, where Lt. Tom Springfield was able to retire to his command post for a little sleep—his first real rest since Sunday night. He had just dozed off when a German half-track, lost and loaded with wounded, blundered past the position at the southern end of the roadblock. Springfield was awakened by the noise of the vehicle, which was halted by his sentries right outside his CP. The sleepy lieutenant leaned out the window and informed the German driver that he and his passengers were now POWs.

The lost half-track was the only vehicle to penetrate Springfield's defenses during the battle. Later that day, a strong infantry attack was launched on the roadblock but was beaten off with heavy losses. Springfield's gunners claimed two half-tracks and five other vehicles on August 10, but for the second day in a row, they didn't see a single German tank.

The 2d Battalion of the 12th Infantry Regiment, still trying to retake St.-Barthelmy, saw several tanks in the predawn hours of August 10, when the Germans launched a counterattack from north of the battalion's position. Several panzers approached to within point-blank range of the battalion CP. The battalion commander was wounded in the face, one arm, and both legs. The battalion exec was wounded in the hand and legs. A radioman was killed.

Sergeant Burick of E Company heard a tank approaching down the road that ran in front of the orchard where the battalion was dug in. Burick grabbed a bazooka, loaded it, and stepped out into the road. He waited until the tank rolled close enough to be identified as a fifty-five-ton Tiger. Then Burick pulled the trigger.

Nothing happened. The safety was stuck.

Sergeant Burick released the safety and raised the bazooka to fire again. The tank was almost on top of him when he pulled the trigger a second time. At almost the same moment, the Tiger's 88mm cannon belched a tongue of flame.

The blast knocked Burick down, but the sergeant reloaded his bazooka, rose, and fired again just as the tank's main gun let loose another round.

Again Burick was knocked to the ground, this time badly wounded. He crawled to his foxhole and found another round for his bazooka. Burick loaded his weapon a third time. Unable to stand, he dragged himself to a firing position and loosed a third shot at the Tiger.

That was enough for the German tank commander. He put his monster into reverse and backed up the road.

"Burick, with utter disregard for his safety, tried to push another injured soldier into his foxhole," reported Lt. William Anderson. "Burick turned and called for more bazooka ammunition, then fell unconscious by the side of the road. Later, he died of his wounds."

The wounded battalion commander and his wounded exec stayed at their posts until the counterattack was beaten off. The German tanks withdrew, leaving behind one burning Panther.

Conditions on Hill 314 were somewhat better on the morning of August 10 than the night before. German pressure eased off until there was little more than sporadic shelling and occasional sniper fire.

The battery problem was becoming more acute, however. The artillery observers had recovered the used batteries they had discarded soon after arriving on the hill and were now trying to use them again. The batteries not in use were set up on rocks in the sunlight, in hopes the heat would regenerate a little power.

"Our batteries were so weak we could hardly hear," said Sgt. Harry Walker, a spotter for Cannon Company attached to Company K on the hill. "Corporal Brown [three miles back with the guns] kept telling me to speak up; he could hardly hear me."

Normally, the 300-series radios in use on the hill were extremely reliable. The dark green sets weighed thirty-two pounds and were designed to be carried on a man's back. The frequencies were preset and code was used because it was assumed that the Germans could listen in. "Oh yeah," Walker said, "and we could hear them talking, too." Lieutenant Woody had the Germans in mind at one point in the battle when he was asked to describe conditions on the hill. "Things are going just great," he said. "We've got plenty of food, plenty of water, and all the ammunition in the world. By the way, you know who I am, don't you? I'm the biggest liar in the U.S. Army."

The radios wouldn't work, however, without the small square batteries. "I can still see that artillery observer taking his batteries out and laying them out in the sun," Pvt. John Weekly said. "He'd stick one back in when he had something to report, then talk a mile a minute, trying to get it all in before the power would fade."

With so little power left, the radios were saved to send messages. Only a limited watch was kept for incoming messages. That was why the men on the hill were surprised just after noon, when a flight of American P-47s roared over Hill 314. The fighters dive-bombed German positions, then returned to strafe the side of the hill, setting off some spectacular explosions. "After they had accomplished their mission, they circled and came in low over the battalion position," Lieutenant Kerley wrote. "The men on the hill jumped for their holes, fearing the fighters had mistaken our position for that of the enemy."

However, the fighter pilots knew who held the hill. They were just scouting the area. At 1600 hours, the P-47s were back, this time escorting a flight of C-47s. "Possibly the most beautiful sight we had ever seen was the multicolored parachutes lazily floating down," Kerley recalled.

Unfortunately, almost all of those pretty parachutes missed the battalion's perimeter. Most landed behind German lines, but the GIs on the hill could see several packages in the no-man's-land swept by rifle fire from both sides.

Captain Delmont Byrn immediately organized a small party to retrieve one group of boxes eight hundred yards outside Company E's perimeter. The Germans began to drop mortar and artillery shells into the field, then opened up with a 20mm antiaircraft weapon as the small group of GIs made their way across the open field. Knowing that his small group couldn't carry everything back, Byrn made the men open the boxes to pick out the most essential items before crawling to safety. Byrn found no radio batteries or medical supplies, but he did find machine-gun and mortar ammunition.

Byrn's party lugged back as much ammo as they could carry, reaching the machine-gun and mortar positions on the forward slope. Byrn then directed fire upon the German positions that had exposed themselves to fire at his expedition.

Lieutenant Woody's men recovered several packages of rifle ammo, but by some bizarre oversight the .30-caliber shells were in clips designed to fit World War I Springfields, not the M1s used by World War II GIs. "We were able to use it," Woody said of the rifle ammo, "but we had to sit there and hand-load our clips."

Sergeant Walker needed radio batteries so badly that he also left the relative safety of the battalion's perimeter in search of supplies. He spotted one bunch of packages in a field seventeen hundred yards from K Company's lines. He had just reached the supplies when he spotted a German tank (he was sure it was a Tiger) sitting at the edge of the field.

"It just sat there," he said. "I don't know why." Either the tankers inside were dead or they were waiting for bigger game and didn't want to give away their position to kill a single GI. The Tiger showed no sign of life as Walker began opening boxes. He was bitterly disappointed by his prize. "I went after radio batteries, but all I found were six boxes of K rations." He didn't have time to ponder his bad luck. Rockets—the dreaded screaming meemies—began to fall on the field (possibly called in by the watching tankers). He grabbed a handful of K rations and raced back for his lines.

The supply drop had to be judged a failure. The few packages recovered by the men on the hill contained food and ammo, both badly needed, but neither as urgently as radio batteries and medical supplies. Lieutenant Weiss reported the results of the drop to the 230th Field Artillery. The battalion's gunners had watched the C-47s go over and were bitterly disappointed to learn how ineffective the supply drop really was. Lieutenant Colonel Lewis D. Vieman, commanding the 230th, decided to take matters into his own hands.

He ordered his operations officer, Maj. Richard Evans, and his medical officer, Capt. Bruce Stern, to prepare medical packages for insertion into artillery shells. Evans prepared fifteen 105mm HC base-ejection smoke shells, which were sometimes used to fire propaganda leaflets. Evans removed the fuses, while Stern packed the insides with bandages, dressings, morphine styrettes, drugs, and plasma.

While they were working, Vieman visited Lt. George Dieser, who was commanding the 743d Tank Battalion's assault gun platoon. "We were working as a six-gun battery with the 230th," Dieser recalled. "Every night, we laid our protective fires on all sides and by day, we fired as we were called. This was a twenty-four-hour business." But Vieman's visit was not business as usual. He gave Dieser a strange order: fill three smoke shells with a half-pound of sand. Dieser's men used a package of sugar to measure the half-pound of sand. The shells ready, they waited until a jeep pulled up and unloaded six of the shells prepared by Evans and Stern.

The tank-mounted 105mm guns of the 743d's assault platoon were chosen because they were more stable, and hence more accurate, than the towed 105s of the 230th.

The observers on Hill 314 were notified of Vieman's plan. At 2210, the first sand-filled shell was fired toward the hill. A correction was made with a second sand-filled shell. At 2240 hours, just before dark, a volley of three carefully prepared "mercy" shells were fired. None were recovered. Dieser's gun crews made another adjustment and launched three more shells filled with medical supplies. The firing continued at five-minute intervals, giving the GIs on the hill plenty of time to spot the incoming shells. After the loss of the first three shells, eight of the next nine landed within American lines.

"They told us to look out for shells with red stripes around the base," Woody said. "The shells would hit, bounce fifteen feet in the air, then bury themselves in the ground. We dug them up. I watched a couple of our guys beating on the base of one, trying to get it off. Hell, it didn't have a red marking. After being fired from a cannon and the shock of landing, whatever markings they had painted on must have rubbed off. I was just hoping they weren't beating on a live shell."

Vieman's innovative relief effort was only partially successful. The shock had destroyed most of the supplies in the shells. Only the bandages and dressings were usable. The containers holding the drugs and plasma were smashed. Disappointed, Vieman promised to try again the next morning. One of his sergeants was working on a plan to mount a radio battery in a 155mm shell. It was worth trying. In addition, another C-47 drop was promised for the next day.

If there was a next day. The men on Hill 314 had held out for four days and four nights. How much longer before relief arrived?

"We could hear the sounds of guns firing far off," Sgt. Charles Herndon said. "Later, the sound seemed a little closer. They told us another unit was fighting to rescue us."

Major Robert Herlong's battalion of the 119th was trying to push through Romagny into Mortain. However, during the previous night, the Germans had succeeded in mining the knocked-out Tiger and covering the approaches to it with machine-gun fire. "As the tank blocked the only road through the village, it effectively blocked the battalion's progress through the town," Herlong said. "Reducing this position took considerable time and cost a number of lives." One of the casualties was an officer who walked forward in response to a white flag waving from the second story of the village church. When he was gunned down, Herlong called in artillery to blast the church. Just before nightfall, the battalion succeeded in pushing through the town and launched an attack, supported by eight Sherman tanks of the 743d Battalion, on the German line east of town. But the tanks broke off in the face of fire from at least two entrenched 88s and the infantry was pinned down and forced to dig in for the night.

On Herlong's right, patrols finally made contact with the left flank of the 35th Division, still slowly moving up the St.-Hilaire–Mortain highway. Although General Baade was still determined to maintain a continuous front, the desperate situation on Hill 314 convinced him to designate one reinforced battalion for a narrow thrust to try and break through to the besieged Americans.

The 1st Battalion of the 320th Infantry Regiment, supported by the 737th Tank Battalion, pushed off at 1500 hours, after a ten-minute artillery barrage. In the first hour, the attack advanced a mile toward the hill, but when darkness fell, the relief column was still short of the hill.

Relief for the men on Hill 314 would have to wait at least another day.

The XV Corps' spearheads made two miles in the first hour of its drive north from Le Mans.

"Advance on the axis Alençon-Sées to the line Sées-Carrouges," General Bradley told George Patton, adding, "Be prepared for further action against the enemy flank and rear in the direction of Argentan."

"Lead with your armor," General Patton ordered Maj. Gen. Wade Hampton Haislip, who had to spend August 9 rearranging his divisions to comply with the order. While his engineers prepared roads and bridges in and around Le Mans, Haislip moved Leclerc's French 2d Armored Division into position in front of the 90th Infantry Division on the left, and Maj. Gen. Lunsford Oliver's 5th Armored Division took station on the right, just ahead of the 79th Infantry. Major General Horace McBride's green 80th Division would protect the left rear of the corps as it pushed north.

The move began just after dawn on August 10. The French tanks pointed toward Alençon, thirty miles north of Le Mans. Oliver's division was to take Mamers, fifteen miles away, then continue to Sées, fifteen miles farther to the northeast of Alençon. Once again, the XV Corps was racing forward on a narrow front with no idea of what enemy forces were in front of it.

Haislip's corps was, in fact, matched against the German LXXXI Corps, which was already suffering from the futile defense of Le Mans. The 708th Infantry Division, chewed up by Maj. Gen. Raymond McLain's 90th Division earlier in the week, was trying to re-form in front of Alençon, but many of its troops were still trapped west of the Sarthe River. The tough, veteran 9th Panzer Division also had units on the wrong side of the river but was better suited to contest Haislip's advance. Backing up these units were the remnants of the shattered Panzer Lehr Division, "of negligible combat strength," and the survivors of another shattered division, the 352d Infantry. A Kampfgruppe from the 6th Parachute Division was en route from central France but had not arrived when the XV Corps jumped off.

Haislip's spearheads found the German resistance sporadic: very fierce in some places, very light in others. Lieutenant Colonel William Hamberg of the 10th Tank Battalion found one extreme. Driving his Sherman across a bridge raked with enemy fire, past the wrecks of two earlier victims, he found an infantry company disorganized by the loss of its company commander. Hamberg dismounted his tank and organized a tank-infantry attack, which cleared the German roadblock and got the column moving again.

The landscape was not ideal tank country. "The hedges, embankments, copses, and winding roads favored the enemy, his ambushes and his retreat," complained a French officer. "They prevented us from deploying and charging as was our custom. We were forced to mark time in endless columns, the van alone fighting."

Nevertheless, both of Haislip's armored columns made spectacular progress, covering fifteen miles—half the distance to Alençon—by nightfall. On the right, Oliver's Combat Command R had outflanked the left wing of the 9th Panzer Division. On the left, Leclerc's artillery was hitting the village of Fresnay-sur-Sarthe, forcing the commanders of both the 9th Panzer and the Panzer Lehr divisions to withdraw their headquarters to the north. Behind the armor, the 79th and 90th infantry divisions kept pace, cleaning up pockets of resistance.

Haislip's spearheads halted for the night, stopping just short of the Forêt de Perseigne, which stretched almost ten miles across the XV Corps' line of advance. The densely wooded area offered the Germans some superb defensive positions. Two divisions could be hiding in the forest, SHAEF intelligence warned.

Back at Third Army headquarters, a newspaper reporter asked General Patton if he was afraid the Germans would stop Haislip before he closed the trap.

"Hell, no!" he shouted. "The Boche can't stop me. The only thing that can stop me are those goddamn phase lines."

Those would turn out to be among the most prophetic words George S. Patton ever uttered.

CHAPTER 19: WITHDRAWAL

G eneral Heinrich Eberbach needed a good excuse—one good enough to convince Hitler to cancel the order for a renewed offensive toward Mortain.

Eberbach had turned over the Fifth Panzer Army to Gen. Sepp Dietrich on August 9 to take over planning for the renewed Mortain counterattack. His transfer was evidence of how strongly Hitler clung to his dream of a breakthrough at Mortain. Eberbach's new command was named Panzer Group Eberbach, but despite the grandiose title, his only assets were a skeleton staff (including von Kluge's son as chief of staff) and the same battered divisions that had failed to crack the 30th Division's lines on August 7.

It didn't take Eberbach long to see that the attack originally scheduled for Friday, August 11, had no chance of success. Only seventy-seven Mark IV tanks and forty-seven Panthers were available for the attack, less than the armored force that had failed to crack the 30th Division's lines in the initial assault. He demanded more tanks, more ammunition, and more fuel supplies. It would take time to assemble an adequate striking force. And time, as Eberbach knew very well, was one thing the German army in Normandy did not have. The Canadians were hammering southward toward Falaise, the American 2d Armored Division was pushing north from Barenton toward Ger behind the battlefield at Mortain, and most dangerous of all, the American XV Corps was driving north from Le Mans toward Alençon. A breakthrough at any one of the three threatened points would be a disaster for the German army in France.

The trick for the German high command was convincing Hitler of the danger. Eberbach had already advanced a clever argument in an attempt to delay his scheduled attack. Given the necessity of avoiding Allied air power, he insisted that his new offensive must be launched after sundown, when darkness and the early-morning ground fog would cover his panzers. His assault forces would thus have at least six hours to achieve their objectives. But to attack after nightfall, he needed the light of the full moon. The next suitable night would be August 20, so Eberbach asked Hitler to delay the attack until then. It is unlikely Eberbach really believed that the front would remain stable for nine more days, but his argument provided a good excuse not to push more forces west at a time when the enemy was threatening encirclement.

Before Hitler could answer Eberbach's request, von Kluge reported the threatening advance from Le Mans and warned that the German forces in that region were not strong enough to stop Haislip's corps. Instead of continuing the attack at Mortain, von Kluge suggested it was "worth considering whether the spearheads of the enemy columns driving north should not be smashed by a swiftly executed panzer thrust."

Hitler wavered. He didn't understand why Eberbach couldn't attack before August 20. He asked questions. What did General Funck think of the situation? What forces did von Kluge propose to use against the threat from Le Mans? Finally, in a message that von Kluge received at 0200 hours on August 11, Hitler conceded that it might be necessary to attack the XV Corps before resuming the advance toward Avranches. It took von Kluge another fifteen hours to obtain final approval for the redistribution of his forces. Hitler agreed that Eberbach should prepare three panzer divisions for an August 14 strike at Alençon, where von Kluge expected to find Haislip's spearheads. In order to free up the forces necessary for this operation, the führer agreed to "a minor withdrawal of the front between Sourdeval and Mortain."

In other words, Hitler finally agreed to admit that his bold gamble to cut the Third Army's lifeline at Avranches had failed. The fighting at Mortain would continue the rest of the day (August 11) and into the night, but the German aim would no longer be to hold ground in preparation for a renewed offensive. Now the enemy was fighting to effect an orderly withdrawal.

Von Kluge could only wonder if the withdrawal would be in time to save the German troops in Mortain from encirclement.

There was another question: Would it be in time to save the encircled American battalion on Hill 314?

Lieutenant Guy Hagen and the six men hiding in the loft of the French barn in Mortain came very close to discovery on the morning of August 11. The Germans searched the bottom of the building, but for some reason didn't come upstairs. A French farmer did.

"He came up to throw down some hay with his pitchfork," Hagen said. "Seeing us shocked him, but he stayed quiet. No one spoke. We tried to signal him to bring us food and water. He left and came back with some water, no food."

Hagen and his companions had had nothing to eat for four days except a handful of raw carrots and beets they'd been able to grab on the journey from the wheat field to the barn. With Germans swarming all around their hiding place, there was nothing they could do about it except live with their hunger.

SHAEF's suspicions about the Forêt de Perseigne appeared to be correct when Maj. Gen. Lunsford Oliver's 5th Armored Division launched its first tentative probes into the forest at dawn.

A column of trucks approaching the woods was forced to slam to a halt when machine-gun fire raked the lead vehicles. One of the drivers, Pvt. Charles McGuire, of the 47th Armored Regiment, grabbed his M1 and crawled down a ditch unobserved to a position where he was behind the troublesome roadblock. Jumping to his feet, McGuire killed every member of the machine-gun crew. Moments later, the column was rolling again. Less than a mile beyond the first obstacle, an 88mm shell ripped into McGuire's truck, killing the heroic driver (who was awarded a posthumous Distinguished Service Cross).

It didn't take many such instances to convince General Haislip that SHAEF intelligence was right about the Forêt de Perseigne. He ordered his two armored divisions to swing around the forest rather than pass through it. To protect his separated columns, he ordered three artillery battalions to interdict the exits from the forest, then requested an air strike to smoke out the Germans with incendiary oil bombs. The attacks were carried out, but contrary to SHAEF's dire predictions, the Germans had already withdrawn most of their forces from the woods. Traffic jams were actually more of a problem than the Germans on the second day of the XV Corps' drive. Both the 5th Armored and General Leclerc's 2d French Armored Division slashed through the French countryside, smashing through lightly defended roadblocks and bypassing heavier enemy concentrations, leaving them to the trailing infantry. General Patton's doubts about Haislip and his corps were erased as he watched their swift advance.

The flamboyant commander of the Third Army spent Friday morning trying to catch up with the fast-moving French tankers. Climbing aboard his jeep, he turned to his aide, Lt. Col. Charles Codman, and ordered, "Be sure to bring along a bag of Bronze Stars for Leclerc's sons of bitches."

Leclerc was at that moment near the head of one of his four armored columns as it seized the village of Bourg-le-Roi. Local inhabitants reported that the Germans had evacuated an hour earlier. But they warned of a formidable defensive position in Champfleur, the next village up the road, and the last before Alençon. Leclerc ordered a table and chair set up in the village square, under some lime trees, where he could direct the attack of the 12th Cuirassiers on the German roadblock.

A column of Shermans headed up the road with a local baker named Louis Martin riding the lead tank to help navigate. He guided the tank's commander down a side road. Three Shermans followed, but the rest of the squadron missed the turn in the dust, inadvertently setting up a two-pronged attack on the German positions in Champfleur. The four Shermans led by Martin entered the town from the west, and the main force entered from the south. Lieutenant Krebs, leading the western thrust, quickly lost two of his tanks, but he succeeded in killing a Mark IV when his Sherman's armor deflected the German's first shot. He pushed on through the town after the retreating enemy forces, killing another panzer as it tried to crash through a hedgerow.

Krebs was ordered to return to the town. It was 1800 hours when he reached Champfleur's village square. Waiting there was a Sherman with the name Tailly painted on the side; it belonged to General Leclerc. Once again, the commander of the French 2d Armored Division ordered a table set up in the open, this time on the steps of the church.

Leclerc spread out his maps and studied them as the delirious towns-people gathered around. An innkeeper asked permission to serve cider to the tankers gathered in the square.

"No more than a couple of glasses each," Leclerc said. "We have work to do."

Patton never did catch up with Leclerc on that busy Friday, but he managed to visit the headquarters of the other three divisions driving north to close Bradley's trap. At Haislip's headquarters, Patton warned the XV Corps commander: "Wade, pay no attention to Monty's goddamn boundaries. Be prepared to push on past Falaise if necessary. I'll give you the word."

At the same moment that Patton was visiting XV Corps headquarters, Field Marshal Günther von Kluge was visiting Alençon to check on the defenses of that vital crossroads. What he saw appalled him.

The rumble of American guns was audible in the early afternoon air. Rear-area service troops were fleeing through the city in near panic. Burning vehicles, knocked out by Allied aircraft and artillery, littered the countryside just out of town.

The headquarters of the LXXXI Corps was in a state of confusion. Von Kluge learned that the units trying to block Haislip's advance had been shattered. The 9th Panzer Division was reduced to little more than a battalion of infantry, a battalion of artillery, and twelve tanks. The only force available to defend the important crossroads of Sées, the immediate objective of Oliver's 5th Armored Division, was a bakery company.

The makeshift defenses would have to hold just a while longer. The 116th Panzer Division, still relatively fresh after its disappointing performance in Operation Lüttich, was already withdrawing from its position north of the Sée River. It should reach Alençon by dawn Saturday.

The observers on Hill 314 were the first to witness evidence of the change in German plans. Soon after the sun came up on Friday morning and burned off the ground fog, enemy traffic was detected moving east—away from Mortain—for the first time. Artillery fire was directed on the retreating vehicles.

"The burning enemy columns could be seen for miles in all directions," Lieutenant Kerley wrote. "The slaughter continued all day."

Unfortunately, the view of the burning enemy convoys was about the only good news for the men on the hill. German artillery continued to hammer away at the American positions. The panzergrenadiers who were dug in at the base of the hill showed no inclination to withdraw, maintaining a dangerous sniper fire, much of it aimed at GIs trying to reach the well they had discovered near their lines. A second airdrop by C-47s proved even less successful than the first. Almost all of the parachuted supplies fell behind enemy lines. Although several more artillery shells packed with medical supplies were recovered, once again the important contents, such as morphine and plasma, failed to withstand the shock of firing. The attempt to load radio batteries in a 155mm shell proved impractical.

"Our biggest concern was just wondering whether they'd get through to us," Lieutenant Woody said. "We were eating raw potatoes and raw cabbages by this time. We'd taken up all the D bars [chocolate ration bars] and given them to the wounded."

A rumor spread among the men on the hill—relief would arrive at noon! No one knew where the rumor started, but for several hours, it was fervently believed. When noon came and went with no relief, there was bitter disappointment.

It wasn't that the troops trying to reach Hill 314 weren't trying. Both the 1st Battalion of the 119th Infantry and the 1st Battalion of the 320th Regiment were closing in on the surrounded battalion.

Major Robert Herlong of the 119th came up with a clever ruse to break the stalemate at Romagny. At 0800 hours, two of his companies followed a heavy artillery barrage forward in a repetition of an attack that had been repulsed the previous evening. While the German defenders were focused on the frontal assault, Herlong's A Company and six Sherman tanks were advancing eight hundred yards south. Within ninety minutes, the flanking attack had forced the Germans out of their defensive line and back to a road junction well to the rear. Herlong's battalion had to halt briefly to let friendly troops catch up on both flanks.

The 117th Infantry's ongoing attempt to retake St.-Barthelmy also ran into fierce resistance. An early-morning attack with the 12th RCT on the right gained just two hundred yards in three hours. A mortarman from D Company of the 12th Regiment's 1st Battalion accomplished the amazing feat of dropping a shell into the open turret of a German tank. But even with that bit of luck and some massive fire support from three artillery battalions, Lieutenant Colonel Johnson's forces were just too tired and too depleted to gain their objective. One battalion reported having just 163 effectives left in its three rifle companies (the normal complement was 212 men in a company) and "some of these were just hanging on by spirit alone."

At 1530 hours, Herlong's advance resumed, with elements of the 320th Infantry Regiment tied in on his right flank, Company F of the 117th Infantry on his left. Progress was very slow as the retreating Germans gave ground grudgingly. By nightfall, the relief force had just reached the outskirts of Mortain. Colonel Birks of the 120th Infantry considered trying to load supplies onto several Shermans and have the tanks attempt a solo dash the last few hundred yards to the hill. However, when asked how desperate the situation was for the surrounded men, Captain Erichson replied, "We can hold out until tomorrow."

With that assurance, General Hobbs elected to halt the relief force until dawn. He suggested that the troops dig in where they were, but Herlong elected to pull back two hundred yards to higher ground. It was a bitter choice to give up such hard-won territory, yet it proved correct. Just after darkness, the Germans poured heavy artillery and mortar fire on the position Herlong's men had just vacated. The relief force didn't know it at the time, but the barrage was designed to cover the withdrawal of the German infantry in and around Mortain.

The men on the hill heard the movement all around them and elected to use the last power in their dying radio batteries to call in fire on the retreating enemy. "Our artillery plastered every available route of withdrawal and was very effective, evidenced by the screams and hysterical cries of the enemy," Kerley wrote. "There was no doubt now relief was certain and the battalion rested, listening to the sing [sic] of outgoing artillery."

General Leclerc was asleep in a meadow outside Champfleur, his headquarters staff sharing the rough ground with the staff of the 12th Cuirassiers, when at 0200 hours, a German shell struck a half-track parked nearby.

The explosion killed two officers and woke up Leclerc—in more ways than one. Within moments, he was stalking the meadow, waving his cane and shouting, "On your feet! Everyone get moving. Forward! Man your tanks!"

The eleven Shermans of the 4th Squadron moved out at 0300 hours, followed by the squadron's other vehicles: tank destroyers, half-tracks, machine-gun carriers, jeeps, and trucks. "An interminable column was en route," one French officer recalled. "We could see nothing. Not a shot was fired. Nothing could be heard except the engines revving at slow speed. The squadron was somewhere in this slow march, in the smoke that thickened the darkness. We passed houses, streets, and more houses. We were in Alençon."

The trip wasn't without incident. The jeep carrying General Leclerc took a wrong turn in the darkness and blundered into a meeting with a German staff car. Leclerc's aide, Lt. Col. Jacques de Guillebon, whipped out his .45 and shot the German driver. Before he could fire again, occupants of the car came piling out with their hands up.

A civilian guided the rest of the column directly toward its prime goal, the Pont Neuf over the Sarthe River. A quick check was made to see if the bridge was mined, then the column of Shermans rolled past, through the sleeping town, to take up defensive positions outside of town.

Leclerc took a seat on the parapet of the captured bridge and watched the pale dawn break over Alençon. "His sons of bitches" had beaten the German reinforcements to the stronghold on the Sarthe.

CHAPTER 20: RELIEF

Sometime during the night, an American artillery shell set afire the building next to the barn where Hagen and his five companions were hiding. The Germans extinguished the fire, but the makeshift hospital was badly burned.

When the sun came up that morning, there were no Germans in sight. Cautiously, the six starving fugitives descended from the loft and began looking for food. Inside the burned-out field hospital, they discovered several jars of jam, six loaves of bread, and a large ham.

"It was a feast," Hagen said. "After we ate, we went out to look for our troops. We knew the Americans must be nearby. We hadn't gone very far when we saw a GI on the street. He pointed the way, and we headed for the regimental CP. Almost the first person we saw when we got there was Colonel Birks. He was so choked up he couldn't speak. He thought the whole battalion staff was gone. He came up and embraced us. He squeezed me real hard."

Two miles to the north, Col. Walter Johnson and Maj. Warren Giles, Johnson's G-2, were the first Americans to reenter St.-Barthelmy. The two officers made a quick survey of the once-quaint little village, now reduced by six days of bitter battle into little more than a heap of rubble.

"That little town—and it was just a small town, really—was totally destroyed," Giles said. "I don't know if there was anything left standing. There were German bodies everywhere. And tanks . . . a world of burnt out tanks."

Johnson wanted to be the first man in town for a reason.

"He had this theory that he needed to be seen up front," Giles said. "He thought it was a real morale booster. He was always up front. It's a wonder he wasn't killed."

Giles almost was. He climbed into a German foxhole to check something and when he climbed out, the foxhole exploded.

"They had booby-trapped everything before they pulled out," Giles said. "A second sooner and I'd be dead."

The Germans left something else in town. The wine cellar of St.-Barthelmy's tiny hotel had first been used as an aid station by the Americans when they were defending the town. The Germans moved out the walking wounded when they took the town, but left the worst cases in the dark cellar, adding their own wounded as they defended the town from the Americans.

When the German troops pulled out of St.-Barthelmy in the pre-dawn hours of August 12, they left behind in the wine cellar all the men—German and American—wounded too badly to be moved. Among them was Cpl. Walter Christianson, Lt. George Greene's No. 1 gunner, who had fired the first shot in the battle for St.-Barthelmy.

The German retreat robbed the relief of Hill 314 of all its drama. When the sun rose on Saturday morning, August 12, the enemy was gone, except for a few snipers left as a rear guard. The relief forces moved in slowly, wary of a possible ambush, but met no real resistance as they advanced through the shattered town and up the steep side of the hill. Just before noon, scouts from the 35th Division's 320th Infantry Regiment reached Company G's position.

Lieutenant Homer Kurtz from Troy, Illinois, and four men from the intelligence section were the first to make contact.

"A guy came up to me and asked for our company commander," Woody said. "Hell, I had my insignia pinned inside my lapel and I looked like a ragamuffin. When he asked for the company commander, I told him, 'This is he.' He said, 'We're relieving you, sir.' I said, 'Allll-rright!' "

The 35th Division's Quartermaster Company had loaded a truck with food, water, and medical supplies to make a quick dash to the top of the hill. Every driver in the company volunteered to make the run. Corporal Verlin Young and T. Sgt. Hans Gehlsen were chosen. Three tanks (two in front, one behind) escorted their truck up the hill. After unloading the supplies, Woody's men loaded twenty of the most seriously wounded onto the truck for a quick trip to the aid station.

More ambulances followed closely behind the leading relief company. Woody got the rest of his wounded off the hill in short order. Meanwhile, Herlong's troops reached K Company. Not long afterward a platoon from the 120th Infantry reached E Company's position on the other side of the hill.

"We knew a lot of those fellows," Sergeant Myers said. "An officer told them to give us all their chocolate bars and bouillon cubes. That's the first time I ever tasted a bouillon cube dissolved in cold water. I didn't know anything could taste so good."

Private First Class Leo Temkin was given some K rations by the relief troops when they reached his position. "Funny thing," he said. "They tasted good. And I didn't like K rations."

John Weekly shared a chocolate bar that his squad leader had been hoarding, then was taken to the rear where he was given hot food. "We were near the divisional artillery. The noise! It was worse than the hill."

All around Mortain, the weary GIs of the 30th Division were given a well-earned rest. It was a time for food, sleep, showers, and clean clothes. And mail.

Especially mail. For Lt. Murray Pulver, it was the first mail to reach him from home since he had joined the 30th Division before St.-Lô. He hurriedly opened the most recent letter from his wife.

"It began, 'The baby is just fine, growing and gaining every day,' " Pulver recalled. "I had to open another letter to learn that the baby was a boy. Wow! Almost three months old already. My prayers had been answered."

For Pulver, victory at Mortain wasn't as important as the birth of his son.

Maybe Col. Hammond Birks, surveying the killing fields around L'Abbaye Blanche with Lt. Tom Springfield that afternoon, realized the extent of the 30th Division's victory. The commander of the 120th Infantry counted forty shattered vehicles littering the roads around the roadblock and declared it "the best damn sight I've seen in the war."

However, it is unlikely that the majority of the men who fought at Mortain shared Birks's enthusiasm that Saturday afternoon. Most were more interested in survival than in victory. Too many didn't survive. The 30th Division's G-1 report covering the six days of the battle listed 1,834 casualties: 165 killed, 1,199 evacuated wounded, 28 nonevacuated wounded, and 442 missing. In all, Old Hickory lost more than 15 percent of its strength in the battle. Many of the missing were in fact dead. Many more were prisoners, including Lt. George Greene, Pfc. Alfred Overbeck, Lt. Col. Eads Hardaway, Chaplain Gunnar Teilmann, his assistant, Jack Thacker, and medic Robert Bradley.

The 117th Infantry, which lost more than 350 men in the first three hours of the attack, ended the battle with an official tally of 24 dead, 299 missing, and 195 wounded. Most were in the 1st Battalion. A postwar count of A Company's 118 casualties (out of 135 officers and men) showed 4 killed, 12 wounded, 87 captured, and 15 missing. (The latter were probably dead as opposed to the missing reported immediately after the battle, which included the many men taken prisoner.) C Company lost almost as heavily, with 11 dead, 16 wounded, 69 captured, and 7 missing. All but 10 of those casualties (4 killed and 6 wounded) came in the first twenty-four hours of the battle.

The 120th Infantry listed only 19 killed, 354 wounded, and 25 missing, almost certainly a gross understatement. More men than that were lost defending Hill 314, not to mention the combat in Mortain, on Hill 285, and in Barenton.

Approximately 700 men reached Hill 314 during the battle. Exactly 357 were able to walk off on August 12. The unwounded survivors included 103 men from Lieutenant Woody's G Company, 100 from Lieutenant Reaser's K Company, 100 from Lieutenant Kerley's E Company, 18 from Captain Byrn's H Company, 24 refugees from C Company, 8 men from Captain Erichson's F Company, 8 refugees from the 823d TD Battalion, 4 refugees from the 120th's Antitank Company, 5 from the Cannon Company, and 6 observers from the 230th FA Battalion. More than 300 men on the hill were killed or wounded.

Whatever the real losses of the 30th Division at Mortain, it is obvious that the Germans suffered much more heavily, although in the chaos of the Falaise evacuation, many of the German unit records were lost, making it difficult to determine exactly how much damage

Mortain's defenders inflicted. Close to a hundred German tanks were counted on the battlefield, although the Americans moved forward so quickly after the battle that an accurate count was never made. However, the German records do yield an interesting clue to the devastation visited on one unit. During General Eberbach's effort to organize a second counterattack at Mortain, he sent a message referring to "the remnants of the 1st SS Panzer Division." Before the battle, the division was one of the strongest and best equipped in the German army.

Counting casualties is not the best way to measure the extent of the American victory at Mortain, however. The original objectives of Operation Lüttich were a very real threat to the Allied position in Normandy. Perhaps Hitler's attempt to strike at Mortain was a gamble, but it was not an impossible one. His professional soldiers, while questioning the strategic sense behind the attack, expected tactical success. Were it not for the determined resistance at St.-Barthelmy, L'Abbaye Blanche, and on Hill 314, von Kluge's panzers could very well have reached Avranches and temporarily cut the supply lines to the Third Army.

Yet Mortain was more than a defensive victory. By maintaining the position without significant reinforcement for five days, Mortain's defenders gave the Allied high command time to spring the trap that would liberate France before the end of August.

General Sir Bernard Law Montgomery, unlike the majority of British historians who have written about the campaign in Normandy, understood the importance of Mortain. In his memoirs, he not only cites the German counterattack as inspiring the idea for the envelopment west of the Seine River, he also labels the result of the Allied trap as "the Mortain-Falaise Pocket."

Von Kluge certainly realized the consequences of his failure at Mortain. In the early morning hours of August 19, soon after being relieved of his command by Field Marshal Walter Model, von Kluge wrote a long, remarkably frank letter to Hitler: "I have been relieved of command . . . The evident reason is the failure of the armored units in their push to Avranches and the consequent impossibility of closing the gap to the sea." Von Kluge accepted blame for the failure, but also criticized Hitler for failing to understand the full measure of Allied superiority. "Rommel and I, and probably all the leaders here in the West,

who have experienced the struggle with the English and Americans
and [witnessed] their wealth of material, foresaw the development that
has now appeared . . . Our views were not dictated by pessimism but
by sober recognition of the facts." Von Kluge closed the letter with
an appeal to end the war.

Soon after leaving his headquarters, von Kluge committed suicide,
swallowing a capsule of potassium cyanide.

Perhaps he should be counted as Mortain's last casualty.

The American high command was generous in passing out honors
to the defenders of Mortain. Six units were awarded the Presidential
Unit Citation. The 1st Battalion of the 117th Infantry Regiment was
honored for its defense of St.-Barthelmy; the 2d Battalion of the 120th
(plus Company K of the 3d Battalion) for its stand on Hill 314; companies A and B of the 823d Tank-Destroyer Battalion for their roadblocks at L'Abbaye Blanche and St.-Barthelmy; and the 1st and 2d
platoons of the 120th's Antitank Company for their part in the L'Abbaye
Blanche roadblock.

Lieutenant Lawson Neel and Lt. Tom Springfield of the 823d were
awarded the Silver Star for their part in the battle. Oddly, Lt. George
Greene, whose platoon performed so heroically in the first hours at
St.-Barthelmy, has never been decorated.

Lieutenant Colonel Ernest Frankland was awarded the Distinguished
Service Cross (the army's second-highest decoration for valor) for his
defense of St.-Barthelmy. So were the five company commanders on
Hill 314: Capt. Reynold Erichson, Capt. Delmont Byrn, Lt. Joseph Reaser,
Lt. Ralph Kerley, and Lt. Ronal Woody.

On the afternoon of August 12, Woody would have traded his DSC—
and his prized Buick sedan—for some rest. His company was marched
off to a little grove where showers and kitchens were set up.

"We had a good place," he said. "When the cooks got to us, the
first thing I told them was to bring us plenty of coffee. I laid down
with a cup of coffee and was starting to open my mail. When a soldier came up and ordered me to report to battalion headquarters, I said,
'There ain't no battalion any more.' But he insisted I go, so I followed
him to a roadblock, where they had these guys from the French un-
derground. They said they knew where there were a bunch of Boche
hiding in a barn."

Woody commandeered a jeep and a driver and sped off, looking for the barn described by the resistance fighters. It didn't take long to find it. Woody approached the building alone, suddenly aware of his vulnerability.

"I was about twenty-five feet away when the barn door swung open and they started coming out with their hands up," he said. "There were thirteen of them and they all had on their cloth hats. That's when I knew it was alright. When they take off their helmets and put on their cloth hats, that's when you know there's no more fight in them. I somehow got them all on the jeep and we rode back to headquarters."

Only then was the battle of Mortain over for Ronal Woody.

CHAPTER 21: CLOSING THE TRAP

G eneral Leclerc didn't rest long on the bridge at Alençon. He was holding in his hands the key to Argentan—the German defense plans for the area, discovered on one of the officers whom Lieutenant Colonel de Guillebon had captured the night before. Strong German forces were rushing to the scene, but on the Saturday morning when the Americans reentered Mortain and St.-Barthelmy, there was still nothing in front of Leclerc except the remnants of the same shattered divisions that had been unable to stop the XV Corps on its wild ride from Fougères to Mayenne to Le Mans to Alençon and Sées. There was, however, another forest between the Allied spearheads and their objective. The Forêt d'Ecouves protected the southern approaches of Argentan, offering the same easily defensible positions as the Forêt de Perseigne south of Alençon.

General Haislip again planned to avoid the unknown hazards hidden in the dark woods. He ordered Leclerc to bypass the forest to the west, while Gen. Lunsford Oliver's 5th Armored Division, which had taken Sées just hours after the French capture of Alençon, was to drive east of the forest, directly toward Argentan.

Leclerc had his own ideas. The lack of discipline that General Bradley feared was to emerge on August 12. Holding proof that the Germans had only weak forces in front of him, Leclerc proposed to send three combat commands racing north. Colonel Dio's column was to follow the 2d Armored's assigned route west of the Forêt d'Ecouves toward Carrouges. Colonel Paul de Langlade's column was to push directly through the forest. Colonel Pierre Billotte's command was ordered to drive east of the forest, to Sées, then to turn northwest toward the village of Ecouche (five miles west of Argentan), the division's assigned objective. There was only one problem with the plan. Sées and the two highways that intersected there belonged to the 5th Armored Division. The results of Leclerc's order were predictable—confusion, anger, and massive traffic problems.

"Those goddamn Frog drivers are crazy as hell," an American MP assigned to a key intersection complained. "One convoy of French trucks came barreling through the intersection at forty-five miles an hour. One truck went straight ahead, one whipped off to the left and another charged off to the right. All I saw were three clouds of dust in all three directions."

On the main square in Sées, the traffic jam degenerated into a shouting match between several high-ranking American and French officers. Leclerc, as always near the front, arrived to join the noisy debate.

"You have no right to be here," Oliver's chief of staff complained.

"We're only passing through," Leclerc explained. "We've decided to bypass the Forêt d'Ecouves."

"Argentan is our business," the American answered. "Our tanks need N 158 [the Sées-Argentan road]."

But Leclerc ordered the American colonel to let Billotte's column through the town, promising that his troops would turn northwest, out of the Americans' way after passing through the bottleneck.

Oliver appealed to General Haislip. The commander of the XV Corps was furious, but when he complained about Leclerc to General Patton, the Third Army commander only laughed. "Hell, Wade, don't get so upset. He's only a baby."

Patton's "baby" was making good speed as his division crawled toward its objective. However, the traffic jam in Sées was to cost the XV Corps dearly. Oliver's Combat Command A, which had passed through Sées before the French arrived, was coiled at Mortrée, just five miles southeast of Argentan, ready to leap forward and seize the undefended prize.

All that Oliver's tankers needed was fuel. But the gasoline trucks assigned to the waiting Shermans were stuck south of Sées. Leclerc's traffic jam was to cause a six-hour delay in Oliver's attack.

*   *   *

Panzer Group Eberbach, originally created to resume the offensive at Mortain, assumed command of the defense in the Argentan sector on the morning of August 12.

Actually, Gen. Heinrich Eberbach was not supposed to be thinking defensively. His orders from Hitler were to "restore the situation at Alençon . . . destroy the enemy forces there . . . then return to Mortain to launch the all-out assault to seize Avranches."

To accomplish these impossible tasks, Eberbach was given the four panzer divisions withdrawn from the six-day battle at Mortain (which contained seventy-four working tanks between them) and the remnants of the battered 9th Panzer Division. The 708th Infantry Division was transferred to the Seventh Army; two new infantry divisions and the long-awaited Kampfgruppe from the Sixth Parachute Army would protect Eberbach's eastern flank.

As usual, there was considerable debate about tactics. Field Marshal von Kluge wanted Eberbach to strike the American spearheads with his arriving panzers. Hitler wanted to strike well behind the XV Corps spearheads. Much of this debate was carried out over radio channels, where it was intercepted and decoded in Hut 3 at Bletchley Park.

The problem for the Germans was time. Eberbach was faced with the same pressures confronting von Kluge before Mortain. He couldn't afford to wait for the forces arriving from Mortain to assemble into an effective striking force, not with Haislip's spearheads within artillery range of the German lifeline at Argentan and the Canadian guns hammering the only other supply route through Falaise.

The only defenders Eberbach found in position to act were the survivors of the 9th Panzer Division. They held a series of roadblocks in the Forêt d'Ecouves. There were no German troops between Oliver's tankers in Mortrée and Argentan.

The first of the Mortain survivors, a strong infantry battalion from the 116th Panzer Division, reached Eberbach soon after noon on Saturday. The general had no choice. He rushed the battalion forward just in time to block Oliver's late afternoon assault from Mortrée.

The six-hour delay caused by Leclerc's traffic jam was to allow the Germans to hold Argentan for eight more days.

General Bradley's "short envelopment" was only a few miles away from reality, but the commander of the 12th Army Group was plagued by doubts about both of the jaws closing the trap on nineteen German divisions.

In the north, General Montgomery's drive toward Falaise was stalled ten miles short of its objective. "The British [actually Canadian and Polish] effort from the north is still mediocre . . ." Bradley's aide, Chet Hansen, wrote on the morning of August 12, "The British effort appears to have bogged itself in timidity and succumbed to the legendary vice of over-caution."

It is only fair to note that Bradley was feeling some of the same cautious impulses as he considered the vulnerability of his southern pincer. His longtime misgivings about the inexperience of the forces comprising Haislip's XV Corps continued to concern him, especially after Ultra revealed the German plans to counterattack Haislip's left flank.

The magnificent performance of the XV Corps over the last week didn't make Bradley feel any better. He discussed the problem with General Eisenhower when Ike visited Bradley's headquarters near Laval. "With Ike's approval, I took steps to reinforce Haislip with the best troops I had in my command: Collins' VII Corps," Bradley wrote. "That afternoon [August 12], I ordered Collins to go all-out to the northeast, inserting his corps between Haislip and the bulk of the Germans withdrawing from Mortain."

"Lightning Joe" Collins had his divisions on the move that night, the Big Red One in the van, followed closely by the 9th Infantry and the 3d Armored.

Neither Haislip nor Patton was disposed to wait for reinforcements. At the same time that Eisenhower was visiting Bradley, Patton was visiting Haislip's advanced command post north of Le Mans. Patton told the XV Corps commander to disregard Montgomery's limits and be ready to drive on past Falaise if necessary.

Falaise did not look like an impossible goal for the XV Corps in the late afternoon of August 12. Despite the 5th Armored's repulse outside Argentan, Haislip's columns were still advancing at many other points, often finding huge gaps in the German defenses.

One of the gaps turned out to be the Forêt d'Ecouves. Haislip had planned to treat the forest as he did the Forêt de Perseigne to the south, by calling on the air force to firebomb it. However, Leclerc's decision to send Colonel de Langlade's combat command through the woods almost caused a tragedy. The bombing attack was barely canceled in time. It took de Langlade's men less than two hours to push the remnants of the 9th Panzer Division out of the forest and onto the open ground in front of Argentan, where Pete Quesada's Thunderbolts became a great help rather than a great threat.

As darkness fell that Saturday evening, the sound of rifle fire was audible to the citizens of Argentan. Leclerc's three columns were converging on Ecouche, just west of Argentan. To the east, Oliver's Combat Command R had reached National Highway 24, the main east-west route through Argentan. Patrols from both the French 2d Armored Division and the American 5th Armored Division were actually scouting routes north of Argentan.

Haislip shifted his forces in preparation for one more leap. He gave Leclerc permission to take Argentan and ordered Oliver to assemble his division southeast of town. Thirty minutes before midnight, he called Patton's headquarters, informed the Third Army commander that he was about to seize Argentan, and mentioned that he had no mission beyond that. Haislip reminded Patton of his earlier order to "be prepared to push on beyond Falaise, if necessary." Should Patton authorize his corps to move northward, Haislip said, the 5th Armored Division was prepared to strike immediately to effect a rendezvous with the Canadians.

Patton could sense the opportunity before him. So he ignored the standing orders to halt at Argentan. Instead, Patton called Haislip at forty minutes after midnight and passed on a different message, telling him: "Push on slowly in the direction of Falaise, allowing your rear elements to close. Road: Argentan-Falaise your boundary inclusive. Upon arrival Falaise continue to push on slowly until you contact with our Allies."

Slowly is a relative term. By Sunday morning, August 13, Haislip's patrols were already eight miles past Argentan and within six miles of Falaise. Although the Germans were still defending Argentan fiercely, there was little resistance beyond the city. Falaise was there for the taking.

But Haislip was not allowed to take it.

The stop order reached Patton at 1130 hours on Sunday morning, August 13. His chief of staff, Maj. Gen. Hugh Gaffney, took the message, reporting to his boss that by order of General Bradley, the Anglo-American boundary in the Falaise-Argentan sector was not to be crossed under any circumstances.

"You're kidding," Patton said, a look of astonishment on his face.

The Third Army commander immediately tried to call Bradley, but the commander of the 12th Army Group was at Shellburst, the code name for General Eisenhower's new headquarters in France. Patton phoned Maj. Gen. Lev Allen, Bradley's chief of staff, and pleaded with him to rescind the stop order.

Allen located Bradley at Shellburst and conveyed Patton's request. Bradley was furious when he learned that Patton had ordered Haislip's corps forward beyond Argentan without his permission. "Patton had knowingly and willingly violated an Allied agreement. He had placed his troops in no-man's-land, where they were exposed to Allied air attack. He had extended Haislip's vulnerable left flank even further, knowing full well Ultra had forecast a German counterattack on that very day."

Bradley discussed the situation with General Eisenhower, who was at first inclined to take the bold course, as he had counseled earlier in the week. Now, however, he was swayed by his subordinate's arguments. Eisenhower stood next to Bradley and listened as he called Patton to break the bad news.

Patton's attitude only made Bradley madder.

"We've got elements in Argentan," Patton reported, stretching the truth a bit. "Let me go on to Falaise and we'll drive the British back into the sea for another Dunkirk!"

"Nothing doing," Bradley replied, trying to restrain his anger. "You're not to go beyond Argentan. Just stop where you are and build up on that shoulder . . . The Germans [are] beginning to pull out. You'd better button down and get ready for him."

Bradley was acting on an intelligence report by Brig. Gen. Edwin Luther Sibert, his intelligence officer (G-2). He estimated that the nineteen German divisions west of the Falaise-Argentan line were already stampeding east.

"I much preferred a solid shoulder at Argentan to a broken neck at Falaise," Bradley later wrote.

Actually, only a few nonessential units had begun their withdrawal from the threatened envelopment. And only Eberbach's grandly styled

"Panzer Group" was rushing to attack Haislip's corps. It was not a formidable force. The bulk of the 116th Panzer Division had joined its advanced infantry battalion in front of Argentan, but Col. Walter Reinhard, who had replaced the disgraced General von Schwerin in command of the Greyhounds, had just fifteen tanks left. The artillery of the 1st SS Panzer Division arrived, but the rest of the battered Liebstandarte would not reach the Argentan sector until the next day. The 2d Panzer Division was even farther behind on the roads from Mortain.

It appeared obvious to the Germans that there was no way they could erect a defensive line in time to prevent Haislip from linking up with the Canadians. On the morning of August 13, at the same moment that Patton was having his argument with Bradley, Gen. Fritz Bayerlein, once the commander of the crack Panzer Lehr Division, now leading a hodgepodge described as "Combat Group Panzer Lehr," saw first-hand just what the Germans were up against. His unit set up a defensive position near the village of Habloville, about four miles northwest of Argentan. But the moment the sun burned off the morning haze, a squadron of fighter-bombers pounced on Bayerlein's position. The Jabos roared in below treetop level, shooting everything that moved. On the next pass, they targeted farms and barns and small clumps of wood—anything that could shelter German troops. Bayerlein and his staff were forced into a slit trench near the burning farmhouse that had been his command post.

"A fighter-bomber roared up from the road towards the orchard," Bayerlein recorded. "Barely thirty feet up, it skimmed over the tops of the apple trees. It banked. The pilot was peering out of the cockpit. I could see his face. The pilot seemed to be laughing and saying, 'Just stay put. I'm coming back in a minute!'"

The P-47 poured 20mm cannon shell into the trench. Two bombs followed, burying Bayerlein and his men in an avalanche of dirt and tree limbs. Those who survived the attack had to dig themselves out. Every one of the survivors was wounded.

Sepp Dietrich, Eberbach's successor as commander of the Fifth Panzer Army, was the first to warn of the danger facing the Germans in France. The Nazi general (he started his career as commander of Hitler's personal bodyguard) told Lt. Gen. Hans Spiedel that morning, "If the front . . . is not withdrawn immediately and every effort is not made to move the forces towards the east and out of the threatened encirclement, the army group will have to write off both armies."

But Dietrich was wrong. The Germans would hold the Falaise-Argentan Gap open for another week—a week that saw perhaps forty thousand of the one hundred thousand men who would have been trapped there on August 13 escape to fight another day.

Patton's earlier prophecy had come true. The Boche couldn't stop him, but Montgomery's "goddamn boundary lines" could and did.

General Bradley never would concede that his stop order was a mistake. Instead, he criticized General Montgomery for not closing the gap. He couldn't understand his colleague's tactics. The Canadians stood still in front of Falaise, while the British mounted an offensive toward the western end of the pocket.

"Rather than close the trap by capping the leak at Falaise, Monty proceeded to squeeze the enemy out toward the Seine," Bradley wrote. "A golden opportunity had truly been lost. I boiled inside, blaming Monty for the blunder. We had done our part, setting the lower jaws at Argentan and restrained Patton from a brash and foolish overextension."

Although Bradley admitted the intelligence estimates that caused him so much concern were "wrong—egregiously wrong," he still argued that Haislip's XV Corps was not strong enough to close the gap. "Patton might have spun a line across that narrow neck, [but] I doubted his ability to hold it."

Patton hotly disputed Bradley's lack of faith in the XV Corps. It is hard to argue with the numbers. As one commentator pointed out, on August 13, when the halt order was given, Panzer Group Eberbach possessed just seventy tanks and a few battered infantry formations, many strung out on the road from Mortain, whereas Haislip "could muster over three hundred Shermans, twenty-two battalions of artillery and two infantry divisions, all with sky-high morale, and under the experienced leadership of [commanders] spoiling for a fight and, adding to these advantages, the complete control of the air."

The latter was Patton's trump card. "If I had worried about flanks, I could have never fought the war," he claimed. "I was convinced our Air Service could locate any groups of enemy large enough to be a serious threat, and then I could always pull something out of a hat to drive them back while the Air Force delayed their further advance."

Bradley also protested that allowing Haislip to advance could have led to a tragic confrontation between Allies: "Any head-on juncture becomes a dangerous and uncontrollable maneuver unless each of the advancing forces is halted by prearranged plan on a terrain objective." Yet Bradley later provided the solution to just that danger when he suggested that the axis of advance of the two armies could be shifted east or west, providing a double (and stronger) barrier across the German escape route.

As it turned out, the barrier was not closed until the night of August 19, when Company G of the 90th Division's 359th Infantry Regiment made contact with a Polish armored regiment in the tiny village of Chambois. The next day, troops from the 80th Infantry Division finally captured Argentan.

Patton's boast that he could push on to Falaise and "drive the British into the sea for another Dunkirk" was to prove an especially apt reference. There were some remarkable similarities between the escape of the British Expeditionary Force (BEF) from Dunkirk in 1940 and the escape of two German armies from the Falaise Pocket—or the Falaise-Mortain Pocket, as General Montgomery called it in his memoirs—in 1944.

Both escapes were made possible by controversial stop orders. Just as Hitler's decision to halt Guderian on May 24, 1940, allowed the Allies time to erect a strong defensive barrier around Dunkirk, so did Bradley's halt order of August 13 allow Eberbach time to build a barrier strong enough to hold open the Falaise-Argentan Gap.

Both escaping armies saved men at the expense of equipment. The BEF, of course, left almost all of its equipment on the beaches and in the sand dunes surrounding Dunkirk. Left behind by the retreating Germans in 1944 were 688 tanks or self-propelled guns and more than a thousand pieces of artillery. In the 21st Army Group sector alone, the Germans abandoned 1,778 trucks and 669 cars, a huge loss for an army so short of vehicles that it was still heavily dependent on horse-drawn transport.

There is no agreement on exactly how many Germans escaped from the pocket. Two large forces broke through the barrier on August 20. Smaller groups continued to slip through the Allied lines as late as August 23. However, the Allies took approximately fifty thousand prisoners and counted more than ten thousand dead Germans in the pocket. Somewhere between twenty thousand and forty thousand Germans escaped the trap, but only a small proportion of that number were combat troops. Most of the escapees were the rear-echelon units, which were the first ordered to withdraw.

Like the British in 1940, the retreating Germans in 1944 were punished from the air, although the Germans suffered much more heavily in 1944, since the Allied air forces had far more firepower—and far less opposition—than the 1940 Luftwaffe.

Hitler's failure to destroy the BEF at Dunkirk was to cost him the war. Bradley's failure to close the Falaise-Mortain Pocket was to cost the Allies a chance to end the war in 1944. The forces that escaped the trap in August were able to re-form in time to man the next German line of that defense, the Westwall along the German border. Units that escaped annihilation in the pocket—units like the 1st and 10th SS Panzers, the 3d and 5th Parachute divisions, and the Panzer Lehr Division—would be reborn to haunt the Allies at places like Arnhem, Aachen, and the Bulge.

Still, as Winston Churchill pointed out in 1940, Dunkirk was a British defeat. And the Falaise Pocket was a German disaster second only to Stalingrad. It broke the enemy's hold on France and allowed the Allies to drive all the way to the German border before supply problems slowed the advance and gave the enemy a chance to recover.

The Allied victory at Falaise has been justly celebrated. But it should be remembered that the entire campaign turned on the Battle of Mortain. The original Overlord plan called for a ponderous straight-front advance across France. Only Hitler's decision to gamble on a counterattack at Mortain allowed Bradley to gamble on an envelopment west of the Seine. That Hitler's gamble failed and Bradley's gamble succeeded was due to the doggedness of the Mortain defenders, who held back the first onslaught, then fought for a week with little help while Patton's armored columns sliced through the German rear.

"Although not highly publicized, the stand made by Hobbs' 30th Infantry Division ranks as one of the more important defensive actions of World War II," the U.S. Army Command and General Staff College concluded in a 1984 report. "Halting the Germans on the first day of the attack proved to be the catalyst of the campaign in northern France."

Bradley acknowledged his debt to the Old Hickory soldiers, whose courage had provided him with "an opportunity that comes to a commander not more than once in a century." The 30th Division, he wrote, "held nobly on the hinge and with such doggedness, we called it the Rock of Mortain."

CHAPTER 22: ROOSEVELT'S SS

The need to maintain pressure on the retreating Germans cut short the rest period that the men of the 30th Division had earned at Mortain. The battle's survivors were given Saturday afternoon and evening off. By Sunday morning, August 13, Old Hickory was attacking again.

"We got one good meal, a good night's sleep, then we were off again at 5:00 A.M.," said Sergeant Myers. "The next three days, we covered sixty-seven miles cross-country."

Private Neidhardt was caught by surprise when F Company was ordered out. "I had found a duck egg and I was going to boil it for breakfast. I never got a chance to eat it." Neidhardt, a raw replacement just one week earlier, was now a combat veteran, lording it over the new replacements who had joined his squad. "After the battle, I was part of the group. But it's not like in the movies, where everybody's real chummy. You're better off if you don't get too chummy with anybody."

Before the movement began, the 30th Division was shifted from General Collins's VII Corps to Maj. Gen. Charles Corlett's XIX Corps. The GIs, not really caring where the division fit in the army's table of organization, boarded trucks for a twelve-mile journey through Barenton toward Domfront. The next day, the 30th advanced four miles on foot. Domfront was defended by a ragtag collection of depot companies, a flak battalion, and labor troops. Many of the German defenders were captured drunk. The GIs took the town on August 15, along with a formidable razorback ridge overlooking the city.

"After making like mountain goats up that very steep hill, which for reasons I'll never understand the enemy did not defend, we finally reached the top," Lieutenant Pulver said. "We felt like dropping in our tracks, but at that moment a salvo of 88 shells whistled over our heads. This gave us some newfound energy to get the hell off the hill."

The 30th continued to push northeast against light resistance, driving past Domfront as the Falaise Pocket collapsed. The division reached the boundary line of the British zone on August 16 and General Hobbs was finally able to let some of his weary battalions rest. Lieutenant Colonel Ernest Frankland's 1st Battalion of the 117th actually got three whole days off, even if they were spent in a field just outside Domfront. A beat-up barn was converted into a movie theater, but more importantly, the bone-weary GIs were allowed to shower and sleep.

The rest period didn't last long. Frustrated by the British failure to close the Falaise Gap, General Bradley had already ordered General Patton to send the XV Corps on another flanking maneuver to the east. The riflemen of the 30th Division climbed aboard the trucks again on August 19 for a 120-mile drive to an assembly area near Dreux, just forty-two miles west of Paris.

"This great move was certainly a triumphal procession," wrote one anonymous officer. "Frenchmen from outlying districts practically lined the route of our advance. They were wild with joy and happiness. They threw flowers and fruit at our vehicles whenever a slight pause was made and offered wine and Calvados . . . One old man had apparently stood by the side of the road all day in order to shout the only words of English he knew. Very slowly and with great emphasis he cried, 'Heeeep! Heeep! Whooray.' "

The GIs riding the trucks were certain they would be called on to help liberate Paris. Instead, Old Hickory was ordered to advance northeast from Dreux, toward the ferries over the lower Seine River.

The next two weeks were a kaleidoscope of experiences as the division raced across France, reaping the harvest of its victory at Mortain. There were still moments of sharp combat. The fast-moving spearheads sometimes bypassed pockets of resistance. Lieutenant Colonel William Bradford, who had commanded the 120th's 1st Battalion for barely a month, was badly wounded in a firefight at a place he nicknamed "Lightning Alley" after watching an unending stream of tracers illuminate the night sky. Near Val David, a small German counterattack almost reached the division command post before it was beaten off with artillery. The 230th FA Battalion captured 343 prisoners after the engagement.

Still, there were far more moments of celebration, similar to the drive from Domfront to Dreux. Lieutenant Pulver remembers one brief stop, when he was invited to dinner with a French family. The farmer led Pulver into his garden, where he dug up a bottle of champagne. "This has been saved for the liberation," he told the young officer. During a dinner of rabbit, the farmer asked Pulver what one food he'd most desire if he were home. Pulver told his host how much he enjoyed a cold slice of watermelon during the hot days of August. The next morning, as Pulver was preparing to leave, the farmer presented his guest with a melon the size of a football.

"One of his farm helpers told me that our host had spent half the night walking a hazardous ten miles to pick up the melon," Pulver said.

Brigadier General William Harrison, along with his driver and his aide, liberated the town of Louviers, reaching the village ahead of the 117th's leading company. "As we drove into town, I could see a French flag hanging out the window," he said. "That told me there were no Germans left. As we approached the center of the town, we were met by a crowd of women and children. There were so many people we couldn't move the jeep."

Two days later, Lt. Raymond Flanner cautiously led a patrol from the 30th's recon troop into Pontoise, which was supposed to be held by a German rear guard. Back at division headquarters, Hobbs and his staff waited anxiously for Flanner's report. It was simple: "One-star general in Pontoise but no Germans." Regulations prohibited identifying a general officer by name, but Hobbs's staff knew that Harrison had liberated another French town on his own.

Harrison's boldness was to have its cost. Shortly after daybreak on September 2, his jeep ran into an ambush near the old World War I battlefield of Cambrai. A 75mm shell flipped the vehicle into a ditch and wounded Harrison in the leg, arm, and shoulder. Harrison managed to get his aide and driver back to safety. He then directed Col. Edwin Sutherland, the commander of the 119th Regiment, to reduce the roadblock. Only after that was accomplished did he allow himself to be evacuated to an aid station. The general was in the hospital for more than a week, but returned to duty on September 16.

When he returned, the 30th Division was still chasing the beaten enemy as quickly as the muddy roads and the long Allied supply line would allow. The American and British advance was still being supplied from the invasion beaches. As the beaches got farther away, more and more trucks were required to move supplies, leaving fewer trucks to move the troops forward. After Dreux, the 30th was allowed only enough vehicles to drive one regiment forward at a time. Hobbs was forced to adopt a leapfrog method of advance, driving one regiment forward, then leaving it to walk, while the other two regiments took their turns as the motorized spearhead.

The 30th Division crossed the Seine at Mantes-Gassicourt on August 27. There, Old Hickory briefly was loaned to the XV Corps to help the 79th Division extend its bridgehead. In a sense, Old Hickory's support for Maj. Gen. Ira Wyche's division could be viewed as partial payback for the way his troops helped take the pressure off the 30th at Mortain. The once-suspect divisions of the XV Corps were again in the forefront of the Third Army's advance. Wade Hampton Haislip's corps had become one of General Patton's favorite combat formations.

And the 30th Division, tough and confident after Mortain, was becoming the premier infantry division in the European theater. That status would be confirmed in September, when Old Hickory raced across the Meuse River and into Belgium. The 117th Regiment crossed the Albert Canal, while the 3d Battalion of the 120th captured the famous Fort Eban Emael. Actually, the German defenders had pulled out of the formidable bastion before the American attack, a bewildering decision that saved the regiment heavy casualties. Instead, the Germans chose to defend the locks of the Maas Canal, another strong position (and vital, because by blowing the locks, the Germans could have flooded the area around Maastricht, greatly slowing the Allied advance). However, a Belgian engineer showed Lt. Col. Paul McCollum two tunnels connecting the fort to the canal near the locks. McCollum and Col. Hammond Birks used the tunnels to get men to the canal just below the enemy position. Their surprise assault captured the locks before the Germans could set off their demolition charges.

To the north, the 117th Regiment pushed across the border into Holland, becoming the first Allied unit to enter that occupied country. Leading the way was Lieutenant Colonel Frankland's 1st Battalion, which was engaged in a fierce firefight soon after it crossed the border. During the "Small-Arms Battle," as it came to be known, a command car carrying a German general's aide was knocked out. The Germans counterattacked to try and reach the vehicle, but Lt. Elwood Daddow of B Company dashed out under fire and reached the car first. He recovered documents showing the location of every important German defensive position in the area.

That knowledge was to prove vital as the 30th Division reached its next obstacle, the Siegfried line. The 1st Infantry Division was already assaulting the German defensive position south of Aachen. Old Hickory's assignment was the segment north of the old German imperial city.

Sergeant Werner Goertz of Pulver's company was born in Aachen and lived there for sixteen years before immigrating to America. As the 30th prepared for its attack on the line, Goertz recognized the main road into the city. "How I wish I could walk down that road and visit my relatives," he told Pulver. "They live just a short distance inside the north side of the city." Goertz didn't get the chance. He was seriously wounded during the attack and had to be evacuated back to the United States.

Aachen would mark the end of the 30th's glorious advance after Mortain. The division had advanced 520 road miles in less than a month. But the miles were about to start coming hard again.

The Nazi propaganda broadcasts proclaimed that the Siegfried line was invincible. Old Hickory's GIs didn't quite believe the boasts. After all, their fathers and uncles had cracked the Hindenburg line, hadn't they? Still, the veterans of the hedgerows and of Mortain weren't looking forward to attacking the belts of pillboxes, minefields, and dugouts that stretched across their front. The northern part of the defenses was protected by the Wurm River, a thirty-foot-wide stream some four to six feet deep with steep banks and a soft bottom. Neither tanks nor tank destroyers would be able to cross until the riflemen secured the area and engineers built bridges. Another problem facing the division was the continuing supply bottleneck, which forced the artillery to ration its expenditure of ammunition.

The veteran infantrymen who would have to make the assault knew exactly what they were up against. Their answer to the problem was meticulous preparation. Lieutenant Robert Cushman, a platoon leader in B Company of the 117th, led one of the first nighttime patrols to probe the German positions.

"He came back dripping wet from the shoulders down, having waded across the Wurm River," Lieutenant Colonel Frankland reported. "He found, by reconnoitering the river on both sides, the best places to cross."

Working on information provided by such patrols, Frankland's intelligence officer, Lt. D. W. Morgan, constructed a sand table, using wooden blocks as houses and cabbage leaves for vegetation, and depicting all the German defensive positions. The company commanders brought their riflemen in every night to study the sand table. Up and down the line, Old Hickory's veterans made sure that they were thoroughly familiar with every detail of the German positions. In addition, every rifle company in the division was given a two-day refresher course in assault tactics.

The saturation bombing that preceded the assault on the Siegfried line turned out to be a major disappointment. Only 324 medium bombers and 72 fighter-bombers were available for the attack, and many of them missed the target due to the overcast. The Germans in their deep, well-protected pillboxes were largely undisturbed by the bombing attack. One prisoner, asked after the attack to describe the effect of the bombing, answered, "What bombing?"

But the training and preparation with the sand table paid off on October 2, when the 30th launched its assault on the Siegfried line. The 117th was on the left, the 119th on the right, and the 120th in reserve. The 117th's riflemen moved out at 1100 hours, taking their first casualties before they ever reached the river. "The result was more speed," one officer reported. The first wave laid a wooden footbridge across the river. The following troops raced forward in the face of heavy fire. Frankland's C Company, rebuilt after being nearly wiped out at Mortain, took eighty-seven casualties in the first hour alone. But the battalion knocked out eleven pillboxes and reached every one of its first-day objectives, then paused to beat off a midnight counterattack.

It took five days of fierce fighting, but the 30th Division blasted a hole in the vaunted Siegfried line "big enough to drive two divisions through," General Hobbs reported. "I have no doubts this line is cracked wide open."

Hobbs was ordered to push southward to make contact with the 1st Infantry Division, which was pushing north to encircle the large city of Aachen. It appeared to be a simple task. The division drove forward on October 8 to within four thousand yards of Crucifix Hill, the assigned boundary between the 1st and 30th divisions. That night, however, a strong German counterattack punched through the 30th's lines and penetrated to the command post of the 117th's 3d Battalion in Alsdorf. It was almost a replay of Frankland's experience at St.-Barthelmy. Lieutenant Colonel S. T. McDowell looked out the window of his CP and saw four German tanks approaching, supported by a strong force of infantry.

"We manned every window and took potshots," McDowell said. "I got four sures and three probables."

The defenders drove off the German infantry and knocked out three of the four attacking tanks, but one Mark V, dubbed the "Reluctant Dragon" by McDowell's men, wandered up and down the streets of Alsdorf for most of the next day. Lieutenant C. M. Spilman managed to shoot two of the tankers as they stuck their heads from the turret, but the Dragon evaded the few tank destroyers and bazooka teams in the town and escaped the next night.

By that time, the Germans were counterattacking all along the 30th Division's front. Over the next three days, intelligence identified elements from the 1st SS Panzer Division, the 2d Panzer, and the 116th Panzer—three of the four divisions involved in the Mortain counterattack. Once again Old Hickory held its ground and beat off everything the Germans could throw at them. Colonel Banner Purdue, who had just replaced Birks (who had been promoted to assistant commander of the 9th Division) in command of the 120th Infantry, got his first look at his Old Hickory veterans in action.

"These are the bravest men you ever saw," he told General Hobbs. "That 1st Battalion fought them off with the outposts. I never did see men going like these have been going. We are as strong as strong can be."

A patrol from the 119th Infantry finally made contact with the 1st Infantry Division on Crucifix Hill late in the afternoon of October 16, completing the encirclement of Aachen and ending two weeks of brutal combat for the 30th Division.

The 1st Division—the regular army's famous Big Red One—sent a formal letter of thanks to the division headquarters for its role in the capture of Aachen. However, the 1st Division commander, Maj. Gen. Clarence Huebner, delivered a more personal tribute about a week later, when he dropped in on an outpost of the 119th Regiment and introduced himself to the surprised GIs.

"I wish you'd get it around to your people," he told them, "that we never could have taken Aachen without your help."

If Aachen was a miniature version of Mortain, the celebrated Battle of the Bulge was a larger replay of the same action. This time the slow Allied advance and the bad winter weather gave the Germans time to assemble a truly formidable striking force in the Ardennes. And just as at Mortain, the Germans were able to attain total tactical surprise for their counterattack.

There were more parallels. The main German effort in the Ardennes was supposed to be made in the north, but it was stopped in its tracks by the fierce defense of Elsenborn Ridge by the 2d and 99th Infantry divisions, just as the main German effort along the ridge at St.-Barthelmy was halted by the 117th Infantry Regiment. The southern wing of the attack achieved a deep penetration in each battle, but in both cases, the failure to eliminate a large pocket of resistance in the rear proved fatal to the German hopes. In a wonderful bit of irony, the capture of Bastogne was attempted by the 17th Panzergrenadier Division, the same unit that tried and failed to capture Hill 314 at Mortain.

The crisis in the Ardennes drew in many of the old Mortain antagonists. The 1st SS Panzer Division was the spearhead for the Fifth Panzer Army. The 2d SS Panzers were also on hand, along with the 2d and 116th panzers. The former bypassed the 101st Airborne at Bastogne and made the deepest penetration of the battle. They reached the outskirts of Dinant before running into the U.S. 2d Armored Division, which checked them with a vicious counterattack at Celles, just three miles short of the Meuse. Just five months earlier, it had been contact with "Hell on Wheels" that stopped the 2d Panzer's drive down the Sée River valley.

When the German assault broke in the predawn hours of December 16, the 30th Division was still north of Aachen. The division's

G-2 summary for December 16 classed the action as a major German counterattack, but it didn't predict how important the faraway fight would be to Old Hickory. The 30th Division was due a long period of rest and refit after leading the Ninth Army's drive to the Roer. Included in the November combat was an assault at Mariadorf labeled by a Ninth Army staff officer as the "perfect infantry attack."

Casualties were not heavy during the month, thanks to the division's growing experience and efficiency. However, the 120th Infantry suffered a major loss when Capt. Ronal Woody was critically injured on the second day of the drive to the Roer. The Mortain veteran took shell fragments in the head and chest, including a piece of metal that punctured a lung and ended up very near his heart. "At the hospital, they were betting I wouldn't make it," said Woody, who beat the odds to return to his family—and his Buick sedan—back in Richmond. He got a promotion on retirement and went home a major.

The Ninth Army commander, Lt. Gen. William Simpson (who had commanded Old Hickory briefly in 1942), pulled the 30th Division out of the line in early December to rest the weary unit. Colonel Walter Johnson, commander of the 117th Infantry, left the afternoon of December 16 for seven days' leave in England. General Hobbs was supposed to fly out the next morning for a week in London. However, his plane was delayed, and Hobbs was still on hand when the new XIX Corps commander called at 1115 hours.

"Just got a call from General Simpson, and he's taking you away from us," said Maj. Gen. Raymond McLain.

Seven months earlier, Hobbs was unhappy to have a National Guardsman commanding his artillery. Now, the former Oklahoma banker, who had turned the 90th Division into one of the best fighting forces in the European theater, was Hobbs's boss. McLain was the only National Guardsman to achieve corps command during the war.

McLain ordered Hobbs to prepare for a rapid movement. Trucks were filled and put on the road as quickly as possible. The 119th Regimental Combat Team was first to depart. Colonel Johnson returned from England just in time to lead the 117th out next. The 120th Infantry, holding a small piece of the Ninth Army's front, had to wait for the 29th Division to take its place before moving out seven hours after the 30th's lead elements.

The move was supposed to be a secret, but as the division's long convoy moved south under the dark, gray December sky, the GIs heard Axis Sally report, "the fanatical 30th Division, Roosevelt's SS troops, are rushing to the rescue of the First Army."

And rushing, it turned out, toward another meeting with Hitler's SS. The last few miles of the journey south were a nightmarish traffic jam, as the advancing convoy had to fight its way though streams of retreating vehicles. It was dawn of December 18 when the 117th Regiment, the first to arrive (the 119th having paused briefly at Hauset, Belgium), reached its assembly area near Malmédy. The GI grapevine was already buzzing with news of the massacre committed nearby, where 140 unarmed prisoners were gunned down (and at least 83 killed) by their captors, SS panzertroopers from an old 30th Division foe, the 1st SS Panzer Division.

Twice before, at Mortain and at Aachen, "Roosevelt's SS" had met and defeated Hitler's SS lifeguards on the field of battle. Now the 30th Division was to do it one more time.

As the troops moved forward, they passed hordes of fleeing refugees, both civilians and GIs from shattered units. Panic and confusion filled the air. But the 30th's GIs, infuriated by the rumors of the Malmédy massacre and confident of their own abilities, went about their duty with grim determination.

The 117th was first ordered to hold the threatened town of Malmédy, but before the soldiers could dig in, General Harrison arrived and told Colonel Johnson to rush a battalion five miles southwest to Stavelot, where the green 526th Armored Infantry Battalion was trying to hold the town and its vital bridge over the Amblève River. The 1st Battalion approached Stavelot on the morning of the eighteenth. Just outside the town, they found a large group of the armored infantrymen sitting around, eating K rations. "The Germans ran us out," one of the 526th's men reported.

That changed the mission of Lieutenant Colonel Frankland's battalion from relief to assault. Without hesitation, the 1st Battalion plunged into the town. Frankland's men wrestled the town square away from the Germans, but without armored support they could go no farther against the King Tigers and Panthers blocking the streets leading to the vital Amblève River bridge.

Hobbs was trying to find help for the embattled battalion, but he was having problems bringing order to his chaotic front. The 119th Regiment was forced to swing west to protect approaches to the First Army headquarters and supply dumps at Spa. When the 120th Infantry reached the assembly area outside Malmédy at sundown on the eighteenth, it was needed to defend that key road junction.

Lieutenant Pulver's company was assigned to construct a roadblock on the Malmédy–St.-Vith highway. About three hours after midnight, while his troops were still fortifying their positions, an American half-track, leading a long column of tanks and other vehicles, approached from the south. The half-track hit a mine that the GIs had laid just minutes before. The explosion blew off the vehicle's front wheels, bringing the column to a halt. A group of German soldiers climbed out of the half-track and approached Pulver's position, their identities obscured by the darkness.

One of them yelled, "Hey, we're American soldiers. Don't shoot!"

Some of Pulver's men hesitated, but two of his veteran sergeants were not fooled. Almost simultaneously, one of them opened up with his BAR, mowing down the approaching German soldiers, while the other used his bazooka to knock out a tank destroyer behind the disabled half-track. The two wrecked vehicles blocked the road, giving Pulver time to call in artillery on the blocked column.

"Things remained pretty hot until daylight," Pulver said. "We could hear the tanks moving around, but our artillery was giving them hell. Soon the tanks backed off, turned around and retreated."

As the foggy dawn of December 19 broke over the Ardennes, the 30th Division was finally in place, stretched along a seventeen-mile front. It was not a connected, fortified defensive line but a series of blocking positions separated by the forest-covered hillsides. The 120th was on the left, protecting Malmédy; the 117th was in the center, clinging to its share of Stavelot; and the 119th was strung out on the right between Stoumont and Spa. Deployed across the division's front was the 1st SS Panzer Division, which was trying to drive west to Liège— the same city whose German name (Lüttich) was the code word for the failed counterattack at Mortain.

The powerful German spearhead, commanded by Lt. Col. Joachim Peiper, was just outside Stoumont (about three miles beyond

Stavelot). The only forces between Peiper and his objective were the 3d Battalion of the 119th Infantry, supported by a company of the 823d TD Battalion and a company of Shermans from the 743d. Unfortunately, the 30th's artillery wasn't yet in position to support Lieutenant Colonel Sutherland's riflemen. Peiper, whose Kampfgruppe contained more than forty Panther and Tiger tanks, hit the American lines at dawn and began to push the outnumbered GIs back towards the tiny villages of Targnon and Stoumont Station (about four kilometers west of Stoumont). With the thick fog and overcast skies protecting the Germans from air attack, and no artillery to protect the infantry, the situation looked desperate.

Lieutenant Tom Springfield, who commanded the roadblock at L'Abbaye Blanche, kept his antitank guns in action even after the withdrawal of the supporting infantry. Springfield saw his guns knocked out one by one, but not before destroying at least one Tiger tank and several other vehicles. Springfield's men abandoned their equipment (losing six half-tracks and eight 3-inch guns) and slipped out of town. Springfield was the last man out of Stoumont.

Sutherland did all he could to help, feeding in his 1st Battalion as reinforcements. Springfield's men returned to battalion maintenance and rearmed themselves with four 3-inch guns and two captured German 75mm guns. They took up positions at the northern end of Sutherland's frail line. Just after noon, the 740th Tank Battalion, fresh from the States, made a dramatic appearance on the battlefield. Their equipment was still en route, but the enterprising tankers raided a supply depot and "liberated" an odd assortment of tanks and antitank equipment. In ten blazing minutes, one of the raw Sherman crews knocked out three Panthers with four shots; another new crew knocked out two more Panthers at 150 yards, then killed a King Tiger at the remarkable range of 1,200 yards.

Still, Sutherland and his men were surprised when Peiper called off his attack just as the Germans were on the verge of breaking into open country. Sutherland didn't know that Frankland's battalion, which had beaten off a major counterattack in Stavelot just after midnight, had renewed its advance at dawn, driving the Germans out of Stavelot and seizing one end of the bridge over the Amblève River. The action cut off Peiper's Kampfgruppe, which was running out of fuel. Unable to capture any of the huge American supply dumps defended by the 30th Division or to draw on supplies from the rear, Peiper's force was left to wither in Stoumont. The Germans tried desperately to reopen the lines of communication. But Frankland's battalion, now strongly supported by the 823d TD Battalion and artillery, beat off six distinct counterattacks on December 20. One platoon of the 823d killed six Tiger tanks trying to cross the Amblève bridge. When panzergrenadiers tried to swim the icy river, Frankland's riflemen calmly mowed them down. Two days later, more than a thousand German bodies were counted lining the banks of the Amblève; eight tanks, fifteen half-tracks, twenty-one trucks, and forty other vehicles in the area were destroyed. Finally, on the night of December 20–21, Frankland ordered his engineers to blow up the bridge, ending any chance for the 1st SS Panzers to reestablish contact with Peiper's group.

It took four more days to wipe out Peiper's force, but Old Hickory—with the help of another old Mortain friend, CCB of the 3d Armored Division—patiently sliced the Kampfgruppe into manageable pieces and swallowed them one by one. Only eight hundred of Peiper's original four thousand men escaped, and even they had to abandon their equipment and slip back through the American lines on foot. On Christmas Eve, at La Glieze, the 119th Infantry Regiment captured the remnants of the once-powerful formation: thirty-nine tanks, seventy half-tracks, thirty-three guns, and thirty other vehicles.

At Malmédy, the 120th Infantry held its position with the same tenacity it had shown at Mortain. Unfortunately, the air force couldn't seem to get the word that Malmédy was in friendly hands. When the weather cleared on December 23, the town was bombed for four successive days and reduced to smoldering ruins.

It wasn't that the Germans didn't try to take Malmédy. Strong assaults were beaten off on December 21 and 23. It was during the latter attack that S. Sgt. Paul Bolden of Company E earned a posthumous Medal of Honor for single-handedly attacking and killing thirty-five panzergrenadiers.

Bolden was one of the three hundred unwounded survivors of Hill 314. Private First Class Leo Temkin was one of his best friends. "He was a farm boy from Alabama," Temkin said. "Paul couldn't read or write, so I wrote letters for him to his parents. They couldn't read either, but they had somebody to write for them and I'd read him their letters. He was a wonderful boy."

The 30th Division remained in the Ardennes for the rest of December and most of January, holding the northern shoulder of the Bulge and joining the 82d Airborne to retake St.-Vith. Still, by Christmas Day of 1944, it was clear that Roosevelt's SS had won its third major battle with Hitler's lifeguards.

Unlike Mortain, the 30th was only one of the many heroic divisions that fought together in the Ardennes to foil the German counterattack. But like Mortain, the full fruits of the GIs' victory in the Battle of the Bulge were to be thrown away by the generals.

When the Germans counterattacked at Mortain, General Bradley had elected to gamble on a bold course that almost turned the crisis into a war-winning victory. General Eisenhower had the same response to the Ardennes counterattack, telling his subordinates, "The present situation is to be regarded as one of opportunity for us and not of disaster."

Unfortunately, Eisenhower made an administrative decision to give Field Marshal Montgomery—he had been promoted in September—control of all Allied forces north of the Bulge, including the U.S. First and Ninth armies. If Eisenhower thought that Montgomery would move with more boldness than he had displayed at Falaise, he was soon to be disappointed.

Bradley, who bitterly opposed the decision, knew what to expect. When Lt. Gen. Courtney Hodges relayed Montgomery's opinion that it would be three months—three months!—before the First Army was strong enough to resume the offensive, Bradley went ballistic. He wrote:

> Although initially Monty had assured Ike that he saw no need to give ground, he was now giving it. Against strong objections from Jim Gavin, Monty ordered Gavin's 82d Division to withdraw farther to the north and "tidy up" the battle line . . . It was the darkest of times for me. Owing to Monty's caution and conservatism, it practically assured that we would fail to cut off the German salient with a bold thrust from the north. The enemy would escape in force as it had escaped from the Falaise Gap. We were going to lose a golden opportunity to destroy the German war machine west of the Rhine.

I prayed for the souls of the dead American GIs, whose stubborn courage had already doomed the German offensive.

It would take more stubborn courage for the Allied armies to finish the job. And there would be many, many more dead GIs in the last four months of combat.

The 30th Division spent two months under British control. It wasn't an experience the division's veterans remember fondly.

"The British moved slowly because their planning was slow," said Maj. Warren Giles, the 117th's intelligence officer. "The Americans moved much faster because they didn't have to stop and plan everything. You could never depend on the British. You couldn't tell what they were going to do. If they wanted to stop in the middle of an advance and have tea, that's just what they'd do."

The 30th Division returned to Ninth Army control on January 27, 1945, and was immediately ordered back to its original staging areas around Aachen. On February 23, after a three-week delay caused by heavy winter rains, the division joined the rest of the XIX Corps in a textbook assault across the Roer River.

The 30th was continuing its tradition of excellence despite the loss of many veteran officers. Reynold Erichson was rotated home in January, returning to Miles, Iowa, to marry the girl next door. Colonel Purdue had another ticket home that month. But he couldn't decide who deserved it more, Capt. Ralph Kerley or Capt. Joseph Reaser. Their records were almost identical: both had earned the Distinguished Service Cross at Mortain; both had been awarded a Silver Star; both had Purple Hearts.

"I can't choose between you," Purdue told the two company commanders. "Cut the cards."

Kerley drew first. He pulled the ace of spades out of the deck. "I always have been lucky," he told Reaser.

Soon after Erichson and Kerley left for home, General Simpson selected the 30th to spearhead the Ninth Army's crossing of the Rhine. Hours before the first wave left its assembly areas on March 23, Simpson and General Eisenhower visited the waiting troops. The Ninth Army commander asked Sgt. LeRoy Sumner of the 117th's B Company if he thought he would make it across all right. "General," the Mortain veteran replied (he earned the Purple Heart on the second day of the battle), "if B Company can't make it tonight, you can give up hope for the whole Ninth Army."

Simpson was putting a lot of faith in the 30th Division. Its reputation was so fearsome that special precautions were taken to mislead the Germans. Old Hickory left its assembly area with all unit patches removed and all vehicle markings obliterated. Meanwhile, a special group of troops emblazoned with the 30th Division insignia moved out in the opposite direction. Similar measures were taken to protect the identity of the 79th Division on Old Hickory's right.

The deep, swift Rhine was more than a thousand feet wide at the 30th's crossing point. The division's attack was preceded by another saturation bombing attack, this time by three hundred Lancasters of the RAF. It is not clear how badly the aerial attack hurt the defenders, but none of the bombs fell on friendly troops, so the Old Hickory veterans counted it a successful prelude to their assault.

In fact, everything went well at first. The division crossed the river without incident, drove more than six miles in twenty-four hours, and captured more than fifteen hundred prisoners. On the morning of March 24, the 30th advanced another four miles, tearing a huge hole through the German 180th Infantry Division and reaching the autobahn that was the division's ultimate objective. The division's drive was halted only when the Germans committed the entire 116th Panzer Division to halt the 30th Division.

In a way, the counterattack of the old Mortain foe was a compliment: the Greyhound Division left its staging area north of the British Second Army, bypassing more than six Allied divisions so it could strike the one that the Germans feared most—Roosevelt's SS. One officer prisoner told his captors that when the 116th left its staging area in Holland, he was told by the division's chief of staff, "We're going to fight the 30th Division."

Old Hickory got another nickname during the Rhine crossing when Associated Press correspondent Wes Gallagher called the 30th "The American Army's work horse division." The 30th lived up to that nickname during the final seven weeks of the war, driving steadily through Germany until the division reached the Elbe River. On April 18, the 117th and 120th regiments captured Magdeburg after a sharp twenty-four-hour action. Leading the way, as it had led almost nine months earlier at Tessy-sur-Vire, was Company B of the 120th.

"A Polish refugee came out of a building waving a white flag," Lieutenant Pulver recalled. "He informed me in broken English that one bridge across the Elbe was left standing. He said it was mined, but he knew where the detonator was."

Pulver called Lt. Col. Ellis Williamson, the onetime trombone player who was now the regimental intelligence officer, and got permission to seize the bridge.

"Sergeant Dale Cloud volunteered to lead the way, and with the Pole, we scrambled over walls, chunks of buildings, and all kinds of carnage. The stench was horrible. Sergeant Cloud and his patrol reached the building where the detonator was. Suddenly, there was an enormous explosion. We dove for cover behind a high stone wall as pieces of steel and cement rained down around us. When the dust cleared, the bridge was no more."

Nobody knew it at the time, but the explosion of that bridge marked the end of combat for the 30th Division. Although some preliminary preparations were made for a dash to Berlin (about eighty kilometers away), the division was instead ordered to halt at Magdeburg. On May 4, the first Russians appeared on the other side of the river.

"The Russians were worse than the Germans," said Warren Giles, who was ordered to coordinate a meeting between American and Russian commanders on an island in the middle of the river. "I had a hell of a time going through Russian lines to reach their headquarters. They were suspicious of everybody."

Not all of the GIs had problems with their Allies. Private First Class Temkin enjoyed a pleasant meeting with some Russian soldiers. "They had some homemade vodka they shared with me," he said. "Boy, was it strong!"

American liquor did in a Russian liaison officer assigned to the 30th Division.

"He had this unpronounceable name," Giles said. "He also had a shaved head, so we nicknamed him Lieutenant Baldheadovich. We took him to a party with some nurses and he had a great time. But he made the mistake of telling his bosses and he never came back."

Going back was on the mind of all the division's soldiers, especially after the German surrender was announced on May 8. In fact, the rotation home started even before the end of the war. Lieutenant Pulver got his ticket stateside and left on May 2.

On that same day, the war finally ended for another Mortain veteran. Lieutenant George Greene, captured following his gallant defense of St.-Barthelmy, was liberated after nine terrible months in captivity. "They took us to Oflag 64 in Poland," he said. "There was nothing there. No food. No heat. On January 15, the Russians were getting close, so they moved us out. We had to walk fifteen hundred kilometers in the dead of winter. In forty-five days, we got thirty-nine bowls of hot water. They called it cabbage soup—that meant every three hundred gallons of water, there was one cabbage leaf. We had to look to each other to survive. We stole rotten potatoes the farmers had put out for their hogs. We stole seed grain. Once we passed some retreating German troops and we were able to trade cigarettes for a loaf of bread and some cheese."

Greene weighed 116 pounds when he was liberated.

The bulk of the 30th Division rode home in style, returning to the United States aboard the *Queen Mary*. Old Hickory was given a tumultuous welcome when it arrived in New York on August 21, 1945.

It wasn't long before the veterans of Mortain were back home, resuming their interrupted lives. Reynold Erichson, already married and back at his family farm, became the father of twin girls. Murray Pulver, who finally got to meet the son he'd never seen, entered college, attending Niagara University to qualify for a job as superintendent of the Gasport (New York) Water District. Delmont Byrn also returned to school, earning a graduate degree and serving for many years as a professor at the University of Michigan. Medic Robert Bradley reenrolled at the University of Maryland and became a physicist.

Hubert Pennington returned to Durham, North Carolina, where he helped re-form the postwar National Guard, rising to the rank of colonel. His prewar company commander, Lt. Dan Edwards, ended up as a major general in command of the North Carolina National Guard unit, which was designated as the 30th Mechanized Infantry Division, one of the successors to Old Hickory. Warren Giles, recalled to service during the Korean War, commanded a regiment in that action and eventually became a major general in command of the 30th Armored Division, the Tennessee National Guard's successor to Old Hickory.

Quite a few Mortain veterans saw action in Korea. Ralph Kerley, who stayed in the army after World War II, commanded a battalion in that conflict. William Kelly Harrison, who rose to the rank of lieutenant general, represented the U.S. Army at the armistice talks that finally ended the Korean War.

By then, Mortain was all but forgotten by the American people. Somehow it got lost in the rush of dramatic events that August—the controversy over the failure to close the Falaise Pocket, the liberation of Paris, the exhilarating rush to the German border. Mortain seemed just another victory in a tidal wave of Allied success. No one was anxious to publicize just how perilous the situation had been in the first hours of the attack, or just how vital the 30th Division's stubborn defense at Mortain was to the rapid reconquest of France.

The 30th Division never received the acclaim accorded units like the Big Red One, the 82d Airborne, or many of Patton's glamour divisions. Yet when S. L. A. Marshall, the U.S. Army's official historian, prepared a rating sheet for General Eisenhower, he picked the 30th as the finest infantry division in the European theater of operations. In a letter to General Hobbs, Marshall said:

> It is the combined judgments of the approximately 35 historical officers who had worked on the records and in the field that the 30th merited this distinction. It was our finding that the 30th had been outstanding in three operations and we could consistently recommend it for citation on any of these occasions. It was further found that it had in no single instance performed discreditably or weakly . . . and in no single operation had it carried less than its share of the burden or looked bad when compared to the forces on its flanks. We were especially impressed with the fact that it consistently achieved results without undue wastage of its men.

Marshall's rating was a tribute to the command team that put the 30th together. General Russell, who brought the National Guard unit into service, deserves a share of the credit. So does General McNair, who purged the guardsman in command and forced the 30th into a new shape. Certainly "Hollywood" Hobbs, despite all his critics, must have done something right, even if it was only letting assistant division commander William Kelly Harrison shape the division with his personality.

However, if the 30th was the finest American infantry division in Europe, the credit should go to the men who fought and bled and died on the front lines. The credit should go to Reynold Erichson and Ernest Frankland and Ronal Woody and Thomas Springfield and George Greene and all the GIs who demonstrated how good the American soldier can be, even when not given overwhelming material support.

The credit should go to the men who defended St.-Barthelmy against impossible odds, the men who manned the roadblock at L'Abbaye Blanche with such deadly skill, the men who refused to surrender Hill 314.

Their forgotten fight at Mortain deserves to be remembered.

SOURCES

The primary source for this book was the interviews collected by the author between September 1989 and December 1990. This project would have been impossible without the help of the veterans who fought at Mortain. Wherever possible, I've let them speak for themselves, without correction. In those rare instances where personal recollections are contradicted by the historical record, I've included notes addressing the discrepancies.

Another important resource is the collection of after-action interviews conducted by Colonel S. L. A. Marshall and his staff in the weeks following the battle. Many thanks to the staff at the National Archives in Suitland, Maryland, for making these materials available, in addition to the official journals and records of the 30th Division.

NOTES

Preface

Page xiii: "In his reckless attack . . . gain us France." Omar N. Bradley, *A Soldier's Story* (New York: Henry Holt and Company, 1951), 371.

Page xiii: "An astonishing failure . . ." *The Stars and Stripes* (Paris edition), June 26, 1945, 3.

Page xv: "On average . . . one German soldier is worth 1.55 Americans." T. N. Dupuy, *Numbers, Predictions and War* (Fairfax, VA: Hero Books, 1985), 104.

Page xv: "They are normal people . . ." Bill Mauldin, *Up Front* (Cleveland, OH: The World Publishing Company, 1945), 15.

Chapter 1: Old Hickory

Page 1: Figures for U.S. Army strength were derived from Mark Skinner Watson, The U.S. Army History of World War II, *The Chief of Staff: Prewar Plans and Preparations* (Washington, DC: Historical Division, Department of the Army, 1950), 16.

Page 2: "the . . . mock combat opened . . ." Russell F. Weigley, *Eisenhower's Lieutenants* (Bloomington: Indiana University Press, 1981), 1.

Page 3: "It is the feeling of the War Department . . ." H. A. De Weerd, ed., *Selected Speeches and Statements of General of the Army George C. Marshall* (Washington, DC: The Infantry Journal, 1945), 86.

Page 4: "During four months of fighting in 1918 . . ." Robert L. Hewitt, *Workhorse of the Western Front: The Story of the 30th Infantry Division* (Washington, DC: Infantry Journal Press, 1946), 2.

Page 5: "Company F . . . was a direct descendant . . ." *History of the 120th Regiment* (Washington, DC: Infantry Journal Press, 1947), 1.

Page 5: "Several of the regiment's companies . . ." *History of the 117th Infantry,* 2d reprint ed. (Baton Rouge, LA: Army and Navy Publishing Company, 1946), 21.

Page 8: "McNair . . . designed and oversaw . . ." Weigley, *Eisenhower's Lieutenants,* 22–24.

Page 8: "the two remaining regiments . . ." Robert R. Palmer, Bell I. Wiley, and William R. Keast, *The U.S. Army in World War II, The Procurement and Training of Ground Combat Troops* (Washington, DC: Historical Division, Department of the Army, 1948), 457.

Page 9: "General Henry Russell . . . ended up as officers." Henry D. Russell, *Purge of the Thirtieth Division* (Macon, GA: Lyon, Marshall and Brooks, 1948), 141.

Page 9: "Of the 108 men . . ." Warren Giles, *Company B, 117th Infantry* (Athens, TN: by the author, n.d.), 26.

Page 10: "Russell, in defending . . . wasn't one of them." Russell, *Purge of the Thirtieth,* 55.

Page 11: "Hobbs . . . had a big, strong jaw . . ." Omar N. Bradley and Clay Blair, *A General's Life* (New York: Simon and Schuster, 1983), 270.

Page 13: "always bragging or complaining." Charles B. MacDonald, *The Mighty Endeavor* (New York: William Morrow, 1969), 323.

Page 13: "strictly a barracks soldier . . ." D. Bruce Lockerbie, *A Man Under Orders: Lt. General William K. Harrison Jr.* (San Francisco, CA: Harper and Row, 1979), 71.

Page 13: "It was Harrison . . . I was on their side." Ibid., 76–77.

Page 14: "I'd known Ike . . ." Ibid., 80.

Page 14: "The General didn't storm . . ." Ibid., 80.

Page 16: "The rest of the division . . ." Hewitt, *Workhorse of the Western Front,* 6–7.

Page 16: "You will remember this day." *History of the 120th,* 8.

Page 17: "The men were issued . . ." William Lyman, *Curlew History* (Chapel Hill, NC: Orange Print Shop, 1948), 10.

Chapter 2: An Expensive Education

Page 18: "One of the first units to cross . . ." *On The Way: A Historical Narrative of the 230th Field Artillery Battalion* (n.p.: by the Battalion History Staff, n.d.), 11.

Page 20: "The 30th's Service Company . . ." Ibid., 9.

Page 20: "The beachhead was still so narrow . . ." *History of the 120th,* 9–11.

Page 22: "The order came down . . ." Lyman, *Curlew History,* 14.

Page 23: "Private Ken Parker . . ." Ken Parker, *Civilian at War* (Traverse City, MI: by the author, 1984), 4.

Page 24: "Pulver got his baptism of fire . . ." Murray S. Pulver, *The Longest Year* (Freeman, SD: Pine Hill Press, 1986), 10–11.

Page 25: "On July 7, a major attack . . ." Hewitt, *Workhorse of the Western Front*, 26.

Page 25: "the 3d Battalion stalled . . ." Lyman, *Curlew History*, 16.

Page 25: "the 3d Armored Division attempted . . ." Weigley, *Eisenhower's Lieutenants*, 131–32.

Page 26: "The 30th Division fought its way . . ." Hewitt, *Workhorse of the Western Front*, 33.

Page 26: "By nightfall of July 17 . . ." *History of the 120th*, 29.

Page 26: "Lieutenant Pulver . . . was forced to take over command . . ." Pulver, *The Longest Year*, 15–17.

Page 28: St.-Lô casualty figures: *St.-Lô: U.S. Forces in Action Series* (Washington, DC: Historical Division, U.S. War Department, 1946), 126.

Page 28: "a monstrous bloodbath . . ." Martin Blumenson, *The United States Army in World War II: Breakout and Pursuit* (Washington, DC: U.S. Army Center for Military History, 1961), 182.

Page 28: "Bradley understood . . ." Dwight D. Eisenhower, *A Crusade in Europe* (Garden City, NY: Doubleday and Company, 1948), 268.

Chapter 3: Cobra

Page 30: "The aerial bombardment . . ." Hewitt, *Workhorse of the Western Front*, 35.

Page 32: "The accident killed 25 . . ." Blumenson, *Breakout and Pursuit*, 229.

Page 32: "The airmen made all kinds of excuses . . ." Bradley and Blair, *A General's Life*, 279–80.

Page 33: "The first bombs fell . . ." Weigley, *Eisenhower's Lieutenants*, 153.

Page 34: "A couple of other generals . . ." Note: Several differing descriptions of McNair's death were related to the author by various witnesses. One veteran claims that the general was in a slit trench; another said that he panicked and was killed running away from the front line. Whitsett's description seems to match official reports that McNair was in a small dugout that suffered a direct hit by an American bomb.

Page 34: "Correspondent Ernie Pyle . . ." Ernie Pyle, *Brave Men* (New York: Grosset and Dunlap, 1943), 299.

Page 35: "Starched lace curtains . . ." Joseph Lawton Collins, *Lightning Joe: An Autobiography* (Baton Rouge: Louisiana State University Press, 1979), 240.

Page 35: "those whistling bombs suddenly sounded different . . ." Pulver, *The Longest Year,* 21–22.

Page 35: Casualty figures from Hewitt, *Workhorse of the Western Front,* 37, and Blumenson, *Breakout and Pursuit,* 236–37.

Page 36: Sergeant Floyd Montgomery's account of Harrison's intervention from a personal interview. Lockerbie claims that Harrison knocked out a German tank with a bazooka soon after the attack as he prodded the 30th Division into action (*Man Under Orders,* 95–96). For his role in the aftermath of the Cobra bombing, General Harrison was awarded the Distinguished Service Cross.

Page 37: Erichson's account from *History of the 120th,* 36–37.

Page xxx: "completely dejected and furious . . ." Bradley and Blair, *A 37 General's Life,* 280.

Page 37: "On the 4th Division front . . ." Pyle, *Brave Men,* 301.

Page 38: "each of these tanks . . ." *History of the 120th,* 37.

Page 38: "Col. Hammond Birks sent his other two battalions . . ." Weigley, *Eisenhower's Lieutenants,* 154.

Page 38: "The reports coming . . ." Ibid., 155.

Page 38: "The divisions were discouraged . . . 2d Armored." Collins, *Lightning Joe,* 242.

Page 39: "The frontline troops . . ." *History of the 120th,* 38.

Page 39: "By midafternoon . . . just north of Le Mesnil-Herman." Weigley, *Eisenhower's Lieutenants,* 155–56.

Page 39: "This thing has busted . . ." Blumenson, *Breakout and Pursuit,* 251.

Page 40: "To say that the personnel . . ." Bradley and Blair, *A General's Life,* 281.

Page 40: "Field Marshal Günther von Kluge . . . was primarily concerned . . ." Blumenson, *Breakout and Pursuit,* 226.

Page 40: "The Americans are to us . . ." Paul Fussell, *Wartime* (Oxford, England: Oxford University Press, 1989), 123.

Page 40: "It was hell . . . Five tanks arrived." Carlo D'Este, *Decision in Normandy* (New York: E. P. Dutton, 1983), 402.

Page 40: "The front has burst . . ." Blumenson, *Breakout and Pursuit*, 240.

Page 42: "I was back at battalion headquarters . . ." Note: This scene, described to the author by a veteran of the 120th Infantry, is unlikely. The 4th Armored Division actually passed through the 1st Infantry Division on the right flank. At this time, the 30th Division was on the far left flank of the breakthrough. Still, it illustrates the moral impact of Patton's arrival at the front.

Page 42: "It's one hell of a mess . . ." Blumenson, *Breakout and Pursuit*, 323.

Page 43: "Lieutenant Pulver's platoon . . . killed by the tankers' mistake." Pulver, *The Longest Year*, 25–26.

Page 44: "Edward G. Robinson . . . wanted to meet a German . . ." Norman F. Fay and Charles M. Kinkaid, *History of the 30th Division Artillery*, 1st reprint ed. (Florida: 30th Division Association, 1971), 26.

Page 44: Figures for 30th Division manpower taken from G-1 Period Chart of August 6, 1944, Record Group 407, Records of the Office of the Adjutant General, World War II Operational Reports, U.S. Army, National Archives, Suitland, MD (hereinafter referred to as *Suitland Archives*).

Page 45: "At first, Hobbs objected . . ." Lockerbie, *Man under Orders*, 105.

Page 45: "Pulver's first job . . ." Pulver, *The Longest Year*, 27–29.

Page 46: "The division orders . . ." 30th Division Training Directive, August 3, 1944, *Suitland Archives*.

Chapter 4: Operation Lüttich

Page 48: "von Kluge . . . tentatively suggested the idea . . ." John Keegan, *Six Armies in Normandy* (New York: Viking Press, 1982), 240.

Page 48: "Hitler's response . . ." Ibid., 240.

Page 49: "On August 2, he sent von Kluge . . ." Blumenson, *Breakout and Pursuit*, 423.

Page 49: "We must strike like lightning . . ." Keegan, *Six Armies in Normandy*, 241.

Page 49: "he told Gen. Adolf Kuntzen . . ." Blumenson, *Breakout and Pursuit*, 457.

Page 50: "the entire corps included less than 190 tanks . . ." Ibid., 461.

Page 51: "On the Dnieper River . . ." Erich von Manstein, *Lost Victories* (London: Arms and Armor Press, 1982), 487.

Page 51: "Das Reich struck like . . ." Ibid., 489.

Page 52: "a superb commander . . ." William Breuer, *Death of a Nazi Army,* 1st paperback edition (Chelsea, MI: Scarborough House, 1990), 177.

Page 52: "His division had performed . . ." Ibid., 177.

Page 52: "Von Kluge's plan, as it finally evolved . . ." Blumenson, *Breakout and Pursuit,* 457–58.

Page 53: "The headquarters . . ." R. von Gersdorff, *Normandy, Cobra and Mortain* (Carlisle, PA: U.S. Army Military History Institute), 12 (mimeographed).

Page 53: "Gen. Paul Hausser . . . felt that the attacking force . . ." Blumenson, *Breakout and Pursuit,* 460.

Page 53: "The German commander received . . ." Ibid., 458.

Page 55: "In order to assure . . ." Ibid., 459.

Page 56: "Von Kluge did not receive final approval . . ." Ibid., 460.

Chapter 5: Mortain

Page 57: Description of Mortain taken from 1944 GSGS maps, prepared by the British General Staff, and from descriptions provided during personal interviews. Note: The southeast peak of the hill east of Mortain is incorrectly identified on the U.S. Army's 1944 maps as 314 meters instead of 317 meters (as shown on the British maps). Most historians have followed Blumenson's lead and identified the hill as 317. Although that number does appear in some records (for instance, the 30th Division G-3 Journal), every veteran I interviewed remembered the position as Hill 314. That number is adopted by both Hewitt (*Workhorse of the Western Front*) and in all the unit histories. Therefore, I've chosen to use Hill 314 throughout my narrative. The same reasoning is behind the adopted spelling of St.-Barthelmy, which is often spelled St.-Barthelemy.

Page 58: "Mortain was liberated . . ." Eddy Florentin, *The Battle of the Falaise Gap,* trans. by Mervyn Savill (New York: Hawthorn Books, 1965), 37–38.

Page 58: "Ralph . . . be sure to get Hill 314 . . ." Blumenson, *Breakout and Pursuit,* 466. Note: Although Blumenson quotes Collins as saying "Hill 317" in both *Breakout and Pursuit* and in *The Duel for France*

(Boston: Houghton Mifflin Company, 1963), in an earlier article ("The Mortain Counterattack: Future Portent?" *Army Magazine,* July 1958, 30–38), he reported the same incident but quoted Collins as saying "Hill 314." Collins relies on Blumenson in his own account of the incident in *Lightning Joe,* published in 1979 (250). However, when Collins described the incident to a group of cadets at West Point in 1947, he reportedly used the designation "Hill 314."

Page 60: "They tell me he's fighting . . ." Bradley and Blair, *A General's Life,* 290.

Page 60: "Let's talk big turkey . . ." Ibid., 290.

Page 61: "There's nothing to speak of . . ." Lyman, *Curlew History,* 26.

Page 62: "On arriving at the hill . . ." *History of the 30th Division Artillery,* 28–29.

Page 62: "The positions prepared by the 18th . . ." Ralph Kerley, *Operations of the 2nd Battalion, 120th Infantry at Mortain, France* (unpublished monograph, U.S. Army Infantry School, Fort Benning, GA, 1948), 8.

Page 62: "Perhaps the battalion was suffering . . ." Ibid., 9–10.

Page 63: "To withdraw to the east . . ." 30th Division G-2 Report, August 6, 1944, *Suitland Archives.*

Page 63: "The movement was executed so rapidly . . ." Kerley, *Operations of the 2nd Battalion,* 8.

Page 64: "Erichson's 1st Platoon . . ." Combat interviews, 30th Infantry Division, Mortain and Domfront, August 6–15, 1944, Record Group 407, Records of the Office of the Adjutant General, World War II Operational Reports, U.S. Army, After-action reports, National Archives, Suitland, MD (hereinafter referred to as *Suitland Interviews*).

Page 64: "Springfield was not thrilled . . ." Lloyd J. Karamales, Charles M. Baily, Victoria I. Young, and Joyce B. Boykin, *U.S. Anti-tank Defense at Mortain, France (August 1944),* Anti-Armor Defense Data Study, McLean, VA, March 30, 1990 (McLean, VA: Science Applications International Corporations, 1990), 67.

Page 68: "Assuming that Barenton was in American hands . . ." After-action interview, *Suitland Interviews.*

Page 68: "The retreating Nazis . . ." Florentin, *Battle of the Falaise Gap,* 38.

Chapter 6: Countdown to H Hour

Page 70: "On August the second, in a long signal . . ." Frances William Winterbotham, *The Ultra Secret* (New York: Harper and Row, 1974), 148.

Page 70: "Bradley was told . . ." Ibid., 150.

Page 70: "This highly-important signal arrived . . ." Ibid., 148.

Page 70: "Hotter news there could hardly be . . ." Ralph Francis Bennett, *Ultra in the West: The Normandy Campaign* (New York: Scribner, 1980), 113.

Page 70: "There appears to be . . ." Ibid., 116.

Page 71: "My recollection is in sharp variance . . ." Bradley and Blair, *A General's Life*, 291.

Page 71: "The first real clue provided by Ultra . . ." Bennett, *Ultra in the West*, 114.

Page 71: "An earlier message . . ." Ibid., 114.

Page 71: "A third message . . ." Ibid., 115.

Page 72: "However, Maj. Melvin Helfers . . . How long has this officer been with us?" Robert A. Miller, *August 1944* (New York: Warner Books, 1988), 69–71.

Page 72: "Patton had received a phone call . . ." Bradley and Blair, *A General's Life*, 292.

Page 72: "Enemy counterattack expected vicinity Mortain . . ." 30th Division G-3 Journal, August 7, 1944, *Suitland Archives.*

Page 73: "Funck telephoned . . ." Hewitt, *Workhorse of the Western Front*, 56.

Page 73: "at La Fantay . . ." After-action interviews, *Suitland Interviews.*

Chapter 7: Out of the Fog

Page 75: "At 0100 hours, Lt. Anthony Ponticello . . ." Combat interviews, 9th Infantry Division, August 6–15, 1944, World War II Operational Reports, Office of the Adjutant General, After-action reports, U.S. Army Military History Institute, Carlisle, PA (hereinafter referred to as *Carlisle Interviews*).

Page 76: "The 39th Regiment's . . ." Ibid.

Page 76: "Company F . . . in the defile." Ibid.

Page 76: "It was not until 0300 . . ." Ibid.

Page 79: "A roadblock manned by a platoon of the 823d . . ." Earl V. Williams, Hobart Churchill, Morris Symons, and Andrew Holmes,

History of the 823rd Tank Destroyer Battalion, 1st reprint edition (Columbia, MO: I. C. Adams, 1951).

Page 79: "Private First Class Lloyd Briese . . . a tight spot." After-action interview, *Suitland Interviews.*

Page 79: "They were screaming at the top of their voices . . ." Kerley, *Operations of the 2nd Battalion,* 10.

Page 80: "His first warning . . ." Hewitt, *Workhorse of the Western Front,* 57.

Page 80: "Lieutenant Smith led his company into Mortain . . ." After-action interview, *Suitland Interviews.*

Page 81: "We are getting an attack . . ." 30th Division G-3 Journal, August 7, 1944, *Suitland Archives.*

Chapter 8: Dawn

Page 85: "Some artillery fire . . ." *History of the 30th Division Artillery,* 30.

Page 86: "Although 30th Division headquarters had assigned . . ." Hewitt, *Workhorse of the Western Front,* 58.

Page 86: "That peace was shattered . . . Hold at all costs." Pulver, *The Longest Year,* 31–32. Note: Both the *History of the 120th Infantry* and the regiment's after-action interviews mistakenly time the attack on Hill 285 as the morning of August 8. Both personal interviews and the division journals make it clear that the hill was attacked soon after dawn on August 7.

Page 87: "The enemy vehicle was so close . . ." Parker, *Civilian at War,* 56.

Page 87: "It was beginning to get light . . . Maybe they were as scared as I was." Pulver, *The Longest Year,* 32–33.

Page 89: "To Pulver's left . . ." After-action interviews, *Suitland Interviews.*

Page 89: "nearby Cannon Company . . . knocked out three more German tanks . . ." Pulver, *The Longest Year,* 31.

Page 89: "A mortar squad from D Company . . ." After-action interviews, *Suitland Interviews.*

Chapter 9: L'Abbaye Blanche

Page 93: "A German recon unit crossed the river . . ." Karamales, et al., *Anti-tank Defense,* 68–69.

Page 93: "The two 3-inch guns expended . . ." Ibid., 69.

Page 94: "A more direct threat materialized . . ." Ibid., 70.

Page 94: "The two 3-inch guns fired . . ." Ibid., 70.

Chapter 10: St.-Barthelmy

Page 97: "Frankland . . . was told that the only German troops . . ." After-action interview, *Suitland Interviews.*

Page 100: "The flashes from the machine gun . . ." Karamales, et al., *Anti-tank Defense,* 25.

Page 100: "During the delay . . . rejoin the Antitank Company." Ibid., 48–50.

Page 101: "When the attack was resumed . . ." After-action interview, *Suitland Interviews.*

Page 102: "If I'd realized the strength . . ." Ibid.

Page 102: "The embattled Able Company . . ." Ibid.

Page 102: "A column of Mark IV . . ." Ibid.

Page 103: "Two privates . . ." Ibid.

Page 103: "Martin's gun claimed . . ." Karamales, et al., *Anti-tank Defense,* 25.

Page 104: "A group of thirteen 2d Platoon men . . . and made his way back to the American lines." After-action interviews, *Suitland Interviews.*

Page 104: "Another refugee . . ." Ibid.

Page 104: "West of the highway . . . was captured." Ibid.

Page 105: "Frankland almost . . . tanks were to the rear." Ibid.

Page 106: "Moments after Christianson . . ." Karamales, et al., *Anti-tank Defense,* 26.

Page 107: "A Panther, supported . . ." Ibid., 53–55.

Page 108: "Greene's No. 3 gun scored its second kill . . ." Ibid., 26.

Page 108: "Greene was trying to move . . . pull the firing pin . . . and withdraw." Ibid., 27.

Page 108: "Greene's No. 2 gun was in similar trouble . . . where it began to burn." Ibid., 27–28.

Page 109: "A member of Greene's . . ." After-action interviews, *Suitland Interviews.*

Chapter 11: Daylight at Mortain

Page 111: "The roadblock accounted for . . ." Karamales, et al., *Anti-tank Defense,* 76.

Page 111: "The defenders were reinforced . . ." After-action interviews, *Suitland Interviews.*

Page 113: "We walked right up . . ." *History of the 120th,* 51–52.

Page 115: "Columns of enemy armor . . ." Kerley, *Operations of the 2nd,* 11.

Page 115: "Whether the enemy . . . could be fired on call." Ibid., 11.

Page 115: "Two batteries of the 197th . . ." After-action interviews, *Suitland Interviews.*

Page 115: "An urgent message . . ." Ibid.

Page 117: "The 197th lost . . ." Ibid.

Page 117: "The drive would have continued . . ." Blumenson, *Breakout and Pursuit,* 462.

Page 117: "A more serious threat . . . the other German tank pulled back." After-action interviews, *Suitland Interviews.*

Page 118: "Lieutenant Colonel Paul McCollum launched . . . without spotting them." Ibid.

Chapter 12: Chateau Nebelwerfer

Page 120: "Two more German tanks approached . . . " After-action interview, *Suitland Interviews.*

Page 122: "Johnson told me . . ." Lockerbie, *Man under Orders,* 106.

Page 122: "We were to organize a movement forward . . . drove away our fear." Ibid., 107.

Page 122: "dubbed the position . . ." After-action interview, *Suitland Interviews.*

Page 123: "With a heavy onion breath . . ." Hewitt, *Workhorse of the Western Front,* 58.

Page 123: "he didn't know if we would need it . . . take it anyway." Telecon, Collins and Hobbs, August 7, 1944, 1550 hours, *Suitland Archives.*

Page 123: "A patrol from one . . ." After-action interview, *Carlisle Interviews.*

Page 123: "Private First Class John Cole . . . as a prisoner." Ibid.

Page 124: "If they had exploited . . . on the ridge." Ibid.

Page 125: "For years historians . . ." Donald E. Houston, *Hell on Wheels* (San Rafael, CA: Presidio Press, 1977), 243.

Page 125: "It was Maj. Gen. J. Lawton Collins . . ." Collins, *Lightning Joe,* 253.

Page 126: "Unfortunately, Col. Truman E. Boudinot's tanks were down . . ." Telecon, Collins and Hobbs, August 7, 1944, 1550 hours, *Suitland Archives.*

Page 127: "The Germans launched . . . the Germans withdrew." Lyman, *Curlew History,* 29.

Chapter 13: Day of the Typhoon

Page 129: "The heavy ground fog . . . off the end of the runway." John Golley, *Day of the Typhoon: Flying with the RAF Tankbusters in Normandy* (Wellingborough, England: P. Stephens, 1986), 123–26.

Page 130: "he was promised that three hundred fighters . . ." Gersdorff, *Normandy, Cobra and Mortain,* 12.

Page 130: "not one German airplane reached the battlefield . . ." Richard P. Hallion, *Strike from the Sky: The History of Battlefield Air Attack, 1911–1945* (Washington and London: Smithsonian Institution Press, 1989), 217. Note: This claim, made at the time by Col. Walter Reinhard (Funck's chief of staff), was not disputed by the Luftwaffe. The German aircraft reported by American GIs on August 7 were almost certainly Allied aircraft.

Page 131: "If Jerry hated . . ." *Spearhead in the West, 1941–45: The 3rd Armored Division* (Frankfurt am Main-Schwarkeim: F. J. Heinrich, 1945), 72.

Page 132: "In four aerial engagements . . . 75 fighters available for combat." Gerritt Zijlstra, *Diary of an Air War* (New York: Vantage Press, 1977), 281.

Page 133: "Broadhurst's ten Typhoon squadrons . . ." Hallion, *Strike from the Sky,* 216–17.

Page 133: "The first Typhoon sorties . . . 1230 hours." Hilary St. George Saunders, *The Royal Air Force in World War II.* Vol. III: *The Fight Is Won* (London: Her Majesty's Stationery Office, 1954), 132.

Page 133: "The northern penetration . . . halted just after dawn . . ." Blumenson, *Breakout and Pursuit,* 463.

Page 133: "The drive by the 2d SS Panzer . . . was brought to a halt . . ." Ibid., 462.

Page 133: "General Funck halted the attack . . ." Ibid., 463.

Page 133: "Brigadier General James Lewis . . . had control . . ." After-action interviews, *Suitland Interviews.*

Page 134: "Wing Commander Green . . . trees alongside the road." Golley, *Day of the Typhoon,* 129–34.

Page 134: "Scott left a vivid picture . . ." Desmond Scott, *Typhoon Pilot* (London: Secker and Warburg, 1982), 318.

Page 135: "The British Second Tactical Air Force flew . . . 54 seriously damaged." Norman MacMillan, *The Royal Air Force in the World War,* Vol. IV (London: George G. Harrap and Co., 1950), 170.

Page 135: "You know, chaps . . ." Golley, *Day of the Typhoon,* 138.

Page 135: "Colonel Birks complained . . ." G-3 Journal, August 7, 1944, 1810 hours, *Suitland Archives.*

Page 135: "Our planes have bombed and strafed . . ." G-3 Journal, August 7, 1944, 1802 hours, *Suitland Archives.*

Page 135: "A Typhoon attacked four Shermans . . ." After-action interviews, *Suitland Interviews.*

Page 136: "Murray Pulver . . . why we weren't all killed." Pulver, *The Longest Year,* 33. Note: Pulver sets the time of this attack at 0900, which was almost certainly too early.

Page 136: "The activities . . ." Florentin, *Battle of the Falaise Gap,* 56–57.

Page 136: "We can do nothing against their . . ." Ibid., 56.

Page 137: "A British Operations Research Group . . ." Forrest C. Pogue, *The Supreme Command* (Washington, DC: Office of the Chief of Military History, Department of the Army, 1954), 208.

Page 137: "perhaps a little too optimistic . . ." MacMillan, *The RAF,* 170.

Chapter 14: The Momentum Shifts

Page 138: "Several 88 shells . . ." *History of the 30th Division Artillery,* 30.

Page 139: "Springfield's gunners continued . . . eight long hours." Karamales, et al., *Anti-tank Defense,* 71, 76.

Page 139: "Lockett led what amounted . . ." After-action interview, *Suitland Interviews.*

Page 140: "The small force . . ." Ibid.

Page 140: "The small task force was a victim . . ." Ibid.

Page 140: "(CCB) of the 3d Armored . . ." Ibid.

Page 141: "Major General Paul Baade's . . . St.-Hilaire and Barenton." *Santa Fe: 35th Infantry Division* (Atlanta: Albert Love Enterprises, 1946), chapter 5.

Page 142: "the men of the 137th . . ." Ibid.

Page 142: "A few miles to the east . . . halted by darkness." Houston, *Hell on Wheels,* 245.

Page 143: "I command the attack . . ." Blumenson, *Breakout and Pursuit,* 464.

Page 143: "Hitler also . . . indulge in . . ." Ibid., 464.

Page 144: "General Hausser . . . blamed . . ." Ibid., 465.

Page 144: "General von Schwerin . . . stopped in its tracks." Ibid., 463–64.

Page 144: "I foresee that the failure . . ." Ibid., 465.

Page 144: "The commander of the American . . . continue its advance toward Le Mans." Bradley and Blair, *A General's Life,* 293.

Page 145: "It occurred to me . . ." Ibid., 294.

Page 145: "Greatest tactical blunder . . ." Ibid., 296.

Page 145: "We silently prayed . . ." Ibid., 295.

Chapter 15: Radio Batteries

Page 146: "*Raus! Raus! Raus!*" Robert Bradley, *Aid Man!* (New York: Vantage Press, 1970), 71.

Page 147: "They were particularly eager . . ." Ibid., 72.

Page 147: "The Germans got in the first blow . . ." After-action interviews, *Suitland Interviews.*

Page 147: "Lieutenant Murray Pulver of B Company . . . with the necessary supplies." Pulver, *The Longest Year,* 34–35.

Page 148: "the security squads covering . . ." Karamales, et al., *Anti-tank Defense,* 72–73.

Page 148: "It was nip and tuck . . ." Karamales, et al., *Anti-tank Defense,* Springfield interview, 38.

Page 149: "Private First Class Robert Vollmer . . . gasoline carrier to his score." *History of the 120th Regiment,* 51.

Page 149: "adding two more Panthers . . ." Karamales, et al., *Anti-tank Defense,* 76.

Page 150: "We made the wounded . . ." Kerley, *Operations of the 2nd Battalion,* 13.

Page 150: "We have to get supplies . . ." G-3 Journal, August 8, 1944, 0110 hours, *Suitland Archives.*

Page 150: "The 30th Division's phone journal . . ." G-3 Journal, August 8, 1944, 0120 hours, *Suitland Archives.*

Page 152: "the 2d Battalion commander . . ." Hewitt, *Workhorse of the Western Front,* 66.

Page 153: "The assault hit . . . almost two dozen men." Lyman, *Curlew History,* 133.

Page 153: "This battalion we got . . ." G-3 Journal, August 8, 1944, 1452 hours, *Suitland Archives.*

Page 153: "That assessment . . . quite jittery." Ibid.

Page 154: "Just about this time . . . so let's go!" Ibid.

Page 155: "The 35th Division . . ." *Santa Fe,* chapter 5.

Page 155: "Two battalions of the 41st . . ." Houston, *Hell on Wheels,* 244.

Page 155: "Birks resolved . . . we can't lose half the regiment." Pulver, *The Longest Year,* 35.

Page 156: "They need batteries . . ." G-3 Journal, August 8, 1944, 2246 hours, *Suitland Archives.*

Chapter 16: The Short Envelopment

Page 157: "who complained . . ." Ladislas Farago, *Patton: Ordeal and Triumph* (New York: Ivan Obolensky, 1964), 527.

Page 158: "I privately worried . . ." Bradley and Blair, *A General's Life,* 296–97.

Page 158: "newly arrived . . ." Ibid., 296.

Page 158: "notoriously undisciplined . . ." Ibid., 296.

Page 158: "we found both Wyche . . ." Ibid., 269.

Page 159: "The division is bad . . ." Weigley, *Eisenhower's Lieutenants,* 190.

Page 160: "a task force commanded . . ." Blumenson, *Breakout and Pursuit,* 428.

Page 160: "accordingly . . . I made the decision . . ." Bradley and Blair, *A General's Life,* 285.

Page 160: "a minimum of forces . . ." Blumenson, *Breakout and Pursuit,* 430.

Page 160: "best troops I had . . ." Bradley and Blair, *A General's Life,* 298.

Page 161: "Nobody knows anything . . ." Blumenson, *Breakout and Pursuit,* 433.

Page 161: "Don't stop . . ." Breuer, *Death of a Nazi Army,* 192.

Page 161: "Weaver could see . . . secured the bridge." Ibid., 192–93.

Page 163: "Push all personnel . . ." Weigley, *Eisenhower's Lieutenants,* 192.

Page 163: "General Simonds's two lead divisions . . ." Ibid., 204.

Page 164: "These were some of Ultra's . . ." Bennett, *Ultra in the West,* 119.

Page 164: "He was curiously cool . . . no weight with Patton." Bradley and Blair, *A General's Life,* 294.

Page 165: "To strengthen the hard tip . . ." Blumenson, *Breakout and Pursuit,* 497.

Page 165: "The two generals met . . . in Bradley's hands." Bradley and Blair, *A General's Life,* 102.

Page 167: "We are holding and getting . . . doing everything in God's power to hold." G-3 Journal, August 8, 1940, 1220 hours, *Suitland Archives.*

Page 167: "The German is either crazy . . ." Bradley and Blair, *A General's Life,* 296.

Page 167: "We didn't expect it . . . heavy heart." Blumenson, *Breakout and Pursuit,* 481.

Page 167: "Hitler's new offensive . . ." Ibid., 481.

Page 168: "The 10th SS Panzer Division had already . . ." Ibid., 481.

Page 168: "too early, too weak . . ." Ibid., 482.

Page 168: "The Gambetta Bridge . . . shots from its 75mm cannon." Florentin, *Battle of the Falaise Gap,* 64–66.

Page 169: "Now I know how . . ." Breuer, *Death of a Nazi Army,* 194.

Chapter 17: Come and Get Us

Page 172: "We made our way cautiously . . . no possible way to get up the hill." Pulver, *The Longest Year,* 35–36.

Page 174: "Here's something for you . . . It's up to G-4 now." G-3 Journal, August 9, 1944, 1305 hours, *Suitland Archives.*

Page 175: "Brig. Gen. James Lewis . . . badly shot up." After-action interview, *Suitland Interviews.*

Page 175: "During one sixty-minute period . . . targets in the north." Ibid.

Page 175: "We had a report . . ." G-3 Journal, August 9, 1944, 2251 hours, *Suitland Archives.*

Page 175: "The light spotting planes . . ." After-action interview, *Suitland Interviews.*

Page 176: "His gunners recorded only . . ." Karamales, et al., *Antitank Defense,* 76.

Page 177: "German artillery damaged . . ." Ibid., 74–75.

Page 177: "A tank force from CCB . . ." After-action interview, *Suitland Interviews.*

Page 178: "Major Robert Herlong . . ." Ibid.

Page 178: "General Baade was forced to commit . . ." Blumenson, *Breakout and Pursuit,* 487.

Page 178: "A counterattack by the 12th SS . . ." Florentin, *Battle of the Falaise Gap,* 84.

Page 179: "One promising breakthrough . . ." Ibid., 84–85.

Page 179: "This is an opportunity . . ." Bradley and Blair, *A General's Life,* 296.

Page 179: "[Bradley] made an excellent . . ." Miller, *August 1944,* 87.

Page 180: "He was a platoon leader . . ." *History of the 120th,* 28.

Page 180: "Attempts by regiment . . . in the minds of the men." Kerley, *Operations of the 2nd Battalion,* 14.

Page 181: "Lieutenant Elmer Rohmiller . . ." Ibid., 14.

Page 181: "He was carrying . . . blown to bits." Ibid., 14–15.

Page 181: "Kerley was directing . . . anything more to say?" Len Guttridge, "Hold Hill 314 Till Dead," *Stag Magazine* (March 1964), 35.

Page 182: "I will surrender . . ." William Smith White, Associated Press, August 12, 1944.

Page 182: "wasn't quite so dramatic . . . unprintable." Kerley, *Operations of the 2nd Battalion,* 15.

Page 182: "Erichson reported . . . move fast." Gutteridge, *Hold Hill 314,* 82.

Page 182: "The 17th Panzergrenadier Division launched a major attack . . ." Kerley, *Operations of the 2nd Battalion,* 15.

Page 183: "Things looked very bad . . ." *History of the 30th Division Artillery,* 32.

Page 183: "Kerley called in artillery . . ." Kerley, *Operations of the 2nd Battalion,* 15.

Page 183: "Kerley noticed the transformation . . ." Ibid., 15.

Chapter 18: Stalemate

Page 186: "It isn't very easy . . ." Blumenson, *Breakout and Pursuit,* 492.

Page 186: "There were thirty-six of them . . . Mowed them down." After-action interview, *Suitland Interviews.*

Page 187: "They draw too much fire . . ." Ibid.

Page 187: "The tanks don't like to mix it up . . ." Ibid.

Page 187: "The tankers of the 2d Armored . . . Capt. Thomas Carothers," Houston, *Hell on Wheels,* 247.

Page 188: "Lt. Tom Springfield was able to retire . . ." Karamales, et al., *Anti-tank Defense,* 75.

Page 188: "a strong infantry attack . . ." Ibid., 75.

Page 188: "Sergeant Burick . . . died of his wounds." After-action interview, *Suitland Interviews.*

Page 190: "when a flight of P-47s roared over . . . lazily floating down." Kerley, *Operations of the 2nd Battalion,* 16.

Page 190: "Captain Delmont Byrn immediately organized . . ." *History of the 120th,* 55.

Page 191: "The supply drop had to be judged a failure . . ." Note: Although Kerley wrote that some radio batteries were recovered in the drop, all other sources agree that no batteries were included. Lieutenant Weiss emphatically states that no fresh batteries were recovered after the drop (p. 32 of the *History of the 30th Division Artillery*).

Page 191: "Lt. Col. Lewis D. Vieman . . . decided . . ." *On the Way,* 26.

Page 191: "Vieman visited Lt. George Dieser . . . landed within American lines." Wayne Robinson, *Move Out, Verify: A Combat History of the 743rd Tank Battalion* (Frankfurt on Main, Germany: by the 743d Battalion Staff, 1945), 73.

Page 192: "relief effort was only partially successful . . ." After-action interview, *Suitland Interviews.*

Page 193: "Major Robert Herlong's battalion . . . dig in for the night." Ibid.

Page 193: "Advance on the axis . . ." Blumenson, *Breakout and Pursuit,* 494.

Page 194: "Haislip's corps was . . . had not arrived." Ibid., 500.

Page 194: "Lieutenant Colonel William Hamberg . . ." Ibid., 500.

Page 195: "Hell, no! . . ." Breuer, *Death of a Nazi Army,* 230.

Chapter 19: Withdrawal

Page 196: "Only seventy-seven Mark IV tanks and forty-seven Panthers . . ." Blumenson, *Breakout and Pursuit,* 483.

Page 197: "Eberbach had already advanced . . . panzer thrust." Ibid., 483–84.

Page 197: "He asked questions . . ." Ibid., 484.

Page 197: "a minor withdrawal . . ." Ibid., 486.

Page 198: "A column of trucks . . . killing the heroic driver." Breuer, *Death of a Nazi Army,* 230.

Page 199: "Be sure to bring along . . ." Ibid., 237.

Page 199: "Leclerc was at that moment . . . work to do." Florentin, *Battle of the Falaise Gap*, 96–100.

Page 200: "Wade, pay no attention . . ." Breuer, *Death of a Nazi Army*, 237.

Page 200: "Von Kluge learned . . ." Blumenson, *Breakout and Pursuit*, 501.

Page 200: "The burning enemy columns . . ." Kerley, *Operations of the 2nd Battalion*, 17.

Page 201: "A rumor spread . . ." *History of the 30th Division Artillery*, 32.

Page 201: "Major Robert Herlong . . ." After-action interview, *Suitland Interviews*.

Page 202: "some of these . . ." Ibid.

Page 202: "We can hold . . ." Ibid.

Page 202: "Our artillery plastered . . ." Kerley, *Operations of the 2nd Battalion*, 17.

Page 202: "General Leclerc was asleep . . . Leclerc took a seat . . ." Florentin, *Battle of the Falaise Gap*, 103–104.

Chapter 20: Relief

Page 205: "The 35th Division's Quartermaster Company . . ." *Santa Fe*, chapter 5.

Page 206: "For Lt. Murray Pulver . . . My prayers had been answered." Pulver, *The Longest Year*, 37.

Page 207: Casualty reports from 30th Division's G-1 report, August 13, 1944, *Suitland Archives*.

Page 207: "A postwar count . . ." Lyman, *Curlew History*, 118.

Page 207: "Exactly 357 were able . . ." *History of the 120th*, 56.

Page 208: "Remnants of the 1st SS . . ." Hewitt, *Workhorse of the Western Front*, 64.

Page 208: "In his memoirs . . ." Bernard Law Montgomery, *Normandy to the Baltic* (Boston: Houghton Mifflin Company, 1948), 162.

Page 208: "I have been relieved of command . . . end the war," Blumenson, *Breakout and Pursuit*, 535–36.

Chapter 21: Closing the Trap

Page 211: "General Leclerc didn't rest . . ." Florentin, *Battle of the Falaise Gap*, 106.

Page 212: "Those goddamn Frog drivers . . ." Breuer, *Death of a Nazi Army,* 231.

Page 212: "You have no right to be here . . . Our tanks need N 158." Florentin, *Battle of the Falaise Gap,* 107.

Page 212: "Hell, Wade . . ." Breuer, *Death of a Nazi Army,* 231.

Page 213: "restore the situation . . ." Blumenson, *Breakout and Pursuit,* 502.

Page 213: "the only defenders . . ." Ibid., 503.

Page 214: "The British . . . effort . . ." Bradley and Blair, *A General's Life,* 297.

Page 214: "With Ike's approval . . ." Ibid., 298.

Page 214: "Patton told the XV Corps commander . . ." Farago, *Patton: Ordeal and Triumph,* 538.

Page 215: "push on slowly . . ." Blumenson, *Breakout and Pursuit,* 504.

Page 216: "You're kidding . . ." Farago, *Patton: Ordeal and Triumph,* 539.

Page 216: "Patton had knowingly and willingly . . ." Bradley and Blair, *A General's Life,* 298.

Page 216: "We've got elements . . . get ready for him." Farago, *Patton: Ordeal and Triumph,* 538.

Page 216: "I much preferred . . ." Bradley and Blair, *A General's Life,* 298.

Page 216: German strength at Argentan, from Blumenson, *Breakout and Pursuit,* 504–5.

Page 217: "A fighter-bomber roared . . . survivors was wounded." Paul Carell (Karl Paul Schmidt), *Invasion—They're Coming,* trans. E. Osers (New York: E. P. Dutton, 1963), 257.

Page 217: "If the front . . . both armies." Blumenson, *Breakout and Pursuit,* 505.

Page 218: "Rather than close the trap . . ." Bradley and Blair, *A General's Life,* 299.

Page 218: "Wrong . . ." Ibid., 300.

Page 218: "Patton might have spun . . ." Ibid.

Page 218: "could muster . . ." John Ellis, *Brute Force* (New York: Viking, 1990), 390–91.

Page 218: "If I had worried about flanks . . ." George S. Patton, Jr., *War as I Knew It* (Boston: Houghton Mifflin Company, 1947), 113.

Page 219: "Any head-on juncture . . ." Bradley, *Soldier's Story,* 377.

Page 220: "Although not highly publicized . . ." U. S. Army Command and General Staff College, Combat Studies Institute, *Military History Anthology*, fall 1984, 122.

Page 221: "held nobly on the hinge . . . the Rock of Mortain." Bradley, *Soldier's Story*, 375.

Chapter 22: Roosevelt's SS

Page 223: "After making like . . ." Pulver, *The Longest Year*, 38.

Page 223: "Lieutenant Colonel Ernest Frankland's . . ." Lyman, *Curlew History*, 34.

Page 223: "This great move . . ." *History of the 120th*, 58.

Page 224: "The 230th FA Battalion . . ." *On The Way*, 104.

Page 224: "This has been saved . . . pick up the melon." Pulver, *The Longest Year*, 42.

Page 224: "As we drove into town . . ." Lockerbie, *Man under Orders*, 112.

Page 224: "Two days later . . . another French town . . ." Ibid., 113–14.

Page 226: "Lt. Elwood Daddow of B Company . . ." Lyman, *Curlew History*, 39.

Page 226: "How I wish . . ." Pulver, *The Longest Year*, 50–51.

Page 227: "He came back dripping . . ." Hewitt, *Workhorse of the Western Front*, 111.

Page 227: "Lt. D. W. Morgan, constructed . . ." Ibid., 111.

Page 227: "What bombing?" Ibid., 112.

Page 227: "The result was more speed . . ." Ibid., 113–14.

Page 227: "Big enough to drive . . ." Ibid., 125.

Page 228: "We manned every window . . ." Ibid., 127.

Page 228: "These are the bravest men . . ." Ibid., 136.

Page 229: "I wish you'd get it around . . ." Ibid., 141.

Page 229: "The division's G-2 summary . . ." Ibid., 172

Page 230: "Just got a call . . ." Ibid., 172–73.

Page 231: "the fanatical 30th Division . . ." Ibid., 173.

Page 231: "The Germans ran us out . . ." Lyman, *Curlew History*, 65.

Page 232: "Lieutenant Pulver's company . . . turned around and retreated." Pulver, *The Longest Year*, 72–73.

Page 232: "The powerful German spearhead . . . at the remarkable range of 1,200 yards." Hewitt, *Workhorse of the Western Front*, 178–79.

Page 234: "Frankland's battalion . . . beat off . . ." Lyman, *Curlew History,* 66–67.

Page 234: Peiper's losses from Hewitt, *Workhorse of the Western Front,* 189.

Page 235: "The present situation . . ." Bradley and Blair, *A General's Life,* 358.

Page 235: "it would be three months . . ." Ibid., 370.

Page 235: "Although initially Monty . . . doomed the German offensive." Ibid., 368–69.

Page 236: "Colonel Purdue . . . I always have been lucky." Harold Boyle, Associated Press, January 8, 1945.

Page 236: "The Ninth Army commander asked . . ." Lyman, *Curlew History,* 85.

Page 237: "We're going to fight . . ." Hewitt, *Workhorse of the Western Front,* 245.

Page 237: "The American Army's workhorse division." Wes Gallagher, Associated Press, March 24, 1945.

Page 238: "A Polish refugee . . . the bridge was no more." Pulver, *The Longest Year,* 124–25.

Page 240: "It is the combined judgments . . . undue wastage of its men." Letter from S. L. A. Marshall to Leland Hobbs, March 16, 1946.

INDEX